Backroads of Central and Northern British Columbia

Backroads of Central and Northern British Columbia

LONE
PINE

Joan Donaldson-Yarmey

© 2000 by Joan Donaldson-Yarmey and Lone Pine Publishing
First printed in 2000   10 9 8 7 6 5 4 3 2 1
Printed in Canada

The Publisher: **Lone Pine Publishing**

10145 – 81 Ave.	202A, 1110 Seymour St.	1901 Raymond Ave. SW, Suite C
Edmonton, AB T6E 1W9	Vancouver, BC V6B 3N3	Renton, WA 98055
Canada	Canada	USA

Canadian Cataloguing in Publication Data

Donaldson-Yarmey, Joan, 1949-
    Backroads of central and northern British Columbia

    Includes index
    ISBN 1-55105-225-3

    1. Automobile travel—British Columbia, Northern—Guidebooks. 2. British Columbia, Northern—Guidebooks. I. Title.
    FC 3845.N67A3 2000   917.11'8044   C99-911263-5
    F1087.7.D66 2000

Editorial Director: Nancy Foulds
Editorial: Volker Bodegom, Randy Williams, Lee Craig
Production Manager: Jody Reekie
Layout & Production: Monica Triska
Book Design: Robert Weidemann
Cover Design: Elliot Engley
Cover Photo: Joan Donaldson-Yarmey, Chilcotin Bridge over the Fraser River
Separations and Film: Elite Lithographers Co. Ltd.

We acknowledge the financial support of the Government of Canada through the Book Publishing Industry Development Program (BPIDP) for our publishing activities.

PC: P6   Canada

Contents

Dedication

To my parents, Oliver H. Donaldson and F. Olive Donaldson.

Acknowledgements

My thanks go to the many friendly and helpful people who gave me information and directions in my quest to explore as much as possible of their beautiful region. It is easy to see that these people enjoy living in this part of the province and, after travelling through it myself, I have found lots of places I know I would enjoy spending time.

I have had many compliments on the attractiveness of the covers of my books and on how well laid out they are. Although I do the travelling and research and take the photographs, it is the people at Lone Pine Publishing who put in the long hours working on the design and poring over the pictures to decide how they and the sidebars will fit in with the text. And before the layout can be done, my editor and cartographer at Lone Pine, Volker Bodegom, must patiently correct my mistakes, edit my wording for better effect and draw the maps. For all this, I thank the staff of Lone Pine Publishing.

Introduction

Although mountains are a common factor throughout British Columbia, each part of the province has its unique scenery, people, climate and attractions. A century ago the search for gold opened up much of the province. Then there were railways and settlers in the southern and central parts of BC. More recently the search for gold and other minerals, as well as the building of the Alaska Highway, during the Second World War, and the Cassiar Highway, helped open up the northern part of the province.

Besides guiding you along the highways and backroads of central and northern BC, *Backroads of Central and Northern British Columbia* will take you on the section of the Alaska Highway that begins in the Peace River area of BC and runs through the province to Watson Lake in the Yukon. (If you wish to tour further north, see my book, *Backroads of the Yukon and Alaska.*) Then you will head south from the border on the Cassiar Highway. These routes are quite long and driving them will give you a sense of the immensity and beauty of the northern part of the province.

Because my books, *Backroads of Southern Interior British Columbia* (Chapter 10) and *Backroads of Southwestern British Columbia* (Chapter 3), have routes that include Kamloops, the first chapter of this book begins at Kamloops. This way you can link the trips in all three of these books together to tour the mainland of the province. If you also wish to visit Vancouver Island, see my book, *Backroads of Vancouver Island.*

Third section of War Falls.

Every road has its lodges, resorts, gift and craft shops, campsites, provincial parks and RV parks, so you are never alone for very long. Nevertheless, one of the best aspects of driving through this part of the province is that there are relatively few signs and other trappings of civilization to disturb your view.

The provincial government has provided plenty of rest areas and pull-outs along rivers and creeks, so take the time to stop and breath deeply of the warm, summer-scented air and listen to the birds and the squirrels and the gurgling waters. Along forestry roads, free recreation areas have been set up by the logging industry. They are 'user-maintained'; leave them clean by taking out your garbage after you enjoy your stay.

Although the logging roads have been constructed by the forestry industry for use by their trucks and equipment, they are generally open to the public. When travelling them, though, remember that a logging truck has the right-of-way at all times. Most of the roads mentioned in this book can be travelled by car or motorhome; those that are not suitable are noted.

Bridge over Chilcotin River at Farwell Canyon.

Salmon Glacier.

Although this book is intended mostly for planning vacations in the summer—the most popular season to visit the area—travellers visiting during other seasons will also find it useful. If you do travel in the off-season, however, be prepared for snowy road conditions and to find many attractions closed.

The chapters in *Backroads of Central and Northern British Columbia* are divided into trips that (with a few exceptions) could be driven in a day, though you may want to travel at a more relaxed pace. The trips in each chapter are as closely connected to the next as possible to make travelling easy and enjoyable. Maps for the roads included at the beginning of each chapter give you an idea of how your trip is laid out. You might want to pick up forest recreation maps, which are available free at most visitor information centres. These maps show the logging roads and recreation sites in the area. Other local maps of various kinds are also usually available.

Tours of mines, sawmills, forests and fish hatcheries are offered during the summer months. Many are booked through the nearest visitor information centre, so ask at these places for times and days. If you like to see Mother Nature firsthand, all towns have hiking trails in their regions. Some are short and easy; some are long and for more experienced hikers. Pamphlets describing them can be obtained at the visitor information centres.

You will be driving up and down many hillsides and mountainsides, some of them quite steep. Make sure that your vehicle is in good condition, especially if you are pulling a trailer. The same goes for your body—because of the terrain, many hiking trails have steep sections; be certain that you are in good enough shape for the climb (on the way out or the way back) before starting out.

This book is designed to lure you to this wonderful part of the province and to give you something to see and do once you get there, but it does not claim to tell everything. If you have the time and the desire, do some exploring and discovering on your own.

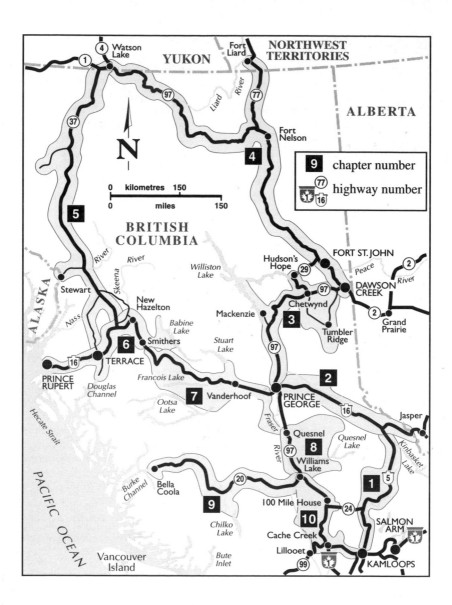

Helpful Hints

If you plan to fish in BC, the Yukon, the Northwest Territories or Alaska, be sure to acquire the correct licence. At the place where you get your licence you can also pick up the current regulations for the area you are in. Regulations for other areas that you might visit are often available at visitor reception centres.

You will be sure to come across animals as you drive along the road. If you encounter large animals while you are in your vehicle, do not get out. Though bears have the most potential to be dangerous, remember that the actions of wild animals of all sizes are unpredictable and that hoofed mammals and smaller animals with sharp teeth can also injure you if they are angry, frightened or hungry.

If you stop to take pictures, park your vehicle off the road as far as possible. Do not encourage animals to come to your vehicle, because they could get run over by another vehicle when they are on the road. And, if they come to your window anyway, do not feed them. Bring binoculars on your trip, for you never know when you will see an animal up a hillside and want to get a better look at it.

When you walk or hike through the bush, always make noise as you walk, so that any bears who might be grazing nearby will notice your approach and have time to leave. If you do come across a bear, back away slowly until you are out of its sight and smelling range. You can return the way you came after it moves on. Visitor reception centres, park offices and ranger stations have more detailed information on how to deal with bears.

Make sure that your vehicle has been tuned up and checked for problems before you leave home. Though you will be able to get service and parts in the cities and larger towns, in many smaller places—if there even is a mechanic there—you may have to wait for parts to arrive from elsewhere. Besides a good spare tire, bring along motor oil, belts and wrenches to fit your car.

Put a deflector on the front of your vehicle's hood to help protect the windshield from bugs and flying rocks. Headlight protectors are also a good idea. Take along a tube of Crazy Glue or a similar product to put on any rock chips in glass to prevent cracks from spreading.

On gravel roads in particular, always drive with your lights on. Top up your gas tank before heading out on long gravel roads, not only because of the greater distances between gas stations, but also because the rougher surfaces, the ups and downs, and the frequent slowing down and speeding up consume more gas than driving a similar distance on the highway would.

In case you get stranded for several days because of road washouts, vehicle breakdown or other problems, carry extra food, especially canned goods, and some extra drinking water. Blankets or sleeping bags are also a good idea. (If you plan to travel through northern BC in winter, consult other resources to find out what else you should take.)

Finally, bring along insect repellent, sunscreen and a first-aid kit.

And don't forget your camera and film.

Dawson Falls.

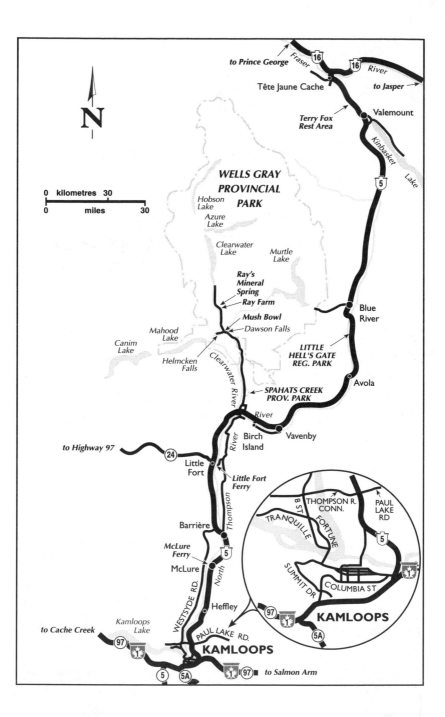

N

0 kilometres 30
0 miles 30

to Prince George

Fraser

16

River

16

to Jasper

Tête Jaune Cache

Terry Fox
Rest Area

Valemount

Kinbasket Lake

5

WELLS GRAY
PROVINCIAL
PARK

Hobson
Lake

Azure
Lake

Clearwater
Lake

Murtle
Lake

Ray's
Mineral
Spring

Ray Farm

Mush Bowl

Dawson Falls

Blue
River

Mahood
Lake

Canim
Lake

Helmcken
Falls

Clearwater River

LITTLE
HELL'S GATE
REG. PARK

Avola

SPAHATS CREEK
PROV. PARK

River

Vavenby

to Highway 97

24

Little
Fort

Birch
Island

River

Little Fort
Ferry

Barrière

Thompson

5

THOMPSON R.
CONN.

PAUL
LAKE
RD.

5

8 ST

TRANQUILLE

FORTUNE

McLure
Ferry

McLure

North

SUMMIT DR

COLUMBIA ST

1

to Cache Creek

Kamloops
Lake

WESTSYDE RD.

Heffley

PAUL LAKE RD.

97

97

1

KAMLOOPS

5A

KAMLOOPS

97

1

5

5A

1

97

to Salmon Arm

1
Kamloops to Valemount

This chapter begins just north of Kamloops, on the South Yellowhead Highway, Highway 5. The scenery of semi-arid hills here will gradually be replaced by trees and mountains as you head north. You will be following the North Thompson River most of the way and can stop to view it at rest areas and viewpoints along the road. If it is a hot day, you will be happy to know that most of the villages and towns mentioned in this chapter have ice cream stands.

There are signs along Highway 5 warning that it is a high mountain road and that the weather can change at any time. If you drive this route just after a spring or fall rainstorm, you might see the pure white of a fresh snowfall on the nearby mountain peaks.

Kamloops to Wells Gray Provincial Park

Kamloops, Heffley and Vinsulla

As you head north from Kamloops on Highway 5, watch on your right for the junction with Paul Lake Road, which goes to Paul Lake Provincial Campground and Harper Mountain Ski Area (to the left is Thompson River Connector Road). Set your odometer to zero at this junction. As you drive along Highway 5, the North Thompson River is to your left. You can stop and fish from its banks for Dolly Varden if you have a BC fishing licence.

You go through the community of Rayleigh and then pass the road to Heffley Lake at kilometre 19.0 (mile 11.8). Heffley Lake, which is 18.0 kilometres (11.2 miles) up that road, is a popular rainbow trout fishing hole. It was named after Adam P. Heffley, who owned property in the area and was involved with the Cariboo camels.

Those black plastic tarps set on stakes that you see out in the fields in this area cover a fairly new type of crop: ginseng (see the sidebar on p. 218). It has been grown in the Kamloops area since 1982 and in the North Thompson Valley since 1988. You pass through Vinsulla, which is an anagram of the surname of a farmer who lived in the area at that time, Michael Sullivan.

As you continue northward, the semi-arid land begins to give way to trees.

The Cariboo Camels

In 1862, a syndicate operating in the Cariboo purchased 25 camels from a San Francisco merchant who had gone to China to buy them in 1860. They were taken to Victoria, where a mother camel and her baby escaped into the wilderness—they were seen in the area for a few months afterward. The rest were then transported across to the mainland. The syndicate had bought the camels as pack animals for the Cariboo because a camel can carry more weight than a horse or mule, can travel faster, has longer legs and can 'live on anything.'

Some of the camels did get used as pack animals for a short time, but their biggest drawback was that they scared the horses of other packers, causing hardships for the syndicate that owned them, such as threats of court action. Also, they became footsore on the rocky terrain and finally their owners decided to turn them loose.

What exactly happened to all of the camels is unknown. Twelve were seen afterward while grazing at Quesnelle Forks (now Quesnel Forks, see p. 187). One was mistaken for a grizzly and shot northeast of 150 Mile House. Some were caught in a blizzard and froze to death; they were buried in a mass grave near 117 Mile House on the Cariboo Wagon Road. One was used at Fort Steele for a couple of years until it died.

Three were turned out to pasture in the Westwold area. Two of these animals were eventually traded to a Native for some horses, and the one camel left died there of old age in 1905.

McLure and Barrière

At kilometre 39.1 (mile 24.3) from Paul Lake Road there is a turn-off to the left for the McLure Ferry, which crosses the North Thompson River. You can drive the 2 kilometres (1.2 miles) to the reaction (current-powered) ferry, which is in a pretty setting. A ferry has been in operation at this site since April 1919.

The ferry is on call from 7 AM to 6:45 PM, between spring thaw and fall freeze-up. Across the river is Westsyde (sometimes known as 'Westside') Road. From there, a left turn would take you back to Kamloops and a right turn would bring you back to Highway 5 just north of Barrière.

Continuing on Highway 5 past the ferry turn-off, you drive through McLure. Just 5.2 kilometres (3.2 miles) from the road to the ferry you reach the Fish Trap Rapids Rest Area, where you can have a picnic overlooking the North Thompson River. The Secwepemc (Shuswap) First Nation used to set fish traps at these rapids to catch spawning salmon.

After the rest area, you drive through the North Thompson River canyon, pass through the settlement of Louis Creek at kilometre 8.6 (mile 5.3) and enter Barrière at kilometre 12.6 (mile 7.8). Barrière, French for 'barrier,' was the name given to the fish traps or weirs used by the Natives of the area to catch salmon. It also became the name of the community in 1828. While the Cariboo Gold Rush was taking place, gold was also being panned from the Barrière River. Although it was not as plentiful here, the gold collected did make a good day's income.

At kilometre 14.2 (mile 8.8), turn left onto Lilley Road to head to the North Thompson Museum. Drive two blocks to the large yellow building, originally a warehouse, on the corner of Lilley Road and Railway Avenue. The museum features local artists and has displays about the mining and ranching history of the area. During July and August it is open Friday to Monday from 9 AM to 5 PM and Tuesday to Thursday from 9 AM to 3:30 PM.

Back on Highway 5, you cross a bridge over the Barrière River and in 0.9 kilometres (0.5 miles) from that bridge you come to Barrière Town Road. If you are here on the Labour Day long weekend, turn right onto this road to go to the Fair

McLure Ferry over the North Thompson River.

and Rodeo Grounds to take in the North Thompson Fall Fair and Rodeo. The event includes a midway, chuckwagon races, and dances, as well as a building full of crafts, baking, vegetables and art displays.

You cross the North Thompson River 0.7 kilometres (0.4 miles) from Barrière Town Road, which puts the river now on your right. You now pass through ranchland, some of it treed and some open, and there are hills all around. Look to your right at kilometre 9.1 (mile 5.7) to see a very wide stretch of the river.

Little Fort and Clearwater

The junction with Highway 24, in the hamlet of Little Fort, is at kilometre 29.0 (mile 18.0) from Barrière. Little Fort was established as a Hudson's Bay Company post in 1850. It was called 'Little Fort' to differentiate it from the larger post at Kamloops.

To see the Little Fort UFO Display, turn left onto Highway 24 and then pull in at the motel immediately on your right. In the yard of the motel there is a roofed-over set of panels with pictures of UFOs (Unidentified Flying Objects). Included are newspaper articles about people who have had contact with them and about some of the other places where UFOs have been seen—such as Switzerland, Mexico and Argentina. There are also some hand drawings of spaceships. Beside the motel stands Out of This World Ice Cream.

To the right (east) of Highway 5 at the junction where Highway 24 goes off to the left (west) is a road that goes down to the Little Fort Ferry. It takes about 30 minutes to cross the North Thompson River on this current-propelled ferry and it is on call from 7 AM to 6:45 PM. On the other side of the river you can turn left to connect with the Dunn Lake Road if you want to either end up back at Barrière or continue northward to Clearwater.

A ferry has been in place here since October 1912. In the 1920s there were 33 ferries on BC rivers. Now there are fewer than 10. This river crossing is one of four in British Columbia that also has a cable-car. Run by the ferry operator, it is in operation only during spring break-up and in the fall until freeze-up is complete,

after which people can walk across the river on the ice. It can carry five foot-passengers at the time. Both the ferry and cable-car are free.

The North Thompson River Provincial Park is to your right at kilometre 25.8 (mile 16.0) from the junction with Highway 24. The campground, where a large Native village stood until most of its residents were wiped out in a smallpox epidemic in the late 1800s, is at the confluence of the North Thompson and Clearwater rivers.

The Clearwater River is a very popular rafting river. If you are interested in taking a trip down it yourself, ask about the rafting companies in the area at the visitor information centre up ahead at the turn-off for Wells Gray Provincial Park.

UFO display at Little Fort.

You cross the Clearwater River and then reach the first of Clearwater's businesses along the highway at kilometre 29.2 (mile 18.1). The old section of Clearwater is on the right side of the highway and the new section is on the left. At kilometre 29.8 (mile 18.5), opposite where Clearwater Village Road goes to your right, turn left onto the Old North Thompson Highway and follow it about 0.5 kilometres (0.3 miles) to the bridge over the Clearwater River. Turn right just before the bridge to enter Reginald Small Park. In the park you can visit the Loggers' Memorial, a log shelter that commemorates the names of local loggers who have lost their lives while on the job. There is also a 46-centimetre (18-inch) thick slab of a 300-year-old Douglas-fir that was cut down in 1986.

Return to Highway 5 and turn left.

Unsolved Mystery #1

In 1900, a man with the first name of Ross and an unknown partner bought the small trading post at Little Fort. Because no one knew his last name and since Ross had moved from Spokane, Washington, to run the business, he was called 'Spokane' by the locals.

A year later, Spokane and all his money disappeared, leaving behind a bloody cabin. No clue was found as to what had happened to the body. And, since there was no body, the police had only rumours to go on as to who had done the alleged killing.

One of the rumours was that Spokane had fallen in love with a Native woman from the Chu Chua Reserve and that another of her suitors had murdered Spokane in jealousy. The second rumour was that his partner had sneaked in from Washington and killed him, taking away his body and his money. Nothing, however, could be proven in either case, and the mystery remains unsolved to this day.

Spahats Creek and Wells Gray Provincial Parks

In 1 kilometre (0.6 miles) from the Old North Thompson Highway, turn left onto Clearwater Valley Road, which goes to Wells Gray Provincial Park. Just after the turn-off, look to your right for the visitor information centre. In the yard there is a full-sized metal sculpture of Jerry, a moose calf that once lived in Wells Gray Park. He became the mascot for the park—and eventually for the whole BC Parks System.

Inside the building there are displays about the Overlanders' journey (see the sidebar on p. 33,), the life of the Simpcw (the local division of the Secwepemc First Nation) and Wells Gray Provincial Park.

Jerry, the replica of a moose at Clearwater.

If you wish to view the park from above, ask about sightseeing charters at the visitor information centre.

You enter Spahats Creek Provincial Park 9.7 kilometres (6.0 miles) from the visitor centre. Turn left into the Spahats Creek Falls Viewpoint and Campground at kilometre 10.4 (mile 6.5). Just after the turn-off, go left again to arrive at the parking area for the falls. Walk to the fence and follow it to the right. Spahats Canyon is to your left as you walk.

In a few minutes you reach a viewpoint where you can look way down into the canyon and see the coppers, greys, yellows, greens and tans of the canyon wall. From here it a short walk to the second viewpoint, from where you can look at the falls. You can see how Spahats Creek has cut its way backwards and downwards through volcanic rock and you can

Spahats Creek Falls.

watch as the water pours out of Spahats Canyon halfway up the face of the rock wall and drops 61 metres (200 feet) to the floor below.

Back on the road to Wells Gray, you leave Spahats Creek Provincial Park in 1.3 kilometres (0.8 miles) from the turn-off for the falls and campground and you have the Clearwater Canyon to your left. Along this road between Spahats and Wells Gray parks there are bed-and-breakfast establishments, trail ride operators, craft shops, campgrounds and a golf course. Watch out for horses and riders as you drive, and pass with caution so as not to spook the horses.

At kilometre 3.2 (mile 2.0) you cross a one-lane bridge over First Canyon. To your right there is a small waterfall, to your left there is a canyon. Second Canyon is at kilometre 3.9 (mile 2.4), but there is not much to see here. As you cross the bridge at Third Canyon, at kilometre 6.0 (mile 3.7), look to your right to see the canyon, or stop at the pull-out just after the bridge and go back to look down into the canyon and at the water flowing into the Clearwater River.

⟩ Volcanic Canyons

A million years ago, the floor of the Clearwater Valley was created when successive flows of lava from erupting volcanoes added about 150 metres (500 feet) to the original elevation of the area. The reds, yellows, oranges, browns and tans of the layers in Spahats Canyon were created by the different lava flows.

When successive periods of glaciers came, they carved the two canyons into the volcanic rock that Spahats Creek and the Clearwater River today continue to deepen. The viewpoint for Spahats Creek Falls sits on the top layer of the lava. The boulders at the viewpoint were pushed this far by the last glacier and left here when it melted.

You enter Wells Gray Provincial Park at kilometre 25.9 (mile 16.1) and kilometre 31.2 (mile 19.4) brings you to the turn-off on the right for the Dawson Falls parking area.

The first part of the trail to the falls is gravel and through the woods, but it soon becomes a dirt path that takes you beside the Clearwater Valley Road and then back into the woods. After a 15- or 20-minute walk you reach the viewpoint. The falls are 91 metres (300 feet) wide and cascade 18 metres (59 feet) over smooth, rounded rocks—you will want to take lots of pictures.

Dawson Falls.

Back on the park's main road, immediately after the Dawson Falls parking area, there is a turn-off to the left for the Helmcken Falls south rim parking lot. From here you can take a half-hour hike to look over the falls. If you want to see the falls without a hike, skip this turn-off and continue along the road.

In less than 0.5 kilometres (0.3 miles) you cross the bridge over the Mush Bowl, also called 'the Devil's Punch Bowl.' Just after the bridge there is a parking area to your left. You can walk back to see where the Murtle River has created the smooth holes of the Mush Bowl in the rock of the river bed.

Mush Bowl.

The road to Pyramid Campground and Pyramid Mountain Trailhead is to your right 0.6 kilometres (0.4 miles) from the Mush Bowl. It is about a two-hour hike, depending on your fitness, to the cinder cones of the Pyramid Mountains. These cones consist of cinders and ash emitted by volcanic vents that erupted beneath glaciers.

At kilometre 1.4 (mile 0.9) from the Dawson Falls turn-off, go left for the Helmcken Falls viewpoint that does not require a hike. The gravel road that continues ahead from this junction goes to the Ray Farm, Ray's Mineral Spring and Clearwater Lake (all described a little later on).

In 3.8 kilometres (2.4 miles) after you turn left, you reach the parking area for the Helmcken Falls viewpoint. Go to the fence and follow it to the left to the wooden viewing platform. From here you can see the Murtle River, which flows across the Murtle Plateau, plunge over the edge of the cliff to the floor of the valley below. Look at the rock wall around the falls to see how the water has made it concave. For a better view and better picture-taking, go to the right along the fence.

Return to the road to the Ray Farm and Clearwater Lake and go left onto it. At 12.4 kilometres (7.7 miles) from the junction, turn right into the parking area for the trail to the Ray Farm.

At the beginning of the trail is a map that shows the 0.5-kilometre (0.3-mile) long route to the farm buildings and gravesite, and the additional 0.7-kilometre (0.4-mile) path to the mineral springs. The trail is wide as it leaves the parking lot and heads through tall trees. About halfway to the farm, you reach a sign that tells about the Ray family—John and Alice Ray and their three children — who farmed here from 1932 to 1946. It also explains about the birds and mammals that now inhabit the buildings and open areas.

From the sign you can see the farmsite in the distance. When you reach it, you find a house, an old barn and the remnants of other buildings. In front of the house there is a handmade plank bench on which you can sit as you look out over a meadow. Inside the house you can see a wooden table, rusted pails with wire handles (which were probably used for berry picking) and a wood stove made from an oil drum.

Past the farmsite you cross a little bridge over a creek, from which the Ray family may have gotten its water. Take a few steps down the Deer Creek Trail, which is marked by sign on a fence here, to visit the Ray gravesite, where John and Alice Ray were buried.

Return to the path, now a narrower dirt trail over rocks and roots, and continue to the mineral springs. There are some steep sections, but it is an enjoyable walk through the forest. Eventually you cross a bridge over a little creek. Further on

there is a bridge over a wet section. Just after the wet section you reach a T junction in the path. The path to the left goes to a second parking lot along the gravel road. Go right a few steps to reach the mineral spring; according to the sign, it is rich in calcium, sodium, magnesium, chlorine and sulphur.

The small spring here has been bubbling away for centuries and the minerals carried by the water have slowly built a cone around it. The cone and the area surrounding it have been coloured a coppery golden yellow by the small amounts of iron oxide in the water.

Ray's Mineral Spring.

After you have seen the springs, you can return by the same path or you can walk for 1.0 kilometre (0.6 miles) to the second parking lot and then a further 1.6 kilometres (1.0 mile) along the road back to your vehicle.

You can turn back to return to Highway 5 or drive further along the gravel road to reach Clearwater Lake, where you can camp, picnic or hike, on trails that range from 2 to 26 kilometres (1.2 to 16 miles) in length. In the winter this road is kept open for people who like to winter camp and/or cross-country ski on the 80 kilometres (50 miles) of ski trails.

Birch Island to Valemount

Birch Island and Vavenby

In 11.3 kilometres (7.0 miles) up Highway 5 from Clearwater Valley Road, take the right turn for Birch Island–Lost Creek Road. You drive through part of the town of Birch Island and, to your left at kilometre 0.8 (mile 0.5) from the highway, is Dee's General Store. This store has been in the family for three generations and the present owners are maintaining its old-time charm while keeping it well stocked. Inside, black-and-white photographs and old advertising posters hang on the walls.

Then you cross the North Thompson River on a one-lane wooden bridge at kilometre 1.3 (mile 0.8) and are in another section of town. There is a walkway on the left side of the bridge for those who want to visit from one side of the river to the other on foot. After the bridge, the road curves left and you are soon on your way out of town and headed toward Vavenby via the quiet, scenic Lost Creek Road.

You are driving through the river valley and in 2 kilometres (1.2 miles) from the bridge you cross railway tracks, then you reach gravel at kilometre 3.3 (mile 2.1). The views switch between open farmland—where you might see

Waterfall Park

Wells Gray Provincial Park, established in 1939, is a wilderness park that covers approximately 530,000 hectares (1.31 million acres) of mountains, valleys, lakes, rivers and forests. It is home to over 150 different species of birds each year and 50 species of other animals, and one of the largest mountain caribou herds in BC lives here. This park was named after the Honourable A. Wells Gray, Minister of Lands for the province from 1930 to 1941.

The park is sometimes called 'the Waterfall Park' because of its abundance of waterfalls. In addition to Helmcken Falls (the best known) and Dawson Falls, you can reach many other waterfalls with a drive and a short hike: Moul Falls, Silvertip Falls and Sylvia and Goodwin falls (both on the Mahood River, on the west side of the Clearwater River), to name just a few. For information about the park, pick up a park brochure at the visitor information centre. An excellent book by Trevor Goward and Cathy Hickson, *Nature Wells Gray* (Lone Pine Publishing, 1996), is also available.

some old buildings—and trees. Occasionally you can see the river and highway to your left. This road has some sharp curves and it gets rougher the farther you go, but it is not so bad that you need to worry.

To your right at kilometre 11.9 (mile 7.4) there is a cairn out in the field. It is for Theodore and Dora Moilliet, second-generation farmers in the area. At kilometre 15.5 (mile 9.6) there is a sawmill to the left. Kilometre 16.7 (mile 10.4) brings you to a junction and pavement. Turn left onto the pavement and in 0.3 kilometres (0.2 miles) you cross a wooden bridge over the North Thompson River and then reach the town of Vavenby on Vavenby Bridge Road.

Originally an important hunting area for the Secwepemc (Shuswap) First Nation, the site of Vavenby was first called 'Peavine Flat' by settlers in the late 1800s. When the post office opened in 1910, the postmaster suggested the name 'Navenby,' after his home in England. However, the 'N' was read as a 'V' and 'Vavenby' was the result.

Follow the road through Vavenby and in 1.7 kilometres (1.1 miles) from the bridge you reach Highway 5.

Vavenby wooden bridge over the Fraser River.

The North Thompson River is to your right as you continue northward and, if you look to your right at kilometre 12.3 (mile 7.6) from Vavenby Bridge Road, you can briefly see the railway bridge over the river. At kilometre 14.6 (mile 9.1) there is a parking area to the right at a viewpoint for the Mad River Rapids. These rapids are on the North Thompson River where the Mad River enters it. You cross the Mad River at kilometre 14.8 (mile 9.2).

Unsolved Mystery #2

'Bunchgrass' Bill Hayworth was rumoured to have had a small fortune hidden in his cabin. The bars that he had placed on the windows and the multiple locks that he had on the metal door fuelled the gossip. But no one checked any further into the idea until one day in 1933, when Bill was found dead in his cabin, from a gunshot.

The police investigated the murder. They interviewed the man's friends and even had a few suspects, but were unable to arrest anyone because of lack of evidence. In the next few years, several people confessed to the killing, but they were found to be lying (and they had also confessed to other murders that they did not commit).

The mystery of who shot Bunchgrass Hayworth is still unsolved, as are the questions about his purported stash of money.

Wire Cache and Avola

At kilometre 28.7 (mile 17.8) from Vavenby Bridge Road you reach the Wire Cache Rest Area, where there is a playground for the children. It is to your right, beside the North Thompson River.

Wire Cache gets its name from the telegraph wire and equipment that was stockpiled here during the building of the ill-fated Collins Overland International Telegraph Line.

You reach Avola Frontage Road at kilometre 13.8 (mile 8.5) from Wire Cache. Avola, named after a village in Sicily, was previously called 'Stillwater Flats' because of the slow-moving river here.

You cross the North Thompson River and are down on the valley floor, with the river to your left and a rock wall to your right. Then you begin climbing and, at kilometre 31 (mile 19.2) from Wire Cache, the road to Little Hell's Gate Regional Park, West Messiter Forest Service Road, is to your left.

Turn onto the side road to Little Hell's Gate Regional Park. When you come to the gates for the park, there is a map that shows the 3.3-kilometre (2.1-mile) road to the parking lot. (Holiday trailers are not allowed into the park so, if you have one, leave it here.) There is a wheelchair-accessible viewing platform about 10 metres (33 feet) from the parking lot. From the platform you can see the North Thompson River as it squeezes between the rock walls of the narrow canyon.

When one member of the Overlanders party (see p. 33) and all of its horses were drowned trying to raft through this section of the North Thompson River, the remaining group made a 14-kilometre (9-mile), three-day detour around them.

Back on the highway, you reach Messiter Summit 1.5 kilometres (0.9 miles)

The Collins International Overland Telegraph

When an attempt to lay a telegraph cable across the Atlantic Ocean failed, Perry Collins, the US commercial agent in Russia, decided to build an overland line that would link the United States with Europe via British Columbia, Alaska and Siberia. Work was begun by Western Union Telegraph in the 1860s.

For two years the company explored the proposed route. The final route went from the US border to New Westminster and from there eastward and northward along the Cariboo Road to the gold-fields and beyond them to Telegraph Creek (see p. 102). Caches of equipment were set up along the route. Then, in 1866, a cable was successfully laid on the Atlantic floor. Work on the overland route—which had reached Fort Stager, near Kispiox (see p. 138)—was suspended a few months afterward and the caches were abandoned. The section of line from New Westminster to the Cariboo was later bought and maintained by the BC government. Under subsequent owners, parts of the line were in use until 1974.

from the turn-off for Little Hell's Gate. With an elevation of 765 metres (2510 feet), it is the highest point on Highway 5. You descend from the summit and then, at kilometre 15.7 (mile 9.8), you cross the North Thompson River again.

Blue River and Valemount

In 20.9 kilometres (13.0 miles) from the road for Little Hell's Gate you pass the sign for the settlement of Blue River. There are services located along the highway and the town is down Angus Horn Street. In addition, if you wish to relax on a beach or go swimming in a lake, turn onto Angus Horn Street, drive to Herb Bilton Way and turn left. You pass a ballpark and come to the playground, picnic area and beach on Eleanor Lake, named after the first white child born in the Blue River area. If you wish to camp for the night, continue past the beach, turn right and cross the railway tracks to the campsite.

Blue River, surrounded by mountains, sits at the confluence of the Blue and North Thompson rivers. It is a logging town that was once the regional railway divisional point, which meant employment for many people—in the station, roundhouse and freight sheds. Land values increased and agricultural settlement occurred because farmers could sell their products to the local stores or send them to larger centres on the train. But prosperity for the area lasted only until a switch-over toward highway travel resulted in cutbacks for the railway.

The road to Murtle Lake (in Wells Gray Provincial Park) is just past the turn-off into Blue River. The parking area is 23.0 kilometres (14.3 miles) down the gravel road and then you have to walk a further 2.5 kilometres (1.6 miles) to a campground on Murtle Lake, the largest lake in North America that is closed to motorized boats.

The North Thompson River is to your right and, as you catch glimpses of it, you can see that it is not as wide as it was near Kamloops, because you are now closer to its source.

Blue River sign.

You cross the Thunder River in 13.8 kilometres (8.6 miles) from the turn-off for Murtle Lake. Between kilometre 39.7 (mile 24.7) and kilometre 44.3 (mile 27.5), you cross the North Thompson River three times. After the third bridge, the river turns away from the highway.

Gosnell Road is to your left at kilometre 44.8 (mile 27.8). The settlement of Gosnell is now just a railway siding, but it began in the early 1900s under the name 'North Thompson' and by 1913 it was a boom town with restaurants, hotels and a mill. It was later named after R. Edward Gosnell, a writer who was secretary to Premier Dunsmuir and who later became the first provincial librarian and the first provincial archivist.

Unsolved Mystery #3

Among western Canada's first 'tourists' were Viscount William Milton and Dr. Walter Cheadle from England. *Northwest Passage by Land*, published in 1865, is the account of their travels across the virtually unpopulated prairies and mountains to reach Fort Victoria. The account tells of how after reaching Fort Edmonton, they headed through the Yellowhead Pass and onward to Kamloops.

South of where Blue River is today, they came upon the headless body of a Native male beside an old fire. Near him were his axe, a cooking kettle and two birch baskets with fish hooks, net and onions. He was wearing pants and a shirt and had been there so long that his skin was like parchment. Although his head was missing, it seemed apparent that he had died of illness and starvation.

Milton and Cheadle searched for the man's head but were unable to find it, so they buried the body without it.

In the 1870s, a railway construction crew nearby found some fishing line, a kettle and a spoon at the site. Along the river bank they also found a skull, which they believed belonged to the headless Native, and they buried it.

Although the head had eventually been found, the mystery of how it became detached from the body still remains.

At kilometre 65.0 (mile 40.4) you pass the road into the settlement of Albreda, also just a siding and a few houses in the trees along the highway. The road to Kinbasket Lake is to your right at kilometre 86.6 (mile 53.8). It is 37 kilometres (23 miles) to the lake, which was formed when the Mica Dam was built across the Columbia River in the 1970s (see *Backroads of Southern Interior British Columbia*, Chapter 11).

To your right at kilometre 88.5 (mile 55.0) is the parking area for Cranberry Marsh and Starratt Wildlife Sanctuary. Cranberry Marsh began as a glacial lake after the last ice age and has slowly dried over the centuries. The wildlife sanctuary was started when over 200 hectares (500 acres) of the wetland was donated to the province by Mrs. Starratt in memory of her husband, Robert, in 1969.

There is a sign at the parking lot that explains the 7.0 kilometres (4.3 miles) of hiking trails, which follow dikes and go through the wetlands and woodlands.

There is also a historic marker for a train wreck that took place on November 21, 1951, 10 kilometres (6.2 miles) south of here. Seventeen soldiers on their way to Fort Lewis, Washington, for training—before heading to Korea—were killed when their troop train collided with the CNR Trans-Continental. Two engineers and two fireman also died.

As you walk down the trail to the marsh, you come to wooden plaques with drawings and names of the trees that grow behind them. There are also information panels that tell you about the sanctuary and about the waterfowl of the marsh.

The sanctuary is on the south end of Valemount. From the parking lot, take the highway the rest of the way into the town. Valemount originated as a logging camp and then became a stop on the railway. Its name means 'valley amid the mountains,' which is appropriate, given that it is situated where the Rocky, Cariboo and Monashee mountain ranges meet. (Monashee is Gaelic for 'mountain and peace.')

In 1.7 kilometres (1.1 miles) from the sanctuary, Fifth Avenue is to your right. Turn onto it and follow it to Main Street (old Highway 5). Turn left on Main and drive to Juniper and on your right is the Valemount and Area Museum, located in the restored 1914 Railway Station. Here you will find antique sewing machines in the sewing room, displays of old lanterns and typewriters, a kitchen with a wood stove, a bedroom with wash-basin and pitcher, and much more. It is open between 10 AM and 8 PM daily, from the end of June to the end of August.

Return to Highway 5. If you are here in August and you want to see spawning salmon—or even if it's not August and you would enjoy a lovely stroll through the park—cross the highway to Pine Road and immediately turn right onto the road to the parking area for the spawning channel in George Hicks Park.

From the parking lot you can walk onto a viewing platform over the channel—or you can walk beside the water—to see the spawning chinook salmon that have taken 10 weeks to travel the 1280 kilometres (800 miles) up the Fraser River to here.

Swift Creek salmon spawning channel in George Hicks Park in Valemount.

When you come back to Highway 5, turn left. You cross Swift Creek and, in 6.0 kilometres (3.7 miles) from the creek, the Terry Fox Rest Area is to your left. Here there is a picture of Terry Fox and the mountain named after him, as well as a sign that explains Terry's Marathon of Hope run in 1980, which was to raise money for cancer research. There is another Terry Fox Rest Area along Highway 16 (see p. 34 to read more about this Canadian hero).

At kilometre 12.7 (mile 7.9) from the rest area there is a road to the left for Tête Jaune Cache. However, you will have a chance to see this town in Chapter 2 (see p. 36). You cross the Fraser River at kilometre 13.2 (mile 8.2) and reach the junction with Highway 16.

You can turn right here and head into Mount Robson Provincial Park, where the trips in Chapter 2 actually begin, or you can turn left and skip that part, and start with the section on Tête Jaune Cache.

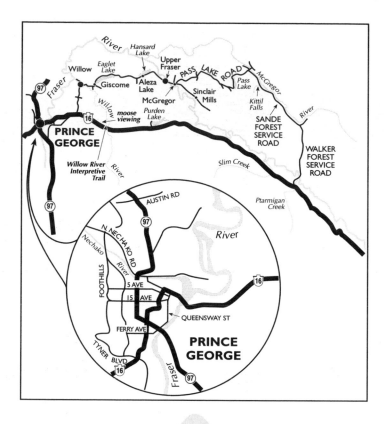

2
Mount Robson Provincial Park to Prince George

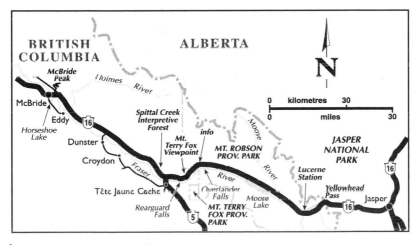

This chapter begins along Highway 16, where Jasper National Park on the Alberta side meets BC's Mount Robson Provincial Park. It then heads westward via Highway 16 and other roads to the city of Prince George. One of the country roads that you will travel on is part of a road that was in use before Highway 16 was built and another takes you through small towns that were once stops along the railway.

Many of the highlights in this chapter come in twos. On this route you can view both the highest mountain in the Canadian Rockies and a mountain named for a national hero; you can drive up to two lookouts for great panoramic views of the Fraser River; and you can hike through two interpretive forests. As for waterfalls, this route boasts not two but four of them.

Jasper National Park is one of Canada's great Rocky Mountain parks. In case you wish to make a side trip into Alberta to see it, here is a brief overview of some of what it has to offer. For more information, pick up brochures at the visitor information centre in the large stone building at 500 Connaught Drive, the main street through the town of Jasper.

Jasper is a tourist town with plenty of gift and souvenir shops and restaurants. You can easily spend a full day browsing through the shops and enjoying the surrounding mountain scenery. To see Maligne Canyon and Medicine and Maligne lakes, go northeast of Jasper on Highway 16 for 1.7 kilometres (1.1 miles) and turn east to cross the Athabasca River and begin following Maligne Lake Road. Each of these three highlights is marked by signs; the last, Maligne Lake, is 44.3 kilometres (27.5 miles) from the highway.

To get to Miette Hot Springs, you need to go 42.4 kilometres (26.3 miles) northeast of Jasper on Highway 16, then a further 17.6 kilometres (10.9 miles) up a side road to the southeast. You can reach the Columbia Icefields, with the famous Athabasca Glacier, by going 103 kilometres (64 miles) southeast of Jasper on the Icefields Parkway (Highway 93). On the way there you pass Athabasca and Sunwapta falls.

Mount Robson Provincial Park

Mount Robson Provincial Park, created in 1913, is the second oldest park in British Columbia and has an area of 217,200 hectares (536,690 acres). The Great Divide separates Mount Robson Provincial Park from Jasper National Park and British Columbia from Alberta. Highway 16 crosses the Great Divide at Yellowhead Pass, which has an elevation of 1131 metres (3710 feet). During the days of the fur trade, Yellowhead Pass was called 'the Leather Pass' because of the large number of moose hides carried from the Athabasca River area westward across the pass into central BC, which was then 'New Caledonia' (New Scotland), a name given by the explorer Simon Fraser.

At kilometre 5.7 (mile 3.5) from the border, stop at the pull-out to your right for a historic site about the Japanese internment camps set up along the Yellowhead Highway during World War II. Men staying in these camps were pressed into service to help build the highway through here.

Yellowhead Lake appears on your right and at kilometre 7.2 (mile 4.5) there is a turn-off for a boat launch. During the time of the fur trade, Yellowhead and Lucerne lakes were thought of as one body of water, which was known as Cow (or Buffalo) Dung Lake.

At kilometre 8.6 (mile 5.3), Lucerne Station Road is to your right. Turn onto this one-lane gravel road that leads to the old Lucerne station and the Yellowhead Mountain Trail. You cross four culverts over the narrows between Yellowhead and Whitney lakes and, at kilometre 1 (mile 0.6), you reach the trailhead, the railway tracks and an old red building with a red fence around it—the Lucerne station.

If you hike the Yellowhead Mountain Trail as far as the viewpoint, it could take you 45 minutes to cover the 1.8 kilometres (1.1 miles). If you decide to go all the way to the alpine meadow at the end of the trail, expect to take at least four hours (one way) for the 10 kilometres (6 miles). Be sure to sign the register at the trailhead and sign out upon your return.

In 3.9 kilometres (2.4 miles) from Lucerne Station Road you come to the Fraser River. It was named for Simon Fraser who, in 1808, followed the river to the Pacific Ocean. Look to your left as you cross the bridge to see the concrete pilings of the old railway bridge. At this river crossing, a drop of water that began at the source of the Fraser River some 50 kilometres (30 miles) upstream (still within Mount Robson Provincial Park) has another 1320 kilometres (820 miles) or so to go before it reaches the Pacific Ocean.

The Yellowhead Name

At one time it was believed that there were three men after whom Yellowhead Pass could have been named. One was François Decoigne, a trapper who ran Rocky Mountain House (later Jasper House and then Jasper) in 1814. The second was another trapper, Jasper Hawes, who took over Jasper House in 1817. The third, Pierre Hatsinaton, was the candidate that most people agree upon as being the most likely. Hatsinaton was a part-Iroquois man who guided a trading party from St. Mary's House, at the outflow of the Smoky River, over the pass and into British Columbia. His blond hair resulted in the nickname 'Tête Jaune,' French for 'yellow head.'

However, in 1984 a Parks Canada historian contended that the name 'Yellowhead' should be actually be attributed to Pierre Bostonais. This blond mixed-blood Iroquois, also known as 'Tête Jaune' and employed by both the North West and Hudson's Bay fur-trading companies during his life, had cached (stored) his furs in the area west of the pass.

When a settlement was begun in the vicinity of the cache, it was called 'Tête Jaune Cache.' When the pass and later the highway were named, they were given the English version of the name, 'Yellowhead.'

Old railway supports at the Fraser River.

In 1911, when the Grand Trunk Pacific Railway was being constructed, a town called Moose City was quickly built at the confluence of the Fraser and Moose rivers. Like most of the instant towns that sprang up around the railway, it had its saloons, bordellos, thieves and gunfights. And, like most of those towns, it died after the advent of the automobile era.

You cross the Fraser River again at kilometre 5.1 (mile 3.2), and at kilometre 15.9 (mile 9.9) you drive over the Moose River bridge. To see Moose River Falls, turn right onto the gravel side road at kilometre 16.3 (mile 10.1).

You cross the railway tracks and start climbing on a one-lane road. At kilometre 1.2 (mile 0.7) the road curves to the left. To your right at the curve there is an area where you can park and take a path that heads into the woods. It will take you to the edge of a canyon (there is no fence, so hike it at your own risk). If you look down from there, you can see part of a smaller waterfall splashing into the canyon below.

If you want to see a larger waterfall, continue around the curve and drive 0.2 kilometres (0.1 miles) further to another spot where you can park. This path climbs up a low hill and into the woods. It too ends at the canyon edge and again there is no fence, so use care. You can see the falls through the trees.

On your way back down to the highway, you have a lovely view of the valley and Moose Lake ahead in the distance. Once you are back on Highway 16, in a

Overlander Falls.

The Overlanders

Word of the Cariboo Gold Rush spread around the world and, in spring 1862, the British Overland Transit Company advertised that it would take passengers from Liverpool, England, to the gold-fields. However, once the gold-seekers reached Toronto, they discovered that their passage ended there.

Determined to continue, 'the Overlanders,' as they were called, went by rail to St. Paul, Minnesota, and then by steamer and wagon to Fort Garry (now Winnipeg, Manitoba), which they reached at the end of May. Here, during a short layover, they were joined by others wanting to go to the gold-fields. These additional travellers included Francis Schubert, his pregnant wife Catherine (the only woman to make the trek) and their three children.

The Overlanders bought horses, oxen and Red River carts for their supplies. They divided into three groups, each with a leader, and left Fort Garry in the beginning of June 1862, on what was expected to be a two-month journey. They reached Fort Edmonton and sighted the Rocky Mountains in the middle of August. Heading over the Yellowhead Pass, they arrived at Tête Jaune Cache at the end of the month. Their supplies were almost depleted and so they traded with a band of Secwepemc (Shuswap) Natives for berries and salmon.

At Tête Jaune Cache they divided again, with most of the travellers heading down the Fraser River to Quesnel. They found that most of the gold-rich rivers had already been staked, so they took jobs working on other people's claims or in town.

The remaining 36, including the Schuberts, decided to go to Kamloops, where Catherine Schubert gave birth to a daughter, Rose. Mrs. Schubert's husband had died on the journey and she subsequently remarried. Most of the other members of the party worked at various jobs for a while, then moved to other parts of the province.

None of the Overlanders made a fortune in the Cariboo Gold Rush.

---

further 2.7 kilometres (1.7 miles) you have Moose Lake to your left. It has a picnic area and a boat launch. The highway follows the lake and you can watch sailboats, motorboats and water-skiers out on the water in summer. During the construction of the railway, a barge loaded with rum sank in the lake. It is believed that the rum has not yet been recovered.

Kilometre 30.9 (mile 19.2) brings you to the pull-out on your left for the trail to Overlander Falls on the Fraser River. The wide trail goes downhill most of the way to the falls, so make sure that you are in good enough shape for the return climb.

These falls were named after 'the Overlanders,' a group who passed by here in late August 1862 on their way to the Cariboo Gold Rush.

In 1.4 kilometres (0.9 miles) from the Overlander Falls pull-out, 3954-metre (12,970-foot) high Mount Robson rises behind the Mount Robson Visitor Information Centre. Mount Robson, the highest mountain in the Canadian Rockies, is usually shrouded in cloud. If you are lucky, the sun will be shining and the white peak will be visible against the blue sky.

You cross the Robson River 1.4 kilometres (0.8 miles) from Mount Robson and at kilometre 2.2 (mile 1.3) you leave Mount Robson Provincial Park.

Mount Robson.

Mount Terry Fox to Dunster

Mount Terry Fox and Rearguard Falls

To your left at kilometre 9.0 (mile 5.6) from Mount Robson is the Mount Terry Fox Rest Area, which has a picnic site with a view of Mount Terry Fox.

Mount Terry Fox and picnic site.

When Terry Fox was 18, his right leg was amputated just above the knee as a result of cancer. Four years later, he started from St. John's, Newfoundland, beginning his Marathon of Hope run across Canada to raise money for cancer research. However, he made only the first 5375 kilometres (3340 miles) before having to quit, because the cancer was spreading to his lungs. He died on June 28, 1981, but his legacy has continued, with Terry Fox runs being held every year around the world to raise money for cancer research. Mount Terry Fox was officially dedicated to his memory on September 22, 1981. There is a cairn on its summit.

The Spittal Creek Interpretive Forest

The Spittal Creek Interpretive Forest is located along Highway 16 at kilometre 6.7 (mile 4.2) from Highway 5. You will pass it if you choose to stay on Highway 16 for the 27.6 kilometres (17.2 miles) between Highway 5 and the side road from Dunster instead of taking the route through Tête Jaune Cache and South Croydon, as is described in the text.

Look for the interpretive forest on the right. Beside the parking lot there is a picnic area. A map here shows the routes for the trails that lead among the tall trees and beside the creek in this 294-hectare (726-acre) forest. There are two choices: the half-hour, 1.3-kilometre (0.8-mile) Creek Trail and the one-hour, 1.8-kilometre (1.1-mile) Pine Trail.

Spittal Creek was named after Bill Spittal, who 'salted' a gold claim (added bits of gold from elsewhere) here and then convinced two Irishmen to buy him supplies in return for being allowed to pan for gold on it. After three days they still hadn't seen a speck of gold. When Bill found out, he is said to have yelled, 'Darn it. There ought to be gold here because I put it here.'

On the left side of the road in 3.2 kilometres (2.0 miles) from the Mount Terry Fox Rest Area, pull in at the parking lot for Rearguard Falls. Follow the path and, just after you begin, you reach a Y. Going right would take you a few steps to the upper lookout, but the best place to see the falls is at the lower lookout, so go left. It is downhill all the way and it is a surprise when you get to the lookout, because you are standing at a fence right on the edge of the falls. The waterfall isn't very high, but the water is forceful and the effect is hypnotic as it churns over the rock at your feet.

At kilometre 3.3 (mile 2.1) from the falls you reach the junction with Highway 5 (to Kamloops). Just after that junction, turn left onto Blackman Road, which goes to Tête Jaune Cache. Go left almost immediately afterward at the T intersection. You cross the Fraser River and reach Tête Jaune Cache at kilometre 1.4 (mile 0.9) from the highway.

Rearguard Falls from Lower Viewpoint.

Tête Jaune Cache, South Croydon and Dunster

Tête Jaune Cache, as was mentioned on p. 31, was named for a blond trapper who cached some supplies and furs here in the early 1800s. The Overlanders (see p. 33) reached Tête Jaune Cache on September 27, 1862, almost out of supplies. Here they traded shirts, needles, ammunition and whatever else they had in exchange for berries and smoked salmon from the Secwepemc.

During the construction of the Canadian Northern Railway (CNR) tracks, Tête Jaune Cache, at the head of navigation on the Fraser River, was a shipping centre to which sternwheelers brought supplies and equipment, having travelled some 640 kilometres (400 miles) up the Fraser from Soda Creek. At its peak it had over 3000 residents, but now it is a small village in the centre of a farming area.

Drive through the community and, at kilometre 3.4 (mile 2.1) from the highway, turn right onto the Croydon–Tête Jaune Cache Forest Service Road. This road is the original one that went from Tête Jaune Cache to Dunster before Highway 16 was built. In August you can see spawning salmon at the Spawning Grounds/Tête Jaune Cache Recreation Site. To get there, turn off to the right 2.5 kilometres (1.6 miles) from where you began on this road. (Note that this very narrow side road is not suitable for a motorhome or large holiday trailer.) Then head left at the Y intersection and in 0.6 kilometres (0.4 miles) you reach the recreation site. Park here and walk down to the river to watch the salmon.

Back at the forest service road, turn right to continue along it and in 2.9 kilometres (1.8 miles) from the salmon-spawning turn-off you reach gravel. At kilometre 4.7 (mile 2.9) you cross a triple set of railway tracks. This crossing marks the old site of

Fraser River and Robson Valley from Croydon–Tête Jaune Cache road viewpoint.

Tête Jaune Cache and, if you look to your left, you can see the CNR's 'Tête Jaune' sign. The road follows a slough, which has lily pads, reeds and ducks, and then begins to climb. Kilometre 11.4 (mile 7.1) brings you to a small pull-out on your right from which you have a view over the Fraser River and the Robson Valley. Across the river you can see an old building site, farmland and mountains.

At kilometre 14.5 (mile 9.0) you pass the junction with the Kiwa–Tête Jaune Cache Forest Service Road, which goes to your left. Continue ahead and at kilometre 14.9 (mile 9.3) you cross Kiwa Creek. Then, at kilometre 24.9 (mile 15.5), you cross a set of railway tracks and the Croydon Cemetery is to your right shortly afterward.

You arrive in downtown South Croydon at kilometre 26.1 (mile 16.2). It consists of The Bears' Lair Studio Gallery, which is in the former post office and store to your right, and the one-room schoolhouse, where the gallery's owners live. Those two buildings are all that is left of the town. Once a bustling logging community with 180 residents, its population is now four. Stop in at The Bears' Lair to see the variety of paintings, jewellery, tatting (knotted lace) and fabric art.

In 10.2 kilometres (mile 6.4) from The Bears' Lair you reach pavement at the community of Dunster. To your right is Hill's Store; to your left is the Dunster Station, one of the few remaining railway stations that were built in this part of the country in the early 1900s. It is not in use and the doors and windows are boarded up. Turn right 0.5 kilometres (0.3 miles) from the station. You cross the Fraser River and at kilometre 3.7 (mile 2.3) you arrive back at Highway 16. Turn left onto the highway.

You cross the Holmes River, known locally as 'the Beaver River,' in 18.5 kilometres (11.5 miles) from Dunster Road. Just after the bridge, turn right into the parking area for Beaver Falls. The falls themselves are not much to see, but the walk through the trees beside the river is lovely. At the falls the water divides around a rock behind which is a jam of old logs and debris.

Beaver Falls on Holmes River.

McBride to Prince George

McBride

In 8.5 kilometres (5.3 miles) from the Holmes River, turn right onto Mountainview Road to go to McBride Peak. (If you are driving a motorhome, it should have a powerful motor for what lies ahead and, if you are pulling a holiday trailer, leave it in the town of McBride, which is a little further along the highway.) When you reach Rainbow Road in 0.5 kilometres (0.3 miles) from the highway, turn right onto it. It is a narrow, rough gravel road that immediately begins to climb. It is a constant climb through tree-lined roads for 6.1 kilometres (3.8 miles) to the McBride Peak Lookout.

At the lookout there are picnic tables and you can enjoy a lunch as you look down on the town of McBride, the Fraser River, the highway, farmland and the mountains across the valley. Look for Horseshoe Lake, named for its shape, near the town. There is a wetland at the lake that you can visit when you reach McBride. On your return trip down the mountainside, remember to use a lower gear.

When you reach Mountainview Road, turn left onto it and drive back toward the highway. Just before the stop sign at the highway, turn right onto Koeneman Road, which runs parallel to the highway. Follow it as it curves right to take you to Koeneman Regional Park in 0.7 kilometres (0.4 miles). Park in the parking area and walk across the large lawn and around the clump of trees to the old log buildings that were constructed by early settler Fred Koeneman in the 1930s. There is also a boat launch on the Fraser River at the park.

View from McBride Peak.

Old log house in Koeneman Regional Park in McBride.

Back on the highway, you soon cross the Fraser River and reach McBride. To get to the Horseshoe Lake Wetland Conservation Project, turn left onto Main Street, drive under the big 'Welcome to McBride' sign and stay on this street to Eddy Road (2nd Avenue). Turn left onto Eddy Road and follow it 0.6 kilometres (0.4 miles) to Horseshoe Lake Road, where you again turn left. In 0.5 kilometres (0.3 miles) is the parking area for the project. Follow the short, wheelchair-accessible boardwalk to a gazebo that overlooks the lake, which was once an elbow of the Fraser River. Watch for birds—such as the blue heron, swans, ducks and geese—and also for moose, deer and bear.

Horseshoe Lake Wetland Conservation Project in McBride.

Walker and Sande Forest Service Roads

As you drive along the highway, watch for Ptarmigan Creek at kilometre 69.5 (mile 43.2) from McBride's Main Street and then continue past it to kilometre 71.6 (mile 44.5), where Walker Forest Service Road goes off to the right. If you would like to drive some of the backroads in this area and perhaps have a picnic beside a pretty waterfall, turn onto it. (If you would rather follow Highway 16 to Prince George, skip ahead to p. 44.)

You will be driving on rough gravel roads with potholes, so plan on taking five to six hours for the drive. Although narrow in places, it is still suitable for a motorhome or to pull a trailer on. The scenery is mainly trees, but with some mountain views.

In 5.3 kilometres (3.3 miles) you cross railway tracks and then a one-lane bridge takes you over the Fraser River. At kilometre 6.6 (mile 4.1) you come to a Y junction, where you go left. Walker Creek is at kilometre 21.2 (mile 13.2). At the end of a bridge there is a very primitive campsite to your left. The road into the campground is a bit further along and you have to make a sharp left turn to get to it. Neither a motorhome nor a truck pulling a holiday trailer could make that turn. The campsite is better suited to more manageable vehicles whose occupants plan to sleep in tents or campers.

At kilometre 32.0 (mile 19.9) you reach Sande Forest Service Road, where you turn left. This road is rougher, and you shouldn't drive it during or just after a rain. You are still driving through the woods and the McGregor River is off to your right. Keep watch for the mountain scenery that shows through gaps in the trees. You climb for a ways and at kilometre 7.0 (mile 4.3) you reach the top of a hill where you have a great view of the McGregor Valley before starting down into it. Watch for glimpses of the river to your right. You cross some bridges and then, at kilometre 33.3 (mile 20.7), turn left to go to Kittil Falls Recreation Site (the sign faces in the opposite direction). From the roadside parking area it is a short walk to the falls, which are high and slim. There is a picnic table at the falls if you wish to carry your lunch along and eat it there.

After the recreation site you have good views of the McGregor River. Kilometre 8.8 (mile 5.5) brings you to the last bridge on Sande Forest Service Road, and at kilometre 9.3 (mile 5.8) you reach a T intersection where you turn left.

You are now on a wide gravel road but it is still bumpy. In 7.3 kilometres (4.5 miles) from the intersection, Pass Lake Forest Service Recreation Site is to your left. At kilometre 41.4 (mile 25.7) you reach a maintenance yard in McGregor, a logging town. Go to the stop sign past the yard and turn left if you want to see the town of Sinclair Mills. Go right if you want to bypass it.

Kittil Falls on Sande Forest Service Road.

Sinclair Mills, Upper Fraser and Willow River

The small towns that you will be travelling through on this section began as stations along the railway. Their populations are supported by the lumber industry and farming.

At kilometre 7.7 (mile 4.8), after turning left at the stop sign, you reach Sinclair Mills, a small place spread out along the road. Look for the sign that marks the Thistle Patch Market Garden, where you can stop to buy vegetables in season, and, further into town, an old, rusted burner from a sawmill.

Return to McGregor and begin measuring distance at the stop sign as you go past it in the other direction. At kilometre 0.9 (mile 0.6) you reach Hansard Bridge, a vehicle/railway bridge across the Fraser River. The traffic over this bridge is controlled by a traffic light. At the other end you make a sharp turn to the right and the railway tracks continue straight ahead. There is a walkway on the side of the bridge if you wish to go back and look down at the river.

After the bridge you are on pavement and by kilometre 8.5 (mile 5.3) you come to Upper Fraser, another mill town. If you look to your right at kilometre 13.0 (mile 8.1) you can see Hansard Lake and at kilometre 14.5 (mile 9.0), also to your right, you can see Aleza Lake. The hamlet of Aleza Lake is along the highway for 2.0 kilometres (1.2 miles) beginning at kilometre 15.8 (mile 9.8).

This road has a few sharp curves and then kilometre 28.5 (mile 17.7) brings you to the beginning of a 12-kilometre (7.5-mile) long stretch of winding road.

Hansard Bridge over Fraser River near McGregor.

You begin driving beside Eaglet Lake, which is much longer than the previous two lakes, and at kilometre 37.2 (mile 23.1) you reach 13-hectare (32-acre) Harold Mann Regional Park, to your left on the lakeshore. This park was named after Harold deWolfe Mann, who brought truck logging to the Prince George area in the 1930s and who worked on many community projects in Prince George after his retirement. It has a picnic area and a small beach with changing rooms.

At kilometre 1.1 (mile 0.7) from the park there is a boat launch on the lake. The road follows the lake until kilometre 4.0 (mile 2.5) and then you pass a school in the community of Giscome and drive through farmland.

Game Fish Habitat Improvement

Within the waters of Eaglet Lake there are three species of game fish: Dolly Varden, burbot (ling cod) and rainbow trout. In order to spawn successfully, the last of these, rainbow trout, need water with a specific oxygen content, a certain depth and the right current speed, and gravel of a certain size and shape.

The first three conditions already existed in Bateman Creek, which flows from the outlet of Eaglet Lake, but the size and shape of the gravel was not suitable. To make the creek a better spawning area for the trout and thus ensuring more fish for anglers, the right kind of gravel was brought from elsewhere and dumped into the creek, and structures were built to hold it from washing away.

At kilometre 12.1 (mile 7.5) you reach the hamlet of Willow River, just 0.4 kilometres (0.2 miles) before you cross a one-lane bridge over the Willow River. Look to your left at kilometre 23.6 (mile 14.7) for Rustic Furniture. You can see all the willow chairs and other furniture set up in the yard and, if there is anything you like, stop in and discuss price with the owners. In 28.3 kilometres (17.6 miles) from the park you reach Highway 16, where you turn right to go toward Prince George.

At kilometre 12.5 (mile 7.8) along the highway you reach the junction with Highway 97, which goes southward to Quesnel. Then at kilometre 14.0 (mile 8.7) you start downhill and can see the Fraser and Nechako rivers and Prince George ahead. If you want to see the sights of Prince George, you can follow the signs for the visitor information centre. Otherwise stay on Highway 16 to where it meets with Highway 97 north and then head for Dawson Creek along the route described in Chapter 3.

Eaglet Lake.

The Highway Route from Walker Forest Service Road to Prince George

From Walker Forest Service Road, continue west on Highway 16. You reach Dome Diner Truckstop and Dome Creek Road at kilometre 15.4 (mile 9.6). A rest area on Slim Creek is to your left at kilometre 18.7 (mile 11.6) and you cross Slim Creek at kilometre 20.1 (mile 12.5).

At kilometre 81.5 (mile 50.6), turn right to go to Purden Lake Provincial Park.

In 2.0 kilometres (1.2 miles) from the highway you come to a set of signs to the right that tell about lakeshore ecology, the plants and animals of Purden Lake and how they help each other, and the life cycle of the rainbow trout.

Purden Lake Provincial Park has a boat launch, a picnic area, a campground and a lovely beach.

In 1976, work was begun to improve the outflow creek of Purden Lake—mostly through the addition of gravel to selected spawning sites—and therefore increase the number of sport fish in the lake. Then, in 1977, 8000 egg-bearing shrimp were transported from Dragon Lake (near Quesnel) to Purden Lake, where they multiplied, thus giving the fish a bigger food supply.

In 24.1 kilometres (15.0 miles) from the turn-off for the park you reach the Willow River. Look down into the canyon below as you cross the bridge. To your

The Mile 141 Bridge

Near the end of August 1913, the *BC Express* was making its usual trip up the Fraser River when it came to a cable stretched from bank to bank, blocking its path. Sternwheelers had by then been plying the Fraser River for half a century. The *BC Express* worked the upper part of the river, earning its owners, the BC Express Company, $5000 in profits per month.

The cable across the river had been placed there by railway contractors laying track for the Grand Trunk Pacific Railway as it forged westward across the country. When deciding on the kind of bridge to build across the Fraser near Dome Creek, the contractors, with the approval of the Board of Railway Commissioners, had, in order to save time and money on construction, intentionally omitted provisions for sternwheelers to continue their upriver journey past this point.

Although the captain of the *BC Express* wanted to stay and fight the railway contractors, he was persuaded to turn around and head downstream.

The shippers protested the lack of a lift span for the bridge and the railway received a court order to build the span. But the railway company, wanting to complete the job quickly without changing the grade of the tracks and the design of the bridge, defied the order and constructed the bridge as originally planned. The courts found in favour of the railway when a lawyer representing the BC Express Company bungled his job, and so the bridge remained, effectively limiting river travel by the sternwheelers.

The Mile 141 Bridge, named for its distance from Lillooet at the headwaters of the Fraser, is to the northeast of the highway near Dome, BC.

How Prince George Came to Be

The explorer Alexander Mackenzie camped at the confluence of the Nechako and Fraser rivers in 1793 on his way to the coast. (Read more about his journey in the sidebar on p. 165.) Simon Fraser spent some time in the area exploring for the North West Company in 1806 and in 1807 the company established Fort George, in honour of King George III, at the junction.

Word of a railway coming through the area in the early 1900s attracted speculators. One was George Hammond, who surveyed land about 3 kilometres (2 miles) from the fort and began to sell lots in his town, which he called 'Central Fort George.' By 1910, an increase of population prompted South Fort George to be founded about 5 kilometres (3 miles) south of Fort George on the shore of the Fraser River. Steamers docked here, passengers disembarked and freight was unloaded. Both towns prospered until 1914, when the railway came through and established its own town, Prince George, between them.

right just after the bridge is the Willow River Rest Area, which features the Willow River Interpretive Trail.

The trail is 1.9 kilometres (1.2 miles) long and it will take you from 45 minutes to one hour to visit the 17 different sites and read the signs. At the beginning of the trail, the first information panel introduces you to the trees—Douglas-fir, spruce, pine, cottonwood, aspen, birch and balsam—that you will see on your walk.

The rest area is also the site of a cairn dedicated to eight teenagers who died in a canoeing accident on May 10, 1974, while trying to navigate an impassable canyon a short distance downstream from here.

Just 3.8 kilometres (2.4 miles) from the rest area there is a place to park if you want to visit a moose observation site. A map here shows you the trail to the viewing tower, which you can reach with a leisurely 10-minute walk. Climb up the steps and look for moose out in the five areas that stretch like fingers into the trees. The trail continues further to the Willow River Canyon.

Back on Highway 16, you pass the road to the town of Willow River and, at kilometre 26.5 (mile 16.5), you begin to go downhill and can see the Fraser and Nechako rivers and Prince George spread out ahead.

View from moose-viewing platform.

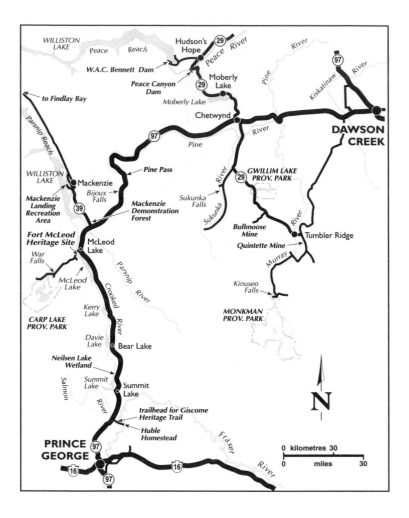

WILLISTON LAKE

Peace Reach

Hudson's Hope (29)

Peace River

River

(97)

W.A.C. Bennett Dam

Peace Canyon Dam

Moberly Lake

(29)

Pine

Kiskatinaw

River

to Findlay Bay

Moberly Lake

Chetwynd

River

DAWSON CREEK

Parsnip Reach

(97)

Pine

River

WILLISTON LAKE

Mackenzie

Pine Pass

GWILLIM LAKE PROV. PARK

(29)

Bijoux Falls

River

Mackenzie Landing Recreation Area

(39)

Mackenzie Demonstration Forest

Sukunka Falls

Sukunka

River

Fort McLeod Heritage Site

McLeod Lake

Bullmoose Mine

Tumbler Ridge

War Falls

McLeod Lake

Parsnip River

Quintette Mine

Murray

CARP LAKE PROV. PARK

Crooked River

Kerry Lake

Kinuseo Falls

Davie Lake

Bear Lake

MONKMAN PROV. PARK

Neilsen Lake Wetland

Summit Lake

Summit Lake

Salmon River

trailhead for Giscome Heritage Trail

N

Huble Homestead

Fraser

PRINCE GEORGE

(97)

River

(16)

(16)

| 0 | kilometres | 30 |
| 0 | miles | 30 |

(97)

3
Prince George to Dawson Creek

With this chapter you begin your journey into northern BC, and the sights and history described here will be very different from place to place. You will see dinosaurs, the first fur-trading post west of the Rockies and two large open-pit mines. You can camp on Williston Lake, Canada's largest man-made lake, and stand beside the world's largest tree crusher.

Along the way you can tour a historic homestead, tramp through a demonstration forest and visit four waterfalls. At one of them you can listen to the sound of war drums. There is truly a lot to see and experience in this area of the province.

Prince George to McLeod Lake

The Huble Homestead

Head northward out of Prince George on Highway 97, the John Hart Highway, and begin measuring your distance at Austin Road. You are in the Salmon River valley and you cross the Salmon River itself at kilometre 15.4 (mile 9.6). Kilometre 29.0 (mile 18.0) brings you to Mitchell Road. Turn right here to visit the Huble Homestead and see the Giscome Portage Trail.

To your left at kilometre 4.9 (mile 3.0) is the Giscome Heritage Trailhead and at kilometre 5.3 (mile 3.3) you enter the 22-hectare (54.4-acre) Giscome Portage Regional Park and reach the parking area for both the Huble Homestead and the Giscome Portage Trail. From the lot, walk down the hill to the homestead. There is a picnic area to your right before you pass through the gates.

The Giscome Portage Trail had been in use for many years already in 1904 when Albert Huble and Ed Seebach formed a partnership and opened a trading post where the Giscome Portage Trail began at the Fraser River. It was on Huble's homestead and soon an agriculture community, Giscome Portage, was established. Steamboats on the Fraser River on their way to Tête Jaune Cache stopped at the settlement. Huble and Seebach revamped the old portage trail to Summit Lake and set up a warehouse there. Giscome Portage died in 1919 as transportation routes changed.

At the homestead, the square-log house, built in 1912, is the only original building. The other farm buildings date from more recent periods in the life of the homestead, when it was leased or had different owners. In 1975 the province bought the property as a community pasture and in 1986 the regional park was established.

The site is open from the Victoria Day long weekend in May to the Thanksgiving long weekend in October and there are guides on site from 9:30 AM to 5:30 PM.

House at Huble Homestead.

The Giscome Portage Trail

Long before the non-Natives arrived, Natives used what became the Giscome Portage Trail to travel between the Fraser River and Summit Lake, which drains into the Crooked River, which in turn flows into the Peace River. When Simon Fraser came through this area in 1806, his Native guides took him over this portage, claiming that it would eliminate having to haul trade goods overland from Fort McLeod (see p. 50) to the newly established Fort St. James. However, the trail itself was low and wet and the Crooked River was too shallow and treacherous for freighting the goods, so the overland haul remained in use.

In 1863, two black men from the West Indies, Henry McDame and John Giscome, headed up the Fraser River to look for gold on the Peace River. (Also see the sidebar 'The Cassiar Gold Rush' on p. 97. Their guide took them over the portage trail, which soon became known to other travellers, as 'the Giscome Portage Trail.' However, it wasn't until the Omineca Gold Rush of 1869–71 took place north of Fort St. James that the trail became popular and the people of Quesnel petitioned the government to build a wagon road over the portage route to make access to the Omineca country easier.

The road was built and it was used for years until the telegraph trail from Quesnel to Fort Fraser became more popular. The Giscome Portage Trail was reconstructed in the early 1900s by Huble and Seebach and used until 1919, when a road was constructed that went directly from Prince George to Summit Lake.

These days the portage has been rebuilt for recreational users—it is about an 8-kilometre (5-mile) hike from the Fraser River to a pull-out on Highway 97 near Summit Lake.

Shortly after getting back on the highway, you come to a pull-out to your right where you can stop and read a write-up about the birds and animals to watch for as you drive through the Crooked River area.

There are two side roads to your left that go to Summit Lake. The first is at kilometre 2.7 (mile 1.7) from the pull-out. Summit Lake Forest Service Recreation Site, which is large and open, is 2.0 kilometres (1.2 miles) down it. The second road, for services, is at kilometre 6.1 (mile 3.8).

Neilsen Lake

To go to Neilsen Lake and the Neilsen Lake Wetland Conservation Project, take the left turn onto Tallus Road at kilometre 2.3 (mile 1.4) from the second road to Summit Lake. Then, in 0.9 kilometres (0.6 miles), turn right onto Caine Creek Forest Service Road and at kilometre 1.7 (mile 1.1) you reach the Neilsen Lake Wetland. Park beside the road and walk out to the marsh. Watch where you step, though, because the geese like walking here and have left their droppings.

Neilsen Lake Wetland.

For years a beaver dam maintained the water levels of the wetland, but in 1994 biologists noticed that the dam was decaying and falling apart. Knowing that about 70% of the wetland would be lost if the dam collapsed, they built a steel weir to preserve the wetland as habitat for the wildlife in the area.

Neilsen Lake is a lovely place to camp, swim, picnic or launch a boat. The road into the campsite on the lakeshore is just past the wetland.

As you drive along the highway after the turn-off for Neilsen Lake, you can occasionally see the Crooked River to your left through the trees. Beginning at kilometre 20.8 (mile 12.9), you pass through the community of Bear Lake, which has an inn, a gas station, a restaurant and RV park.

After the community of Bear Lake, you can see Davie Lake to your left at kilometre 22.6 (mile 14.0) from Neilsen Lake. Then comes Kerry Lake, at kilometre 43.7 (mile 27.2). Both of these lakes have forest service campsites and boat launches. McLeod Lake at kilometre 68.0 (mile 42.3) is next, and there are two provincial parks on its shore. These lakes are all connected by the Crooked River. The road follows McLeod Lake until you enter the hamlet of McLeod Lake at kilometre 85.7 (mile 53.3).

McLeod Lake

As you come into McLeod Lake, watch for the general store to your left. In the yard there is a cairn that commemorates Fort McLeod. Fort McLeod, also called 'the McLeod's Lake Post,' was established in the fall of 1805 by Simon Fraser. It

Workshop and house, built in 1929, at Fort McLeod Heritage Site.

was the North West Company's first fort west of the Rockies. After the Hudson's Bay and North West companies merged in 1821, the Hudson's Bay Company retained the fort as one of its posts into the 1950s.

To see the buildings at Fort McLeod, drive 0.4 kilometres (0.2 miles) along the highway from the cairn to Carp Lake Road. Turn left onto it and in 0.5 kilometres

(0.3 miles) you enter McLeod Lake Indian Reserve 1. At kilometre 0.8 (mile 0.5) there is a small black-and-white sign that says 'Heritage Site.' Turn left onto the narrow road and in 0.2 kilometres (0.1 miles) you reach the McLeod's Lake Post.

There are four buildings in a small meadow. The workshop, house and warehouse date from 1929 and the icehouse dates from 1944. At the Fort McLeod Heritage Site there is also an old cemetery. Two signs, one in the TseK'ehne language and one in English, tell the cemetery's history and explain how the burial customs of the TseK'ehne people changed with the arrival of Roman Catholic missionaries in the mid-1800s.

To go to War Falls and Carp Lake, return to Carp Lake Road and turn left. The road is narrow, winding and rough with potholes as you drive through tall trees. You pass the Warhorse Lake Recreation Site in 8.2 kilometres (5.1 miles) and the Sekani Lake Recreation Site at kilometre 15.0 (mile 9.3). You enter Carp Lake Provincial Park at kilometre 22.5 (mile 14.0). To your right there is a parking area. A map shows the park's trails, as well as the campground and the boat launch, which are at Kettle Bay on the large lake.

To reach the falls, take the trail that leads from this parking area and walk with the river to your left. There are three sections to the falls. As you come to the first one, listen: Can you hear the sound of thumping war drums that gives these falls their name? Continue onward to a set of steps that takes you down to another viewing area. Another set of stairs and a downhill path lead you past some small cascades to the second section of the falls and then you reach the end of the path at the viewpoint for the third section.

If you continue along the road for about 9 kilometres (6 miles) from the parking area, you will reach the Carp Lake campground. Carp Lake was named by Simon Fraser in 1806 for the carp-like fish that the Dakelh-ne (Carrier People) caught in the lake.

Return to Highway 97 and turn left to continue north.

Third section of War Falls.

Mackenzie to the W.A.C. Bennett Dam

Mackenzie

You cross the Parsnip River in 16.0 kilometres (9.9 miles) from Carp Lake Road and at kilometre 16.7 (mile 10.4) you turn left onto Highway 39 to go to Mackenzie. Just after the turn, look to your right for the first of eight self-guided trails in the Mackenzie Demonstration Forest.

The road to Mackenzie Landing on Williston Lake is to your left at kilometre 26.7 (mile 16.6) from Highway 97. If you wish to camp on Williston Lake at a place close to where Alexander Mackenzie camped in early June 1793 on his journey to the Pacific Ocean, turn onto this road and in 0.6 kilometres (0.4 miles) you reach a T intersection. Go right and you are on the Parsnip West Forest Service Road. At kilometre 6.2 (mile 3.9), turn left for the Mackenzie Landing Recreation Area, where camping is free. This part of the lake was a river in Mackenzie's time.

Because of the W.A.C. Bennett Dam (see p. 58), the main part of the lake now extends about 200 kilometres (125 miles) to the northwest from this campsite. The longest arm, Peace Reach, extends approximately 110 kilometres (70 miles) to the east from about the midpoint of the lake to just past the dam.

Past the turn-off for the recreation site you enter the town of Mackenzie and, to your right at kilometre 1.6 (mile 1.0) from the turn-off, the world's largest 'tree crusher' is on display in Tree Crusher Park. This huge yellow machine was built in Texas and brought to Mackenzie in 1964. It was used to push over and crush the trees of what was to become Williston Lake.

 The Mackenzie Demonstration Forest

Each of the eight loop trails in the Mackenzie Demonstration Forest is about 300 metres (1000 feet) long and takes about 30 minutes to walk. They are spaced along Highway 39, mainly on the right, and are marked by numbered signs of blue-and-white painted metal or unpainted wood.

Each of the trails has a display panel with a particular focus. At the first stop you find out about the plants, animals, water and soil of a mature forest. The second one, at kilometre 1.6 (mile 1.0) from the first, explains about replanting to grow a new forest. Number three, to your left 5.3 kilometres (3.3 miles) from the first one, shows you a managed forest.

The fourth panel is at kilometre 7.3 (mile 4.5) and it explains the difference between white spruce and pine. The parking for number five is to your right at kilometre 8.3 (mile 5.2), but the walk is across the highway on your left. The overmature forest of panel number six is at kilometre 10.3 (mile 6.4). 'Brushing,' or weeding, of a forest is explained by the seventh, at kilometre 13.6 (mile 8.5). Number eight at kilometre 19.1 (mile 11.9) takes you along Gagnon Creek and from a pine forest to an old-growth spruce forest.

The total length is 17 metres (56 feet) and the height to the top of cab is about 6.4 metres (21 feet, 3 inches). It weighs 159 tonnes (175 tons) and can travel at a speed up to around 4 kilometres per hour (3 miles per hour).

Mackenzie is a relatively new town. Construction began in 1965 and the first residents moved in the next year. It was named after Alexander Mackenzie (see the sidebar on p. 165) and is supported by the forestry and mining industries.

You can continue on this road for some 93 kilometres (58 miles) to Finlay Bay on Williston Lake. The forest recreation site there has a boat launch onto Peace Reach and is said to be the most scenic place on the lake. It is not usually open until late June or early July and your vehicle should have four-wheel drive if you intend to launch and pull out your boat with it. Watch for floating debris on the lake and for quick weather changes.

Williston Lake at Mackenzie Landing Recreation Site.

Bijoux Falls and Pine Pass

Back on the Hart Highway, you travel with views of mountain scenery ahead. The parking and picnic area for Bijoux Falls is to your left at kilometre 32.8 (mile 20.4) and the high waterfall itself is just off the highway.

Past the falls, the highway climbs and you drive beside a row of peaks in the Rocky Mountains. You reach Pine Pass 9.7 kilometres (6.0 miles) from the falls. At the pass, although you are 874 metres (2868 feet) above sea level, you are on the lowest highway pass in the Rockies.

At the pass there is a pull-out from which you have a lovely view of beautiful Azouzetta Lake below. As you continue along the highway you pass a campground to your right on the lakeshore. Between kilometre 32.8 (mile 20.4) and kilometre 35.2 (mile 21.9) you cross the West Pine River three times.

The road follows the Pine River most the way to Chetwynd and you can see it occasionally to your right. You begin to get into some farmland and the mountains are gradually replaced by foothills. At kilometre 78.1 (mile 48.5) there is a pull-out to your right that has a picnic site, a view of farmland along the Pine River and an area map.

The Pine River valley is to your right for a ways and you arrive in Chetwynd at kilometre 105.3 (mile 65.4).

Bijoux Falls.

Chetwynd

Chetwynd's visitor information centre is between 53rd and 52nd streets. Next to the building there is a sign that says 'Welcome to Chetwynd' and beneath it stands a chainsaw sculpture of three bears. In 1990, to commemorate Chetwynd's participation in the Alaska Highway's 50th anniversary celebration, the businesses of the town decided to commission those three bears. Since then, businesses and private residents have ordered more than 20 other sculptures from various artists. Some sit in front of, or inside, businesses, parks, private homes and offices. You can pick up a location guide to these sculptures at the visitor information centre, though not all of them are accessible to the viewing public.

Moberly Lake and the Peace Canyon Dam

To reach Moberly Lake, the Peace Canyon Dam, the W.A.C. Bennett Dam and Hudson's Hope, turn onto Highway 29 at the junction with Highway 97 in Chetwynd. As you leave Chetwynd, you climb above a valley and its farmland to your right. You curve away from the valley and pass through the Saulteau Indian Reserve, beginning at kilometre 16.9 (mile 10.5). To your left at kilometre 19.6 (mile 12.1) is the road to Moberly Lake Provincial Park, which offers a boat launch, a picnic area, a campground and swimming.

You cross the Moberly River at kilometre 20.1 (mile 12.5) and, if you look left, you can see the lake. The highway follows the lake and you can see it and the foothills on the other side through the trees. Centennial Road is to your left at kilometre 26.0 (mile 16.2). Turn onto it and then immediately go right into a little park with a cairn that commemorates the 'discovery' of Moberly Lake in 1865. A sign at the park welcomes you to 'Moberly Lake, a Resort Town on the Lake.'

After the cairn are some roads along the highway that take you down to the town of Moberly Lake or to lovely picnic and camping areas by the lake.

In 24.7 kilometres (15.3 miles) from the turn-off for the cairn, you begin a long, steep descent to the Peace River and you can see its valley spread out before you. You reach the Hudson Hope Bridge over the Peace River at kilometre 32.7 (mile 20.3). There is a pull-out to the right before the bridge where you can park if you want to look at the pictures carved in the concrete totem pole located here (it is duplicated at the other end of the bridge). One is of Henry Fuller 'Twelve Foot' Davis, a legendary miner and trader of the north country in the 1800s. (To read more about Davis, see the 'Peace River' section of my book, *Backroads of Northern Alberta*.) Another has a moose, beaver and bear, and others show Native people and Alexander Mackenzie looking for the Pacific Ocean in 1793. (There is more about this explorer in the sidebar on p. 165.)

As you cross the bridge, the Peace Canyon Dam is to your left and to your right you can see the river flowing through its canyon. Heinz Leber Knives, where you can look at and buy homemade knives, is to your right in 1.2 kilometres (0.7 miles) from the bridge.

Peace Canyon Dam.

For a closer look at the Peace Canyon Dam, turn to the left opposite the knife shop. In 0.7 kilometres (0.4 miles) from the turn-off there is a road to a viewpoint, which you reach in less than 0.5 kilometres (0.3 miles). Here there is a picnic area and you can see the Peace River flowing from the Peace Canyon Dam.

At kilometre 0.3 (mile 0.2) from the road to the viewpoint you can turn to the right to go to a boat launch, picnic area and public camping area on Dinosaur Lake, a widening of the Peace River formed by the Peace Canyon Dam. A further 0.6 kilometres (0.4 miles) past that turn-off brings you to the dam's visitor centre. It is open from 8 AM to 4 PM.

Inside the centre you can see a replica of a hadrasaur, a type of dinosaur whose fossilized footprints have been found in the area, although no skeletons have been discovered. The staff will give you a map and explain some of the features of the dam and then you can take a self-guided stroll through the centre. On the tour you visit the control room, the powerhouse and the 'switchgear station' and then go out onto the observation deck to see the dam, the reservoir and the river downstream. If you wish, you can even walk on the 50-metre (165-foot) high dam itself, which was constructed between 1975 and 1980.

Back on Highway 29, the road to Alwin Holland Memorial Park is to your right at kilometre 2.9 (mile 1.8) from the turn-off for the dam. To walk through part of the Peace Canyon, turn down the road to the park. If you camp in the park, which is free, you are asked to keep the grounds clean. You reach the park in 0.5 kilometres (0.3 miles). At the bottom of the hill, to your left, there is a track with two poles blocking it. Follow the track on foot to reach a section of the Peace River Canyon that the river once churned through but is now high and dry. You can walk between these walls carved by the river to the current edge of the river itself, where you see more of the beautiful canyon.

The Hadrasaur

Dinosaurs ('terrible lizards') are divided into two orders: Saurischia ('lizard-hipped') and Ornithischia ('bird-hipped'). The vegetation-eating Ornithischia are further subdivided into four suborders: Ornithopoda, Stegosauria, Ankylosauria and Ceratopsia.

The hadrasaur is a member of the *Ornithopoda* group, whose members could walk on just their hind legs and had long tails. The mouth of a hadrasaur was broad like a duck's—hence its nickname of 'duck-billed'—and it had no front teeth. Hadrasaurs ranged from North America to South America and through Europe and Asia. Half of the hadrasaur fossils found have been in Alberta. Nests of hadrasaur eggs have been discovered in both Alberta and Montana.

Peace River canyon at Alvin Howard Park.

Hudson's Hope and the W.A.C. Bennett Dam

King Gething Park, where you can also camp at no charge, is to your right in 4.9 kilometres (3.0 miles) from the turn-off for Holland Park. Then you are in Hudson's Hope. As you come into town, just follow the road as it curves and at kilometre 6.2 (mile 3.9) you come to 94th Street. To your left is Beattie Park, with 'Dudley the Dinosaur' sitting in front of the log building that houses the visitor information centre. To your right is the Hudson's Hope Museum. To visit these places, turn left at 94th Street to park.

At the museum, which is set on a cliff overlooking the Peace River, you can see a large collection of fossils, as well as displays on the early days of the trapping and the mining industries. The museum also includes St. Peter's Anglican United Church, a log structure built in 1938 and still in use as a church today.

St. Peter's Anglican United Church at Hudson's Hope Museum.

Across 94th Street from the museum there is a cairn that marks the site where James Laurence Ruxton and Helen Rand Ruxton settled in the 1920s.

Drive back to the intersection and continue along the main road. In one block you reach a junction. A right turn here would take you to Fort St. John on the Alaska Highway (see Chapter 4). Turn left instead to go to the W.A.C. Bennett Dam.

You have views of the Peace River with the Rocky Mountains in the distance as you drive. Kilometre 17.0 (mile 10.6) brings you to a parking lot for the Trapper's Cabin picnic area. There *is* a trapper's cabin here, but there is no sign explaining its history. Its doors are locked and the windows have screens on them and there is no furniture inside.

You reach the parking area for the W.A.C. Bennett Dam 4.0 kilometres (2.5 miles) from the trapper's cabin. At the parking lot there is a viewpoint to look down on the dam, along with a visitor centre. Signs describe how the reservoir collects and stores water from rain and melted snow in an area the size of New Brunswick. You can read how the penstocks, turbines and generators are used to create electricity that is sent out through the province.

There are also some covered display areas at the viewpoint. One of the displays features the Straub Stamp Mill, which was bought by the Peace River Mining and Milling Company in 1926 for grinding ore 19.3 kilometres (12.0 miles) downstream from Finlay Forks, north of where Mackenzie is today. However, no gold was found and the mill was abandoned. It was removed from the area before the flooding of Williston Lake.

The W.A.C. Bennett Dam

The Bennett Dam was named for William Andrew Cecil Bennett, who was premier of British Columbia from 1952 to 1972. The dam was built between 1962 and 1967, with the first power being sent south in September 1968. The first step in building the dam was to temporarily divert the Peace River from its normal path, using three tunnels that had been blasted in the canyon wall. Each tunnel was 14.6 metres (48 feet) in diameter and 805 metres (2641 feet) long, and the river began flowing through them on September 13, 1963.

Fill, 43.7 million cubic metres (57.3 million cubic yards) of it, was brought in to create the dam, which is 800 metres (2625 feet) thick at its base and 9.1 metres (30 feet) thick at its top. It stands 186 metres (610 feet) high and is 2068 metres (6785 feet) long.

Power from this generating station and the one at the Peace Canyon Dam goes to Prince Rupert, Nanaimo, the Vancouver area and other parts of southern BC.

There are also replicas of fossilized duck-billed dinosaur footprints found during the excavation of the powerhouse, and a coal car that was used by the Peace River Coal Mine between 1944 and 1951. The mine is now covered by the dam.

Inside the visitor centre you can book a free guided bus tour of the underground powerhouse. Tours begin on the half-hour, starting at 9:30 AM, with the last one at 4:30 PM. The centre itself is open from 9 AM to 6 PM daily.

Return to Chetwynd and turn onto the Hart Highway in the direction of Dawson Creek.

The W.A.C. Bennett Dam.

Chetwynd to Dawson Creek

Sukunka Falls and Tumbler Ridge

Drive 2.9 kilometres (1.8 miles) east of the junction of Highways 97 and 29 in Chetwynd until you get to Highway 29 southbound, where you turn right to head for Tumbler Ridge. By about kilometre 11 (mile 7) you are following the Sukunka River. You can see it beside the highway in a number of places until kilometre 23.0 (mile 14.3), where you can turn right onto Sukunka Forest Service Road, still following the river, to go to Sukunka Falls.

The forest service road is narrow and very rough and you have to watch for logging trucks. There are yellow-and-black kilometre signs posted, with numbering that starts at 200 and counts up, '201,' '202,' etc., but do not expect them to exactly match your odometer. When you reach the Y junction at kilometre 17.0 (mile 10.6), go to the left. At kilometre 21.7 (mile 13.5), turn right when you reach one end of the loop road that goes past Sukunka Falls. If you miss it, just ahead you will see the yellow sign with a black '221' on it that marks the other end of the loop road to the falls.

The waterfall is a series of cascades and you can look down on them from the loop road. There is a steep, almost sliding type of path down to them, but you will probably be content to view them from the road.

Back at the highway, turn right to continue toward Tumbler Ridge. You reach the boundary of Gwillim Lake Provincial Park in 23.0 kilometres (14.2 miles) and then you crest a hill and can see Gwillim Lake ahead. The turn-off for the Gwillim Lake Provincial Park campground is to your left at kilometre 24.3 (mile 15.1). It is a lovely place to relax and enjoy the scenery or fish for arctic grayling, Dolly Varden, northern pike and mountain whitefish.

After the park, you can see the peaks of the Rocky Mountains ahead. You pass the road to Moose Lake 18.6 kilometres (11.6 miles) from the turn-off for the park and road to Bullmoose Mine is to your right at kilometre 20.7 (mile 12.9). The plant is 15.0 kilometres (9.3 miles) along this paved road.

In 1968, exploration for coal was begun in the area and the building of the plant started in spring 1982. Production began in November 1983, with 10 million tonnes (11 million tons) being taken out in the first six years. Coal from the mine is transported to two 70-metre (230-foot) high silos at the rail-loading facility, where it is loaded into railcars. It is taken to the Ridley Island deep-sea port at Prince Rupert (see p. 124), as is the coal from the Quintette Mine, which is closer to Tumbler Ridge. From there it is shipped to Japanese steel companies.

At the mine you can see a slide show and then take a bus tour of the pit. Summer tours, between June 2 to August 28, are on Tuesdays and Thursdays at 10 AM. Children must be at least six years of age to go on the tour.

Sukunka Falls.

You drive through Bullmoose Flats at 1.2 kilometre (0.7 miles) from the mine road. At kilometre 12.2 (mile 7.6) you round a curve and can see Tumbler Ridge way ahead of you, surrounded by trees and hills. You cross the Murray River at kilometre 22.1 (mile 13.7) and then Flatbed Creek at kilometre 23.3 (mile 14.5). To your left after the bridge there is a picnic and camping area along the creek. From there you can hike to Flatbed Falls in about one hour; there is another, shorter trail to the falls that begins just past Tumbler Ridge. At kilometre 25.1 (mile 15.6) you turn left to go into the town of Tumbler Ridge. (If you want to bypass the town and go directly to Quintette Mine and Kinuseo Falls, continue straight ahead.)

From the highway, go to Southgate Road and turn right to reach the city centre. On the corner of Southgate and Front Street is the visitor information centre, in a BC Rail caboose. If you wish to tour the Quintette Mine, you have to book here. You are advised to arrive 15 minutes early for the mine tours, which begin at 1:30 PM on Wednesdays, Saturdays and Sundays. The Sunday tour goes to different pits and takes about two and one-half hours, an hour longer than the other two.

Tumbler Ridge was established in the early 1980s as a housing and service area for the workers at the Bullmoose and Quintette Mine. It has quickly developed into a modern town, with a golf course and trails for hiking, cross-country skiing and snowmobiling.

Note: If you are pulling a holiday trailer and plan to visit Monkman Provincial Park Campground, you should take into account that the road becomes rough so, unless you plan on spending the night there, it is better to leave your holiday trailer in Tumbler Ridge. Ask at the visitor centre.

The Quintette Mine, Kinuseo Falls and Dawson Creek

Return to the highway and turn left. In 1.2 kilometres (0.7 miles) you reach the second trail to Flatbed Falls and from here it is a 20-minute hike. The creek is a popular place to swim, but diving from the falls is not advised.

You arrive at the Heritage Highway (not numbered) at kilometre 2.2 (mile 1.4). Turn left here if you wish to go to Dawson Creek without first seeing the Quintette Mine or Kinuseo Falls. Otherwise continue ahead and you cross Flatbed Creek at kilometre 5.7 (mile 3.5). Turn right when you get to Murray River Forest Service Road at kilometre 13.6 (mile 8.5). At kilometre 3.8 (mile 2.4) you reach the parking area for the Quintette Mine tour on the right.

After your tour, if you went on one, continue along the forest service road past the parking area. As you drive, you can see the coal-processing plant, mounds of coal and a conveyor belt that brings the coal from the distant reserves. At kilometre 1.1 (mile 0.7) from the parking area you reach a viewpoint that overlooks the plant. If you didn't take a tour, stop in here to read the signs about where the coal comes from, how it gets to the plant and some of the history of the mine.

In 0.4 kilometres (0.2 miles) from the viewpoint you go through a short tunnel and at kilometre 2.2 (mile 1.4) there is a second one. At kilometre 3.6 (mile 2.2)

Kinuseo Falls.

Canoeing the Murray River

Beginner and intermediate canoeists may want to paddle the Murray River from below Kinuseo Falls to the bridge on Highway 29, just west of Tumbler Ridge. The 52-kilometre (32-mile) trip can be made in one long day or two shorter ones. It is normally Class II water all the way, but you should not attempt this trip during spring thaw or just after a heavy rain, as the river could be swollen and fast.

If you wish to take out sooner, there are bridges that mark take-out places where the access road for Monkman Provincial Park or a side road crosses the river. They are at about 16 kilometres (10 miles), 25 kilometres (15.5 miles) and 38 kilometres (23.5 miles) from your starting point.

There are three campsites, the first at approximately 1 kilometre (0.5 miles) from the put-in point, one at kilometre 12 (mile 7.5) and the last at kilometre 23 (mile 14.5).

To put in, go to the beginning of the upper falls viewpoint trail, where there is a sign that says 'Murray River, 1.5 km.' Portage over the trail that it indicates to the river and put your canoe in there. Do not put in at the base of the falls, as the water is too turbulent there.

there is a bridge over the Murray River and the road curves through the Quintette property and becomes quite rough, especially if you are pulling a holiday trailer.

The scenery is great, with mountains visible above the trees. You have glimpses of the Murray River, which you cross again at kilometre 24.2 (mile 15.0). At kilometre 41.0 (mile 25.5) you arrive at the entrance to Monkman Provincial Park.

To see Kinuseo Falls, go right at kilometre 45.1 (mile 28.0) and drive 1.0 kilometre (0.6 miles) to the parking area. One trail leads along a fence to the wheelchair-accessible lower viewpoint. From here you look down at the top of the falls. To see the full falls, take the upper viewpoint trail, which is across the parking lot from the fence. It climbs uphill most of the way, about 0.5 kilometres (0.3 miles).

From the upper viewpoint you can see the churning water as it plunges 69 metres (226 feet) down the rock wall. The water that passes over the falls here eventually flows into the Peace River south of Fort St. John.

From the falls parking lot, return to the main road and continue 0.5 kilometres (0.3 miles) to the Monkman Provincial Park Campground.

Return past the Quintette Mine to the junction with the road to Dawson Creek (the Heritage Highway). Turn right onto it and you begin climbing. Starting at kilometre 17.5 (mile 10.8) along this road and continuing for quite some distance, you can see a long way and have a great view of a valley, hills and mountains. At kilometre 22.7 (mile 14.1) you reach the Heritage Highway Summit, with a posted elevation of 1264.5 metres (4149 feet).

Between the summit and Highway 97 you travel through a varying landscape of hills, trees, meadows and mountains. Notice how poplar and spruce trees grow on the richer soils, but pine predominates in the sandier areas.

Monkman Pass and the Highway That Wasn't Built

Alex Monkman was a jack-of-all-trades. In 1899, as a fur trader, he built a house and set up a store at Saskatoon Lake, near Grande Prairie, Alberta. He tried a little farming, ranching, trapping and exploring.

On his explorations he discovered a pass through the Rockies that lay between Beaverlodge, Alberta, and Prince George, BC. Other travellers followed in his footsteps in the early 1930s and rough maps were drawn. But the railways weren't interested in establishing a line and the Alberta government refused to build a highway through it. The residents of the area between Beaverlodge and Prince George decided to construct their own road. They were promised funding to improve it by the Edmonton Chamber of Commerce, but not until they could drive a car over the route.

A path was blazed in 1937. The following year, men, women and children began cutting bush and trees, levelling the land and installing culverts on the 212-kilometre (132-mile) road from Rio Grande, Alberta to Hansard, BC.

On September 3, 1938, a Model-T and driver started across the partially completed trail to Hansard. Late supplies, bad weather and the freezing of Herrick Creek forced the suspension of the trek for the winter. Support money was slow in coming in 1939 and then World War II began. Soon, the car and the idea were totally abandoned.

In 1967, the Grande Prairie River Rats Association located the old car, carefully disassembled it and loaded it onto five jet boats, ferried it to Prince George, and then hauled it to Grande Prairie. The car has been restored, but the Alex Monkman Highway is still just a dream. Monkman's name, however, is commemorated in the name of a provincial park that surrounds the pass on three sides.

There are farms in places, beginning at kilometre 55.0 (mile 34.2), and they become more plentiful as you go. You pass the Cutbank Community Hall to your right at kilometre 70.5 (mile 43.8) and reach Highway 97 at kilometre 77.8 (mile 48.3). Turn right to go to Dawson Creek.

Look to your left just after you turn onto the highway to see the banks of the Kiskatinaw River. You cross it in 0.3 kilometres (0.2 miles). You pass through farmland on your way to Dawson Creek, which you reach at kilometre 17.8 (mile 11.1). The junction with the Alaska Highway is at kilometre 19.9 (mile 12.4). To get to the beginning of the Alaska Highway (Alaska Avenue through Dawson Creek), turn right onto it. In 1.9 kilometres (1.2 miles) you arrive at Northern Alberta Railway (NAR) Park and the Mile 0 Cairn, both on your left, where the trips in Chapter 4 begins.

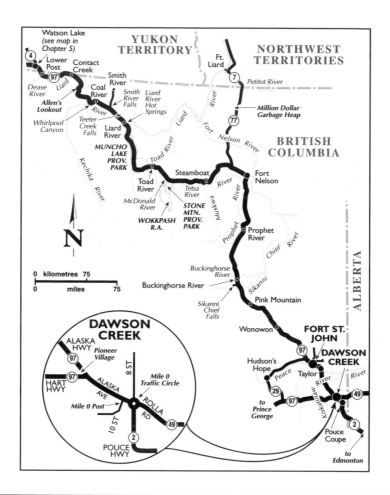

Watson Lake
(see map in
Chapter 5)

YUKON
TERRITORY

NORTHWEST
TERRITORIES

Ft.
Liard

Lower
Post

Contact
Creek

Smith
River

Petitot River

Dease
River

Coal
River

Smith
River
Falls

Liard
River
Hot
Springs

Million Dollar
Garbage Heap

Allen's
Lookout

River

Liard
River

BRITISH
COLUMBIA

Whirlpool
Canyon

Teeter
Creek
Falls

Kechika River

MUNCHO
LAKE
PROV.
PARK

Toad River

Liard

Steamboat

River

Fort
Nelson

Toad
River

Tetsa
River

Muskwa

Fort Nelson River

McDonald
River

STONE
MTN.
PROV.
PARK

WOKKPASH
R.A.

Prophet River

Prophet
River

N

Chief River

ALBERTA

0 kilometres 75
0   miles   75

Buckinghorse
River

Buckinghorse River

Sikanni

Pink Mountain

Sikanni
Chief
Falls

Wonowon

FORT ST.
JOHN

DAWSON CREEK

ALASKA
HWY

Pioneer
Village

8 ST

Hudson's
Hope

Peace

Taylor

DAWSON
CREEK

HART
HWY

ALASKA
AVE

Mile 0
Traffic Circle

29

to
Prince
George

Kiskatinaw River

River

HART
HWY

Mile 0 Post

10 ST

ROLLA
RD

Pouce
Coupe

POUCE
HWY

to
Edmonton

4
Dawson Creek to Watson Lake

This chapter takes you along the Alaska Highway (also sometimes called 'the AlCan (Alaska–Canada) Highway') from Dawson Creek to Watson Lake in the Yukon, with a side trip into the Northwest Territories. On this trip, for which you should allow at least three days, you will see ever-changing scenery and learn about the history of the highway and this section of British Columbia. As a bonus, if you do this trip in summer, you will have many hours of daylight each day.

In 1992, the 50th anniversary of the building of the highway, North West Highway System (NWHS) signs were put up to mark the original construction camps, airfields, army camps and telegraph stations along it. Some sites have only a small black-and-white marker at the spot, and others have a huge NWHS sign and a write-up about the site. These signs are scattered along the highway, and each is worth reading. As you travel this part of the Alaska Highway and read the signs, you will learn about the difficulties and the good times experienced in building it. If you want to locate all of these sites in British Columbia, ask at the visitor information centre in Dawson Creek for a copy of *Alaska Highway Historic Milepost*, a pamphlet that lists the mileposts and gives a bit of their history.

There are also other point-of-interest signs that tell about the people, the wildlife and the land of northern British Columbia.

Dawson Creek to Fort Nelson

Dawson Creek and Pouce Coupe

Dawson Creek, in the northeastern part of British Columbia, is at 'Mile 0' of the Alaska Highway. If you just finished the trip in Chapter 3, you will have arrived from the southwest via Highway 97, (the John Hart Highway), which continues to the northwest as the Alaska Highway. There are two other highways that enter Dawson Creek: Highway 2 comes from the southeast, through Grande Prairie, Alberta; and Highway 49 comes from the east, also out of Alberta.

The Mile 0 Cairn that marks the official beginning of the Alaska Highway is in Northern Alberta Railway (NAR) Park. At one time the cairn stood in the centre of the traffic circle in front of the park but, because tourists would risk their lives dashing across the road to pose beside it, it was moved to its present site.

Dawson Creek's visitor information centre and the Station Museum are also at NAR Park, inside a railway station that was built in 1931. If you would like a tour of the Louisiana-Pacific Waferboard plant just north of town, book it at the visitor centre. The tall grain elevator beside the visitor centre has been renovated to hold the Dawson Creek Art Gallery, which displays works by local artists and travelling collections. The railway car in front is a 1903 model called 'the Blue Goose Caboose.'

Blue Goose Caboose in NAR Park in Dawson Creek.

Visitor information centre, museum and art gallery in the NAR Park in Dawson Creek.

Across the Alaska Highway from the front of the information centre is 10th Street. To see the Mile 0 Post that attests that Dawson Creek is the beginning of the Alaska Highway, go one block down 10th Street. The Mile 0 Post is in the centre of the Mile Zero Square. The original buildings on the block that you walked down were destroyed when fire ignited 60 cases of dynamite on February 13, 1943.

The History of Dawson Creek

The Dawson Creek area was first settled, as an agricultural community in the Peace River Country, in 1912. In 1930 the town was moved to its current location from its original site 3.2 kilometres (2.0 miles) to the west to become the railhead for the Northern Alberta Railway. The town grew quickly when the United States, fearing attacks from the Japanese during the Second World War, decided to construct the Alaska Highway to provide land access to Alaska.

Work on the 2288-kilometre (1422-mile) 'pioneer road' between Dawson Creek and Delta Junction began in March 1942, and was completed on November 20 of that same year. During that time, Dawson Creek's population swelled from 518 to over 10,000. More than 5000 train-car loads of materials for construction and equipment for the troops arrived in Dawson Creek during 1942. Today, the industries in and around Dawson Creek include a waferboard (oriented strand board) plant, oil production and tourism.

Flowerbeds on 49th Avenue in Pouce Coupe.

Before heading north on the Alaska Highway, take a few minutes to go south on Highway 2 to the town of Pouce Coupe, only 9.3 kilometres (5.8 miles) from the Mile 0 traffic circle. As you drive into the village, continue straight ahead on 50th Street when Highway 2 curves left. In one block, turn left onto 49th Avenue. This extra-wide avenue has long log flower boxes down the middle of it. The individuals or groups in the village who look after each flowerbed have their names on it.

Pouce Coupe's first settler, Hector Tremblay, arrived in the area in 1898. Ten years later he opened a trading post that served the influx of pioneers to Pouce Coupe—from their starting points they first went to Edson, Alberta, and then followed the Edson Trail here in 1912. In 1998 Pouce Coupe celebrated the 100th anniversary of its founding and the 25th anniversary of the opening of the Pouce Coupe Museum, which is to your left halfway down 49th Avenue. Tour it to see displays about Pouce Coupe's history.

Return to the Mile 0 traffic circle in Dawson Creek to begin your journey north on the Alaska Highway. Just after you pass the junction with the Hart Highway (Highway 97), look for the left turn for the Walter Wright Pioneer Village. In the village you can see old buildings from Dawson Creek as well as from surrounding communities. The attractions include a general store, antique farm machinery, a tea house and 'Gardens North,' which consists of nine flower beds and a rose garden. The flowers are best seen in July and August.

Old building in Walter Wright Pioneer Village in Dawson Creek.

The first historic NWHS sign on the highway, on the left after the village, is Historic Milepost 2, which is about US Army Station 2. Then, to your right at kilometre 2.2 (mile 1.4) from the Walter Wright Pioneer Village, is the Louisiana-Pacific Waferboard plant. Tours of this plant are booked through the visitor centre in Dawson Creek.

As you drive the winding highway through farmland and hills, look to your left at kilometre 18.8 (mile 11.6) from the pioneer village to see a driveway lined with burls. At kilometre 21.6 (mile 13.4) there is a sign that says that you are entering Farmington and then you start downhill into a valley. A store on the left of the highway in Farmington has a huge replica of a bear in front of it.

The Kiskatinaw River

After Farmington, you come out of the treed valley into open farmland. Then, at kilometre 4.3 (mile 2.7) from the store, turn to the right for the old Kiskatinaw Bridge. You immediately come to a stop sign, where you turn left. You are now driving on an old section of the Alaska Highway that was bypassed during upgrading in 1978.

The pavement here is broken in places, but it is passable by all vehicles as you begin working your way down into the valley of the Kiskatinaw River. At kilometre 4.5 (mile 2.8) from the stop sign you pass the entrance for Kiskatinaw Provincial Park. Continue ahead to the old bridge, which you reach almost immediately. There is a pull-out to the right before the bridge where you can park and take pictures. This white wooden bridge, built in 1942–43, is 163 metres (534 feet) long and curves to the right at a 9° angle. From the bridge you have a lovely view 30 metres (100 feet) down to the river.

No longer a part of the highway, this bridge is still used by the area's residents. Although the bridge is supposedly two lanes wide, it is best to wait if you see a bus or large truck coming the other way when you are about to drive across. After the bridge, the road follows alongside the river for a ways and, in 5.4 kilometres (3.4 miles) from the bridge, you reach the highway again.

If you wish to see the new bridge, with its single support system, turn left and it is 2.3 kilometres (1.4 miles) back towards Dawson Creek. Park at the near end and walk to the edge of the bank. The one V-shaped support has its bottom sitting on a concrete pillar in the middle of the river.

New Kiskatinaw Bridge.

Head northward once again and, 15.4 kilometres (9.6 miles) from the bridge, you come to a pull-out and rest area on your right. Here you can check your brakes and read a sign that describes the descent that you will be making over the next few minutes as you approach the Peace River and the town of Taylor. As you drive down into the valley, the great views include farmland, the town of Taylor, the Peace River and both the blue bridge and the red-and-white gas pipeline that cross the river.

Taylor

At kilometre 5.2 (mile 3.2) from the pull-out there is a sign that welcomes you to Taylor. Just past that sign, but before you cross the Peace River Bridge, there is a sign that marks the left turn for Peace Island Park, where you can picnic, camp or hike on an island in the river.

On your right, just 0.7 kilometres (0.4 miles) from the highway, you reach the entrance to Peace Island Park. As you follow the road, you can see the island to your right and then you cross a causeway to it. The park is open from 7 AM to 11 PM. Dogs are welcome, but must be leashed.

Back at the highway, turn left and cross the bridge over the Peace River. This bridge, like many on this trip, has a metal deck and your steering may be affected. Look to your right as you cross to see the red-and-white gas pipeline as it comes out of the river bank, crosses the river and enters the other bank.

As you come off the bridge, you are in the main section of Taylor. Founded in 1912, the town was named after Herbie Taylor, a Hudson's Bay Company trader. Continue along the highway to the visitor information centre, located in a 1932 pioneer cabin on the left. In its yard there is a large replica of a fur-trade canoe of the type used by Alexander Mackenzie on his 8835-kilometre (5490-mile) journey from Montreal, Quebec, to Bella Coola, BC, in the 1790s. He was the first non-Native to cross the North American continent (see the sidebar on p. 165 and also p. 201).

On the long weekend in August, Taylor holds an annual World Invitational Class 'A' Championship Gold Panning Competition that attracts professional gold-panners from around the world. Other activities during the weekend include a parade, gold-panning for everyone, claim-staking and bannock-baking.

Spanning the Peace River

During the construction of the Alaska Highway, two ferries were used to transport workers and vehicles across the river. The crossing was slow and time-consuming. The workers tried three times to build trestles to support a bridge, but each time the pilings were washed out by the river. Finally, a 650-metre (2130-foot) suspension bridge was completed in July 1943—it was one of two such bridges on the highway. It collapsed in 1957 and the current cantilever-and-truss bridge was built in 1960.

Continue along the highway. To see what is said to be the world's largest golf ball, look to your right at the railway crossing. The giant golf ball is sitting in an open field near the Lone Wolf Golf Club.

World's largest golf ball, at Taylor.

After Taylor, you climb out of the Peace River Valley. Take note of the 'Thank You, Come Again' sign as you leave Taylor, because in 7.4 kilometres (4.6 miles) from it you reach the Honey Place—turn left and drive in. Bees are constantly flying through the yard but they are busy and generally ignore you if you leave them alone. Enter the building. Inside, along the right wall, there are three large glass display cases full of working bees. Each case has a clear plastic pipe running from it through the wall to the outside, so you can watch the bees as they enter and leave the hives.

You can buy a variety of honey products here. If you would like to sample something unusual, try the flavoured honey sticks, which come in cinnamon, peppermint, strawberry, raspberry, root beer, apple and cherry.

Fort St. John and Charlie Lake

At kilometre 4.1 (mile 2.5) from the Honey Place you pass the sign that welcomes you to Fort St. John. Follow the road into town to the traffic lights at 100th Street. Turn right here, go two blocks and turn right again to enter Centennial Park, which contains the city's visitor information centre and museum and other features of interest. The church here, the Chapel of the Holy Cross, was built in 1934 by Monica Storrs, an Anglican missionary. The one-room trapper's cabin is a replica constructed by the members of the Trappers' Association. Inside are a bed, a little table and a stove. The local oil industry is commemorated here by a pump-jack, a wellhead and a 46-metre (150-foot) tall, black oil derrick.

Fort St. John is one of the two oldest non-Native settlements on BC's mainland (in a tie with Hudson's Hope), having been established in 1794, just after Alexander Mackenzie explored the region in 1793 during his trip to the coast. It was originally situated 16 kilometres (10 miles) to

Fort St. John's Centennial Park.

the south, on the banks of the Peace River at its confluence with the Moberly River, but it was moved several times before the current location was chosen.

A large oil- and gasfield was discovered in the area in 1955 and Fort St. John became known as the oil capital of the province.

If you wish to get some exercise walking, turn right when you come out of the park and go 2.7 kilometres (1.7 miles) to the East By-pass Road and turn right. Then turn left and park in the lot for Northern Lights College. Beside the college is the Fish Creek Community Forest, where there are three self-guided trails, ranging from 30 minutes to 2.5 hours in length. Signs along the trails will help you learn about the insects, birds, animals and plants of the area.

For a view of the Peace River, head back south on 100th Street past Centennial Park and cross the Alaska Highway at the lights. After you pass businesses and acreages, the road becomes gravel as you work your way down a long hill. In less than 3 kilometres (2 miles) the road curves to your left and you are overlooking the Peace River at Lookout Park.

Back at the set of lights on 100th Street, turn left onto the Alaska Highway. You begin by travelling through an industrial area as you leave town. Then, at kilometre 7.0 (mile 4.3) from the lights, you enter the community of Charlie Lake, which is spread out along the highway, At kilometre 11.4 (mile 7.1) you come to a junction. To the left, Highway 29 goes to Hudson's Hope and the W.A.C. Bennett Dam (see Chapter 3). The short road to the right goes to Charlie Lake Provincial Park. There is good fishing for walleye, perch and northern pike on this 16-kilometre (10-mile) long, 3.2-kilometre (2.0-mile) wide lake. During highway construction, while crossing the lake on pontoon barges, 12 soldiers drowned; their bodies were subsequently recovered.

From the junction, continue along the Alaska Highway and in 13.2 kilometres (8.2 miles) from it you pass a giant statue of a logger on the left at the Clarke Sawmill.

Peace River from the Peace River Lookout at Fort St. John.

Building the Alaska Highway

Construction on the section of the Alaska Highway between Dawson Creek and Delta Junction began on March 8, 1942—less than three months after the bombing of Pearl Harbor. With an agreement that the Canadian section of the Alaska Highway would be turned over to Canada at the end of the war, the Canadian government gave the United States permission to build a road through the northeastern section of British Columbia and the southwestern part of the Yukon.

Thousands of soldiers were sent to the area to begin construction. The road followed Native trails, winter roads and rivers. Where there was nothing to follow, surveyors marked out a route. The routing of the road was designed to follow a line of airfields, 'the Northwest Staging Route,' which ran from Edmonton, Alberta, to Fairbanks, Alaska. Simultaneously, highway construction crews began work in Dawson Creek, Fort Nelson, Whitehorse and Delta Junction (then known as Big Delta). Fort St. John and Whitehorse were the sites of the two largest construction camps.

On September 25, the crews from Whitehorse and Fort Nelson met at Contact Creek and vehicles began travelling that section three days later. On November 20, 1942, the official opening ceremony was held at Soldiers Summit at Kluane Lake, where the crews from Delta Junction and Whitehorse had met on October 29.

This initial construction effort built the 'pioneer road' and the next year it was upgraded to an all-season road by civilian construction crews.

Charlie Lake.

Wonowon, Pink Mountain and Sikanni Chief Falls

Wonowon, formerly 'Blueberry,' is 75.2 kilometres (46.7 miles) from the junction at Charlie Lake. Blueberry was one of many military checkpoints on the Alaska Highway during the war. When the highway was transferred to Canada's Department of National Defence in 1946, the Royal Canadian Mounted Police took over staffing the gate. They required that anyone travelling this road carry extra fuel, tire chains, spare parts for their vehicle, tools, food, and at least $200. Anyone not in possession of everything on the list was turned back.

In the early 1960s, Blueberry's name was changed to 'Wonowon,' a bit of wordplay that reflected its location at 'Mile 101' of the highway.

At kilometre 64.5 (mile 40.1) from Wonowon you reach the settlement of Pink Mountain. It has two service stations, a motel, a grocery store and an RV park. In 24.3 kilometres (15.1 miles) from Pink Mountain you pass a pull-out for truckers to check their brakes before beginning a steep (9%) descent with curves posted at 50 kilometres per hour (30 miles per hour). The Sikanni Chief River and its canyon are to your right as you descend. At kilometre 29.9 (mile 18.6) you reach the bridge over the Sikanni Chief River. Look to your left and you can see pilings in the river, all that is left of the original bridge. Completed in 1943, it was the first permanent bridge on the highway. It was burned by vandals in 1992.

To see Sikanni Chief Falls, watch for the turn-off for the Grassy Gas Field to your left in 15.6 kilometres (9.7 miles) from the bridge over the Sikanni Chief River, as there is no sign for the falls itself. Turn left onto the gravel oilfield road and in 3.8 kilometres (2.4 miles) you reach a Y junction. Take the right fork, which does have a sign for the falls, and at kilometre 14.7 (mile 9.1) you come to a three-way branch in the road. Keep to the left here and you should see a brown sign for the falls hiking trail. You arrive at a small parking area with picnic tables in 17.0 kilometres (10.6 miles) from the highway. The 1.5-kilometre (0.9-mile) hiking trail begins from the parking lot. Much of the trail is downhill, so be sure that you will be able to climb back up. The path is narrow and there are roots underfoot as you walk through the woods.

Soon you come to a sign that points the way back to the parking lot. Just step to your left for a view of the falls. If you want to get closer, follow the path along the ledge to your right. Tread carefully here as part of the trail is along the top of a drop-off. You soon come to a sign cautioning you about the steep cliffs. If you continue, you will arrive at the edge of a cliff, but the trail is quite wide and does lead to a great view of the falls.

Sikanni Chief Falls.

Buckinghorse River, Prophet River and Muskwa Heights

From the turn-off for the Sikanni Chief Falls, it is 7.0 kilometres (4.3 miles) to the community of Buckinghorse River, which has a service station, a cafe and a campground.

At kilometre 72.2 (mile 44.8) from Buckinghorse River, you reach Prophet River Provincial Park campground and picnic site, which are on the left. Here you can walk the first of many self-guided Forest Ecology Tours, called 'Ecotours,' in the Fort Nelson area. They were established by the Fort Nelson Forest District to give visitors an idea of local landscapes and forest management practices. Pamphlets are available in Fort Nelson, from the forest district office and from the visitor information centre. Each Ecotour is indicated by a sign with a number on it and the word 'site' printed four times around the number. If you miss the Ecotours between here and Fort Nelson, there are many more along the section of highway between Fort Nelson and Liard River and also along the Liard Highway.

The settlement of Prophet River, at kilometre 88.0 (mile 54.6), is your last chance to buy fuel until you reach Fort Nelson.

At kilometre 79.0 (mile 49.1) from Prophet River you reach Muskwa Heights, a mainly industrial area outside Fort Nelson. Then you begin going downhill into the Muskwa River valley and cross the Muskwa River bridge, which, at 305 metres (1000 feet) above sea level, is the lowest point on the Alaska Highway. When you climb out of the valley you are in Fort Nelson.

Straightening the Alaska Highway

As agreed upon at the time of building, the Canadian part of the Alaska Highway reverted to Canada in 1946. It was opened to the public in 1948.

Though there were many twists and curves in the original road, new construction over the years has taken most of them out. For example, in a length of 56 kilometres (35 miles) between Prophet River and Jackfish Creek, 132 curves were removed. The highway is now about 60 kilometres (40 miles) shorter than the first all-season road and about 160 kilometres (100 miles) shorter than the pioneer road pushed through in 1942.

Fort Nelson

As you enter Fort Nelson, watch for Simpson Trail (a road) to your right. To visit Fort Nelson's community forest, turn onto it and drive five blocks to Mountain View Drive, where you turn left. Drive past the school to the parking area for the community forest. From here you can hike on two trails, one about 1 kilometre (0.6 miles) long and the other about 2 kilometres (1.2 miles) long.

Return to the highway, but turn right just before your reach it to park at the visitor information centre, which is in the same building that houses the arena.

Fort Nelson Museum.

The Fort Nelson Museum is in a log building across the highway from the visitor centre. In addition to all the displays inside, artifacts outside the museum include an oil derrick, old buildings, old tractors, Model-T cars, road graders, bulldozers and some wooden culverts that were put in during the highway construction and used for 50 years before they were removed in 1992. There is also a 6.7-metre (22-foot) long crankshaft from BC Hydro's Fort Nelson operations. It was new in 1957 and was in use for 111,722 hours (12 years and nine months) before failure. The museum is open daily from 8:30 AM to 7:30 PM, from May until the end of August.

On Monday, Tuesday, Wednesday and Thursday nights there is a 'Welcome Visitor' program that runs at the Phoenix Theatre in the Town Square, located one block east of the recreation centre, along the Alaska Highway at 54th Street. Each night a different person gives a talk. You might hear from a resident about past and present life in the area, or from a firefighter or trapper. If you are staying more than one day, go each night to hear a new talk. Stop in at the visitor centre for more information.

The Five Sites of Fort Nelson

The first Fort Nelson was established by the North West Company, a rival of the Hudson's Bay Company, in 1805. It was named after Lord Horatio Nelson, the English admiral. The post was moved to a spot south of the original one and in 1813 it was attacked by the Dene-Dhaa Nation (Slavey People) and destroyed by fire. The eight company employees at the post were killed in the attack.

In 1821, the North West Company merged into the Hudson's Bay Company. In 1865, a third Fort Nelson was built by the company on the banks of the river 1.6 kilometres (1.0 mile) downstream from the present-day airport. It was erected to purchase the furs of the area before the Natives could be persuaded to sell them to the newly arriving free traders, who were offering a higher price.

The rising of the Fort Nelson River in the spring of 1890 destroyed the third fort. The fourth fort was constructed across the river on higher ground. When the present (fifth) site was established, the fourth fort became known as 'Old Fort Nelson.'

In 1755, the Slavey (pronounced 'slay-vee') Natives, now known as the Dene-Dhaa Nation, arrived in the Fort Nelson area from the Great Slave Lake area, with fur traders following in the early 1800s. Until 1922, rivers were the only long-distance routes through this area. In that year, the Godsell Trail was completed from Fort St. John to Fort Nelson. Then, in the 1940s, the Alaska Highway brought much more of the outside world to the area.

Forestry and oil are the main industries in the Fort Nelson area, with agriculture coming in third. The Northwest Energy Plant in Fort Nelson is one of the largest natural gas producers in North America.

Especially if you are planning to take a side trip to Fort Liard, make sure to gas up before you leave Fort Nelson, since the only services along the Liard Highway are at Fort Liard.

The Liard Highway to Watson Lake

The Liard Highway

At kilometre 28.0 (mile 17.4) from the Fort Nelson Museum, you reach the junction with the Liard Highway (Highway 77). Turn right here to take a detour off the Alaska Highway to head for the Northwest Territories and Fort Liard. Note that there are no services for the next 175 kilometres (110 miles). Highway 77 is a gravel road that is wide enough for two vehicles to pass. The speed limit is 80 kilometres per hour (50 miles per hour).

In 40 kilometres (25 miles) from the Alaska Highway, you begin a downhill descent to the Fort Nelson River, which you cross on a one–lane bridge at kilometre 42.3 (mile 26.3). At 4.0 metres (13.1 feet) wide and almost 0.5 kilometres (0.3 miles) long, it is believed to be the longest Acrow (or Bailey) bridge in the world. After the bridge there is a rest area. The local First Nations people have described on a sign posted here how they monitor changes in the river because of the fishing and hunting they do along it.

Concrete beams at the Million Dollar Garbage Heap on the Liard Highway.

Look to your left through an opening in the trees at kilometre 97.2 (mile 60.4) to see some long concrete beams almost overgrown with grass. This site is known locally as 'the Million Dollar Garbage Heap.' These concrete beams fell off a truck during the construction of the Petitot River bridge; this accident delayed the completion of the bridge by a year. The beams, which are about 9 metres (30 feet) long, have rusted cables sticking out of the ends.

At kilometre 36.5 (mile 22.7) from the beams, you reach an 11% descent that leads to the Petitot River. This river, called *Meh Cho La* by local Natives, was renamed to honour Father Émile Petitot (1838-1917) of the Oblates of Mary Immaculate, who travelled throughout the North in the mid-1800s teaching the written form of the Dene language. It was at the Petitot River bridge that the ceremonies for the opening of the Liard Highway were held on June 23, 1984. However, instead of cutting the ribbon with scissors, a 1926 Model-T Ford was used; the ribbon was stretched 6 metres (20 feet) along the road before it broke.

Just before the bridge there is a pull-out; a road from it leads down to a boat and canoe launch on the river.

After you cross the river and begin to climb above it, look to the right to see the river valley. In 3.6 kilometres (2.2 miles) from the bridge there is a green sign that announces the border between BC and the Northwest Territories (NWT), where there is a time-zone change. From the border, it is a further 38.2 kilometres (23.7 miles) to Fort Liard.

Fort Liard has a long, warm summer and produces bountiful gardens. It is one of the oldest continually occupied places in the NWT. Although the Dene-Dhaa Nation (Slavey People) live here now, for 9000 years before them the Small Knife Native culture occupied the area.

As you drive into Fort Liard, watch on your right for Acho Dene Native Crafts. Here you can buy birch-bark baskets, snowshoes, moose-hide glasses cases, bead and quill jewellery and moccasins trimmed with rabbit, beaver or wolf hair. Each piece is individually designed and handcrafted by the artist.

Steamboat and Stone Mountain Provincial Park

Back on the Alaska Highway, as you travel toward Watson Lake you are driving through the Muskwa Range of the Rocky Mountains. It is 32.5 kilometres (20.2 miles) from the junction with the Liard Highway to Steamboat Creek and the beginning of the climb up Steamboat Mountain. At kilometre 49.0 (mile 30.4) you reach the settlement of Steamboat, which is marked by a service station and store on the left. As you continue climbing after Steamboat, you can look down on the valley of the Muskwa River.

In 6.8 kilometres (4.2 miles) from Steamboat you begin descending. Look straight ahead and up at about kilometre 15 (mile 9) to see Indian Head Rock, named for its resemblance to a Native's head in profile.

You then descend into the Tetsa River valley and, to your left at kilometre 39.0 (mile 24.2), you reach the entrance to Tetsa River Outfitters. There is a craft shop here that sells moccasins and mitts and home-made sourdough bread.

The road is narrow and winding as you follow the Tetsa River. Watch for falling rock and curves posted at 40 kilometres per hour (25 miles per hour). At 13.3 kilometres (8.2 miles) from the outfitters, you cross the Tetsa River Bridge #1. In 1.6 kilometres (1.0 mile) from the first bridge you cross the Tetsa River Bridge #2. At kilometre 9.6 (mile 6.0) you enter Stone Mountain Provincial Park. You reach the community of Summit Lake at kilometre 12.0 (mile 7.5). Just past the lake itself you reach Summit Lake Pass. The highest point on the Alaska Highway, with an elevation of 1295 metres (4250 feet), it experiences sudden weather changes.

At kilometre 3.7 (mile 2.3) from the pass, look to your right to see erosion pillars up on the hillside. There a pull-out on the left, across the highway from a 0.5-kilometre (0.3-mile) hiking trail to the pillars. Shortly after the pull-out, you round a curve and have a better view of the pillars on the right. Watch for stone sheep—a blackish colour phase of white (Dall) sheep—in this area, especially around kilometre 5 (mile 3).

You have a great view of the MacDonald River valley below, with mountains above it, at kilometre 6.2 (mile 3.8). After following the MacDonald River awhile, you cross it at kilometre 30.8 (mile 19.1). Kilometre 49.7 (mile 30.9) brings you to the community of Toad River.

Toad River and Muncho Lake Provincial Park

Toad River has a lodge, a service station, a cafe, a store and a campground. Walk inside the lodge and look at some of the baseball caps hanging on the walls and from the ceiling. Although there are more than 5500 in the collection, some of the caps are packed away because there isn't enough space to display them all at the same time. Many of the caps were left here one at the time by visitors who came by, but others are from people who donated their entire cap collections. One such collection came from a man who, with his wife, had planned a trip north. He had decided that he would bring his assortment of caps to leave at the lodge. Unfortunately, he passed away before they could make the trip, so the widow came on her own with her late husband's collection of 500 caps.

You enter Muncho Lake Provincial Park 7.1 kilometres (4.4 miles) from Toad River. Look up at kilometre 9.7 (mile 6.0) to see Folded Mountain. The layers of rock look like the mixture for marble cake when you swirl the chocolate and the

Alluvial Fans

You are in flash-flood country. A flash-flood results when a heavy summer downpour falls on the mainly bare mountainsides. The water washes soil, pebbles, vegetation and even boulders down the ravines between the mountain peaks, to be deposited on the valley floor. Over the centuries, 'alluvial fans' (from a Latin word that means 'wash' and a word to describe their shape) have formed at the bottoms of these ravines, where the water spreads out, slows down and begins to seep into the ground, leaving the solid material behind.

Each time a flash-flood occurs, the streams take a somewhat different route down the mountain, thus distributing this debris, called 'alluvium,' evenly over the ground and building up the fan.

There is a good example of an alluvial fan across the highway from Centennial Falls.

white batters together. There is a viewpoint for Folded Mountain to your left at kilometre 11.2 (mile 7.0).

Folded Mountain is a result of the North American continent pushing westward, catching what was then the continental shelf between it and offshore islands. The flat layers of the shelf buckled upward into the folds that you see on the mountain.

At 8.9 kilometres (5.5 miles) from the viewpoint, watch to your left for Centennial Falls—a long, slim line of water that comes down the hillside to a roadside ditch that empties into the Toad River.

At about kilometre 29 (mile 18), you begin to see the Sawteeth, part of the Sentinel Range, which were formed when huge slabs of dolomite were pushed up during the formation of these mountains.

Centennial Falls.

At kilometre 41.1 (mile 25.5) you come over a hill and beautiful, emerald Muncho Lake is in front of you. There are service stations, lodges, cafes and campgrounds beside the highway as it curves along the lakeshore. As with Summit Lake Pass, watch for sudden weather changes in this area.

Muncho means 'big lake' in the language of the Tagish First Nation. The lake, which is 12.0 kilometres (7.5 miles) long, is up to 60 metres (200 feet) deep and reaches a temperature of 10°C (50°F) in the summer. Its colour comes from rock particles that are ground by glaciers and brought down to the lake by mountain streams. This fine, flourlike glacial silt remains suspended in the lake's waters and reflects the blue-green part of the light spectrum for viewers to see.

At kilometre 54.4 (mile 33.8) a viewpoint overlooks Muncho Lake and has some information panels about it. At 15.5 kilometres (9.6 miles) from that viewpoint there is a road that goes to a natural animal mineral lick. Turn left onto this road and drive 0.2 kilometres (0.1 miles) to the parking area. Take the gravel path that leads from the parking area and choose the right fork when you come to a Y junction. The descending path, well used by humans and animals, has been fitted with steps in places. Look down through the trees to your right to see a ridge of erosion pillars. When you reach another Y junction, take the left fork and you soon arrive at the mineral lick, which is at a fenced area overlooking the Trout River and its valley.

Muncho Lake.

Essential Minerals

The sediment at this mineral lick is mainly rock flour ground off the mountains by the movement of glaciers centuries ago. This rock flour contains calcium, phosphorus, sulphur, sodium and magnesium—elements essential to the development of teeth, bones, antlers and hair.

During the spring and summer, female animals who are nursing their young will come here for the minerals, and so will male animals who are growing antlers. The best times to watch for moose, caribou and stone sheep around the lick are the early morning and the evening. You may see smaller animals using it too.

Back on the highway, in 5.7 kilometres (3.5 miles) from the turn-off for the mineral lick, you cross the Trout River. At 10.5 kilometres (6.5 miles) you leave Muncho Lake Provincial Park. You descend into the valley of the Liard River. The name 'Liard' came about because the French Canadian fur traders travelling through this country called the poplars along the river 'liards.' The Liard River is beside you at kilometre 19.4 (mile 12.0). After a lovely drive through the valley, you reach a bridge that spans the Liard River. This 348-metre (1143-foot) long bridge is now the only suspension bridge on the Alaska Highway.

Liard River Bridge.

Liard River Hot Springs

Just past the Liard River bridge you enter Liard River Hot Springs Provincial Park and reach the community of Liard River. Downstream from the bridge is the Grand Canyon of the Liard River, which can be reached by boat or by helicopter. A third option, a 12.8-kilometre (7.9-mile) path along the river bank, is not recommended by area residents.

During the construction of the Alaska Highway, the engineers decided that it would be easier to build if they avoided the Grand Canyon of the Liard and instead followed the Toad River, routed the road beside Muncho Lake and then followed the Trout River to the upper Liard River.

To your right, less than 1 kilometre (0.6 miles) from the bridge, is the Liard River Hot Springs Provincial Park Campground. Signs in the parking area direct you to a boardwalk trail that leads to the two pools. Although the changing rooms and both pool areas are wheelchair accessible, there are no special arrangements for wheelchair users to enter the water. Along the boardwalk through the warm-water swamps and the forest are signs that tell you about the plants that grow in the warm climate created by the hot springs, the animals that come to eat them, and the small fish that swim in the waters beneath the boardwalk.

Watch for moose: they are frequently seen eating or walking through the bush. Take a deep breath as you stroll and enjoy the warm forest smell. The area was known as 'the Liard Tropical Valley' during the 1940s. Orchids, luxuriant ostrich ferns and cow-parsnip are a few of the more than 250 plant species that grow here. Many of these plants survive only because of the warmth of the hot springs.

The first pool that you reach is Alpha Pool. There are three different sets of steps into this rectangular pool, which has benches in the middle where you can sit as you enjoy the warm water. Take it slow getting into the pool, because the water temperature averages about 45°C (113°F). On a cool day you can see steam rising off the waters.

When you are done here, follow the signs along the boardwalk toward Beta Pool. On the way, you reach the steps to the hanging gardens, where you can see mosses and wildflowers, some usually not found this far north, growing over a rock face. Climb up to the second viewpoint to see the gardens from above.

Alpha Pool at Liard River Hot Springs.

Continue along the boardwalk, at an uphill slant, to Beta Pool. The little streams, flowers and other plants along the way create a setting reminiscent of a rainforest. Beta Pool, round and smaller than Alpha Pool, is 3 metres (10 feet) deep. There are no benches and the temperature is about the same as at Alpha Pool. Look down to see the water bubbling up from the bottom.

The Liard River Hot Springs

The Kaska Natives, who lived and hunted in the region of the Liard River Hot Springs, used the waters to soothe and heal. The first recorded account of the springs is in the 1835 journal kept by Hudson's Bay Company explorer Robert Campbell. In the 1920s, the area was homesteaded for a few years by a man named John Smith.

During construction of the Alaska Highway, a camp, a sawmill, a hospital and a fuel depot were situated at the nearby crossing of the Liard River. Because of the dust in summer, mud in fall and cold in winter, the workers who lived in the camp spent much of their free time in the hot springs. They built the first boardwalk to the pools but, after the highway was completed, the hot springs were left to nature. In the 1950s, renovations and repairs were made to the site by nearby residents. Liard River Hot Springs Provincial Park was dedicated in 1957 and these days up to 150,000 people visit the site every year.

Teeter Falls and Smith River Falls

For a relaxing stroll in the forest, and to see the falls on Teeter Creek, watch for a gravel road to your right at 8.1 kilometres (5.0 miles) from the turn-off for the Liard River Hot Springs. This road goes to a small, circular area just below the highway. Follow the easy, level trail along Teeter Creek through the tall shade trees. In 10 minutes you reach a bridge over Teeter Creek, on which you can stand to take pictures of the small falls. The brown box and numbered stick beside the falls are for measuring the water level.

What you see from the bridge, however, is only a part of the falls. You may want to cross the bridge to the opposite bank and climb the steep trail for a better view of some other cascades of the falls. However, it is a very steep climb on the edge of the cliff, so you do so at your own risk.

Teeter Creek Falls.

Back on the highway, you immediately drive over the Teeter Creek culvert and, in 19.7 kilometres (12.2 miles) from that culvert, you cross a bridge over the Smith River. A short distance beyond, at kilometre 20.1 (mile 12.5), there is a one-lane gravel road on your right that leads to Smith River Falls.

At 2.0 kilometres (1.2 miles) from the highway you reach a parking area. The trail to the falls begins at the far end of the parking lot. It is a steep descent on steps and then on a path. You get your best view of the falls when you come to an unfenced viewpoint on a cliff.

To reach the river's edge, continue down more steps into a canyon with black, ochre and grey walls. Here you can see only the bottom part of the falls. The water roars as it plunges over the rock—the force of the falls creates a mist at the bottom and produces waves that lap up onto the narrow, gravelly beach.

If you have to choose between seeing this waterfall or Teeter Creek Falls, pick this one. It is more spectacular and the walk, though steeper, takes about the same amount of time.

Smith River Falls.

Coal River, Whirlpool Canyon and Contact Creek

The settlement of Coal River is 33.3 kilometres (20.7 miles) from the turn-off for Smith River Falls. Then you cross the outflow of the Coal River. Look to your left to see it flowing into the Liard River. At kilometre 39.3 (mile 24.4) you reach a turn-off to your left for Whirlpool Canyon, known to some people as 'Mountain Portage Rapids.'

Whirlpool Canyon.

Turn off here and park in the campground. Then walk across the huge pile of driftwood and rock to reach the path to the top of the canyon wall. Follow the path along the edge of the canyon with care, as there is no fence. The water sometimes carries logs as it churns and swirls around huge rocks and islands in the middle of the river below.

At kilometre 46.3 (mile 28.8) from the canyon, you can stop in on the left at Allen's Lookout. During the late 1800s, a band of robbers watched from this vantage point for boats travelling on the river. When they spotted one, they hurried down to their own boat, overtook the other boat and relieved the travellers of their goods. More recently, a cairn dedicated to the surveyors of the Alaska Highway was placed here.

You reach Contact Creek 27.3 kilometres (17.0 miles) from the lookout. It is here that soldiers of the 340th Regiment of the United States Army Corps of Engineers, working simultaneously from the southeast and the northwest, met. The creek was named to commemorate the completion of construction on the southern section of the Alaska Highway pioneer road.

In 1957, the original bridge across Contact Creek was torn down and a second one built. The second bridge was then replaced in 1997.

On the other side of Contact Creek you enter the Yukon. You pass Contact Creek Lodge and Iron Creek Lodge and then, at kilometre 47.0 (mile 29.2) from the border crossing at Contact Creek, you reach the left turn for Lower Post.

Contact Creek Bridge #2.

Lower Post

Just 1.0 kilometre (0.6 miles) from the highway, the hamlet of Lower Post, British Columbia, is billed as 'the Home of the Kaska Dena Nation.'

Lower Post, at the junction of the Liard and Dease rivers, was a Native village site that became a stop for miners and trappers travelling the rivers. A Hudson's Bay Company trading post was built here in the 1800s. The settlement had the names 'Sylvester's Lower Post' and 'Liard Post' before becoming 'Lower Post.'

In an effort to make an overland route from Edmonton, Alberta, to the Klondike during the gold rush, the North-West Mounted Police cut a trail that ran through this area, but it was abandoned because it took too long and the country was too rugged. A wagon trail to Watson Lake was constructed and it eventually became part of the original Alaska Highway. During highway construction, the military set up a sawmill here to cut bridge timbers.

From Lower Post you can drive toward Watson Lake for about 2 kilometres (1.2 miles) along the old pavement that was bypassed by new highway construction in 1985. Park when you reach a berm pushed up to stop traffic. Walk around the berm to a bluff from which you can look down on the traffic on the new part of the highway. Return through Lower Post to get onto the highway again.

At kilometre 17.1 (mile 10.6) from the turn-off for Lower Post, a sign at the Yukon border says 'Welcome to Canada's Yukon.' You reach the Liard Canyon Recreation Site, situated to the left on the shore of Lucky Lake, at kilometre 39.8 (mile 24.7). Nearby is the Watson Lake–Lucky Lake Waterslide Park.

Lucky Lake, a 'kettle lake,' was created by a huge piece of glacial ice that was left buried in glacial till as the glaciers around it melted away. When this piece finally melted too, it left a hole in which the lake formed. Some people say that the lake got its name during highway construction when a 'lady of the evening' set up a tent on its shore. Her visitors liked to say that they were getting a change of luck when they went into her tent, therefore 'Lucky Lake.'

Liard Canyon near Lucky Lake.

For an easy hike through the trees to the beginning of the Liard Canyon, walk into the park from the parking lot. To your right there is a map of the Liard River Canyon walking trail. It is a 2.2-kilometre (1.4-mile) self-guided trail that descends gradually to the Liard River.

You begin walking past picnic tables on a sandy path between pine trees. The further you go, the wetter the soil. The pines gradually give way to spruce and poplar. It is a lovely walk among these trees, which are some of the tallest in the Yukon, thanks to the rich soils of the Liard River basin.

When you reach the river, stand on the platform there. To your right are trees right down to the river bank and to your left is the 400- to 500-million-year-old rock wall that marks the beginning of the Liard River Canyon. The water that flows past you goes to the Mackenzie River and will eventually end up in the Beaufort Sea.

Watson Lake

In 5.8 kilometres (3.6 miles) from Lucky Lake, a sign welcomes you to Watson Lake (incorporated in 1984). Watson Lake, on the 60th parallel, is called 'the Gateway to the Yukon.' The town began as a trading post in Kaska Dena First Nation territory. The official history is that the settlement was named after a trapper and prospector named Frank Watson, who homesteaded in the area of the lake with his Kaska Dena wife. Another story states that it was named for Bob Watson, who had a store here in the 1930s. Since the Alaska Highway was built, Watson Lake has grown into a major centre that supplies and serves the logging, mining and tourism industries of the region.

Continue up the highway until you come to the visitor information centre at the junction with Highway 4, the Robert Campbell Highway, which goes past Ross River. Turn right to visit 'the Sign Post Forest' to contribute a sign of your own.

On the same property as the signs there is some old machinery that was used in the building of the Alaska Highway. One of the pieces is an orange tractor called Gertrude. This 1938 TD 35 International tractor came to the Yukon with its owner, Ed Kerry, in 1942. It worked all over the Yukon for 40 years and was then donated to the Yukon government by the Kerry family in memory of Ed Kerry.

The Sign Post Forest

'The Sign Post Forest' began with one sign put up during the construction of the Alaska Highway. A soldier was given the task of repainting the direction sign on the highway. Being lonely for his home town of Danville, Ohio, he added a sign for it.

Other soldiers joined in and the practice was continued by visitors, who have been adding home-made signs or ones from their towns as they pass through. There are now long rows of sign-filled posts and the forest is growing every year.

There is also a model of a Bell P-39 Airacobra plane. More than 8000 of these planes stopped in at Watson Lake between 1942 and 1954. During World War II (when the Russians were on the same side as the Americans), these American P-39s were painted with Russian military insignia and then flown from Great Falls, Montana, to Fairbanks, Alaska, refueling at airfields along the Alaska Highway. Russian pilots then flew them to Nome, Alaska, and across the Bering Sea to Siberia. From there they were sent to the Russian front.

The aurora borealis (northern lights) phenomenon is best seen in the winter and the further north you are, the clearer and brighter the lights appear. However, most people visit Watson Lake in the summer, when there are nearly 24 hours of daylight. To allow summer visitors to see this magnificent light phenomenon, the state-of-the-art Northern Lights Centre, across the Alaska Highway from the visitor centre and one block south, puts on several shows every day between 2 PM and 10 PM, from May into September. Just sit in your chair while the northern lights dance overhead.

From Watson Lake you can head west to the Stewart-Cassiar Highway (Highway 37) and back into British Columbia, as described in Chapter 5. (As an alternative, you could first tour more of the Yukon and Alaska. For a description of the area, pick up just after Watson Lake in Chapter 1 of my book *Backroads of the Yukon and Alaska*.)

'Gertrude' at Watson Lake Sign Post Forest.

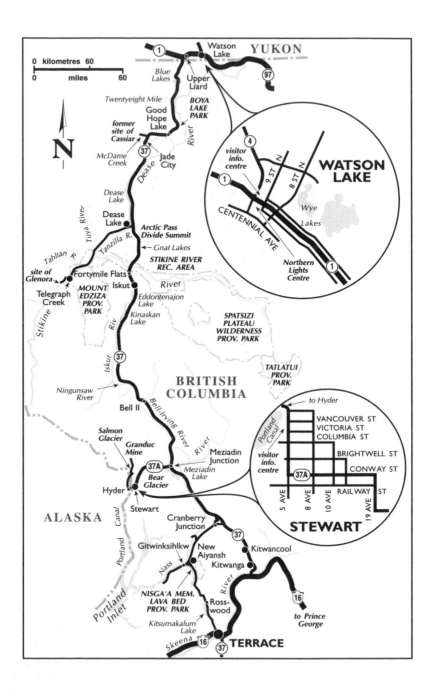

5
The Cassiar Highway

In this chapter you begin in Watson Lake, Yukon, and head almost straight south until you get to Terrace, BC. For most of the trip you will be on the Cassiar Highway (sometimes called the Stewart–Cassiar Highway), Highway 37. This highway has had a bad reputation over the years for its roughness and isolation. However, work has been ongoing to pave it and its condition has greatly improved. There are resorts, lodges, motels, souvenir shops, ranches, guided tours, campgrounds (both private and public) and rest areas along this road. It is not the long, lonely drive that some people may think.

If you are travelling Highway 37 in the evening, watch for black bears alongside the pavement, or perhaps even on it.

Watson Lake to Telegraph Creek

Watson Lake, Good Hope Lake and Jade City

Beginning on the Alaska Highway at Watson Lake, it's 10.1 kilometres (6.3 miles) from the Sign Post Forest until you cross the Upper Liard River bridge and reach the hamlet of Upper Liard. To your right is Our Lady of the Yukon Church.

This church was built in 1955 by members of the local Kaska Dena community. In the yard there is a four-sided building, each side with a mural on it. The murals depict the story of White Calf Woman receiving from Medequdihte—the Creator of the Lakota Sioux and other Native nations—the sacred pipe, which she is to take to her people.

At kilometre 9.8 (mile 6.1) from Upper Liard you reach the junction with the Cassiar Highway (Highway 37), where you turn left to head into BC. Gas up at the service station on the corner.

In 3.3 kilometres (2.0 miles) you cross the 60th parallel, where you leave the Yukon and enter British Columbia. For the next while, the highway has some sharp curves and you pass lakes, ponds and open areas. You cross rivers and creeks and can occasionally see the tops of the Cassiar Mountains ahead of you. For your convenience there are pull-outs with garbage barrels and rest areas with toilets. There are some forest service roads that branch off the highway and you can explore them if you wish, but remember that logging trucks have the right of way.

At kilometre 26.3 (mile 16.3) there is a pull-out beside the Blue Lakes where you can fish for grayling and pike. After you cross Twentyeight-mile Creek at kilometre 46.4 (mile 28.8), you are headed into the Cassiar Mountains.

At kilometre 54.1 (mile 33.6) you round a curve and go downhill; the Dease River is now to your left. The rivers and creeks that you will cross between here and Dease Lake flow into this river.

The Beaver Dam Rest Area is to your right at kilometre 74.0 (mile 46.0) and you cross Beaver Dam Creek at kilometre 75.4 (mile 46.9). To your left at kilometre 84.8 (mile 52.7) there is a short road that goes to Boya Lake Provincial Park, which has a boat launch, campsites and a picnic area.

The mountain scenery gets better as you head south, and you reach the Native village of Good Hope Lake at kilometre 96.7 (mile 60.1). There is a gas station and store, as well as the Dease River Band Council and Good Hope Lake Band Office along the highway, and the rest of the village is off the highway to your left.

You cross 1st North Fork Creek at kilometre 7.0 (mile 4.3) from Good Hope Lake, 2nd North Fork Creek at kilometre 11.3 (mile 7.0) and 3rd North Fork Creek at kilometre 13.7 (mile 8.5). Then, at kilometre 19.3 (mile 12.0), McDame Creek is to your left.

At kilometre 20.9 (mile 13.0) there is a Y junction in the road. The branch to the right goes to the former townsite of Cassiar and the Cassiar Asbestos Mine. In 1992, after 40 years of operation, the mine shut down and the town of 3000 disappeared.

The Cassiar Gold Rush

The Cassiar Gold Rush began in 1872, when gold was discovered on Dease Creek. A few years later, Henry McDame, a black man from the West Indies, and his partners made a gold discovery on what became McDame Creek (also see the sidebar, 'The Giscome Portage Trail,' on p. 49).

In 1877, a 2.0-kilogram (4.5-pound) nugget was found in McDame Creek by Alfred Freeman but by 1878 the rush was over. Though there is still active mining in the area, the miners of today use front-end loaders, dump trucks, bulldozers and huge sluices.

The site is now a reclamation project to which there is no admittance and there are no services. Go left to continue to Jade City, which you reach at kilometre 22.7 (mile 14.1).

In spite of its name, Jade City is little more than a jade souvenir store and RV park beside the road. However, it is worth a visit. Huge boulders of jade line the service road to the store. In the yard you can see some of the large saw-blades used for cutting the jade and you might even see a demonstration of jade cutting. The cut jade is sent to artisans who make the jewellery and figurines that are sold in the store. You can buy either raw jade or finished products here.

Large chunks of jade at Jade City.

Dease Lake

Just 0.5 kilometres (0.3 miles) from Jade City you can look up a road to the left to see buildings associated with the Cusac Gold Mine in the hills. At kilometre 9.8 (mile 6.1) you pass between the Twin Lakes and over the creek that connects them.

At kilometre 56.1 (mile 34.9) you lose your mountain scenery and, when you cross Beady Creek at kilometre 66.5 (mile 41.3), you leave the Cassiar Mountains. You then follow Dease Lake, which is to your right, and reach the town of Dease Lake at kilometre 108.9 (mile 67.7). Dease Lake was named for Peter Warren Dease, an explorer and fur trader. He was first with the XY Company (which explorer Alexander Mackenzie later joined), then the North West Company and finally the Hudson's Bay Company, as these companies merged. When gold was discovered in the area in 1872, the town of Dease Lake boomed for a few years. Now it is an important commercial centre for this part of the province.

In the centre of town, at kilometre 114.0 (mile 70.8), you come to Boulder Street, which goes toward Telegraph Creek. Visit some of the gift and souvenir shops here before heading to Telegraph Creek.

Telegraph Creek

Turn right onto Boulder Street to go to Telegraph Creek. Note that parts of the road ahead are not suitable for motorhomes or for holiday trailers, which should be left in Dease Lake. There is a gas station on the right if you need to top up your tank. In 1.3 kilometres (0.8 miles) you reach a T intersection. Turn left and by kilometre 5 (mile 3) you are on gravel.

Telegraph Creek Road, constructed in 1922, has been upgraded over the years, but it remains rough, very steep in places and with many sharp curves. At one point it has a very tight 180° turn that is impassable to motorhomes and vehicles with trailers.

You cross Sixteenmile Creek at kilometre 25.8 (mile 16.0) and begin the first of a series of three sharp curves at kilometre 26.8 (mile 16.7). You soon cross Nineteenmile Creek and Twentymile Creek, pass through Moosehorn Swamp and then enter the Stikine River Recreation Area at kilometre 60.2 (mile 37.4). A warning sign at kilometre 74.9 (mile 46.5) marks the beginning of an especially steep descent. Be sure that you can make that 20% climb on the return before continuing.

Use a lower gear on this winding, very steep descent as you work your way down to the Tuya River. You, or at least your passengers as you should be concentrating on the road, have great views of the canyon as you descend. The road narrows, with a wall to your right and a drop-off on the left. If you look down you can see the Tuya River snaking below you. You reach the river at kilometre 77.9 (mile 48.4) and cross it on a one-lane bridge.

After the bridge you follow alongside the Tuya awhile before you climb out of its canyon and leave it behind. But you soon have the Grand Canyon of the Stikine to your left.

Tuya River on the road to Telegraph Creek.

At kilometre 90.1 (mile 56.0) the road curves to your right. Go straight ahead to a rest area that overlooks the Grand Canyon. If it's lunch-time—or even if it isn't—stop here for a gorgeous view of the canyon. However, since there is no fence, do be careful.

In 2.6 kilometres (1.6 miles) from the rest area you are on a narrow lava-rock promontory high above both the Grand Canyon of the Stikine (to your left) and

Lava rock beside Telegraph Creek road.

Tahltan Canyon (to your right). You then come to a yellow-and-black checkerboard sign with an arrow that points downward, showing you that the road is going to curve 180° to the right and descend. To your left at the checkerboard there is a pull-out. Park here and take the path leading from it over the loose, uneven lava rock to see the Grand Canyon of the Stikine and the confluence where the waters of the Tahltan flow into the Stikine.

The Grand Canyon of the Stikine River

The Stikine River, which is about 540 kilometres (335 miles) long, begins in Spatsizi Plateau Wilderness Park. It travels westward across the Stikine Plateau and then heads southward to the Pacific Ocean near Wrangell, Alaska. Along the way it has cut a deep, narrow gorge through volcanic rock, forming the Grand Canyon of the Stikine, said to be Canada's largest canyon. This canyon is 97 kilometres (60 miles) long and in places the walls rise some 450 metres (1475 feet) above the river.

Grand Canyon of the Stikine River.

As you drive away from the checkerboard, make that sharp right-hand curve slowly and carefully as you cannot see if anyone is coming the other way. The one-lane road hugs the side of Tahltan Canyon as it descends to the river, where you enter the Tahltan Indian Reserve. The land on the reserve is private property, so please respect it. You follow beside the river to its confluence with the Stikine. Then you begin climbing up the other side of the Grand Canyon of the Stikine, with a drop-off to your left giving you a great view. When you reach the highest point you are 122 metres (400 feet) above the Stikine River.

You follow the river and canyon and reach Tahltan's school

The Tahltan Bear Dog

The area surrounding the Tahltan Reserve was formerly the home of the Tahltan bear dog. It was black and white in colour and had a head like a fox, with its ears pointed up. The end of its tail was like a shaving-brush. Although it was only about 0.3 metres (1 foot) high and weighed about 7 kilograms (15 pounds), it was used to hunt bear and lynx.

This unusual dog was first recorded by a person from the outside world, Samuel Black, a Hudson's Bay Company explorer, in 1824. In 1940 the Canadian Kennel Club recognized the breed, but by then this dog was dying out and only nine of the animals were registered. No Tahltan bear dogs survive today.

at kilometre 23.5 (mile 14.6). Continue past the school and the Native community and then you can see the older section of the community of Telegraph Creek across a canyon formed by the creek itself. The road descends and you cross Telegraph Creek. Just after the creek you reach a Y junction. The road straight ahead goes to the ghost town of Glenora, starting point of an attempted railway to the Yukon. Take the left to go into the community of Telegraph Creek.

Tahltan River canyon.

The History of Telegraph Creek

Placer gold was discovered on the Stikine River in 1861, beginning a minor gold rush, and a community was established soon afterward. It was later called 'Telegraph Creek' after the adjacent creek, which received its name on account of the ill-fated Collins Overland Telegraph line that was put through a few years later (see the sidebar on p. 23).

In the 1880s the settlement became the trailhead for a trail inland. Paddlewheelers from Wrangell, Alaska, would come up the Stikine to the town, where the passengers disembarked. At Telegraph Creek they began their overland trip by pack train to Dease Lake, and then by boat again on the Dease River to Lower Post, which can now be reached from the Alaska Highway.

This trail was popular during the Klondike Gold Rush at the end of the 19th century, with prospectors heading north to Teslin and then down the Teslin and Yukon rivers to Dawson City. The town was also a supply depot for the Yukon (or Dominion) Telegraph Line, completed in 1901, which ran from Vancouver to Dawson City and included part of the former Collins Overland Telegraph Line. Mail from Atlin, to the northwest, was carried by dog sled in winter and pack dogs in summer.

After the building of the Alaska Highway in the 1940s, the route to the North through Telegraph Creek fell into disuse and the population dwindled.

St. Aidan's Church in Telegraph Creek.

You are following the creek, which you cross again before reaching a T intersection at kilometre 25.5 (mile 15.8). Ahead is the Stikine River. One block to your right is the Riversong Cafe, where you can book riverboat tours or hikes into the Grand Canyon of the Stikine. The cafe is located in the former Hudson's Bay Company store, which was built in 1898 and is now a BC heritage building. One block to your left from the T intersection is historic St. Aidan's Church. There are some old homes on the hillside above the church and there is a Royal Canadian Mounted Police (RCMP) detachment just down the road from the church. Telegraph Creek runs beside the church, under the road and into the Stikine River.

From the Y junction where you turned left to visit Telegraph Creek, it is 19.0 kilometres (11.8 miles) to Glenora, but nothing is left of the town, which

Mount Edziza Provincial Park is situated on over 230,000 hectares (568,000 acres) of the Tahltan Plateau to the east and southeast of Telegraph Creek. Inside the park there are volcanoes, of which Mount Edziza is the dominant one. It began erupting 4,000,000 years ago, with each successive eruption adding to its height above the plateau and spreading lava over an area of 1625 square kilometres (627 square miles). It last erupted 10,000 years ago and today it is 2787 metres (9143 feet) high. Other eruptions within the past 1300 years have formed about 30 smaller cones on the plateau.

For centuries, the Tahltan Natives mined obsidian—rapidly cooled lava that has crystallized into hard, black volcanic glass—from the Tahltan Plateau below Mount Edziza. Pieces of this obsidian were sharpened into cutting tools, some of which were traded with other Native bands, from Alaska to the Queen Charlotte Islands.

Moose, caribou, mountain goat, stone sheep, grey wolf, black bear, grizzly bear and smaller mammals roam throughout the park. There is also a large population of shorebirds and waterfowl.

You cannot reach the park by road. Access is on foot, by plane or by horseback. The trails in the park are not maintained and only the hardy, skilled hiker should attempt them. For more information, contact BC Parks in Dease Lake at 250-771-4591.

was built about the same time as Telegraph Creek and once had a tent population of 10,000. When the Hudson's Bay company moved its headquarters into Telegraph Creek in the early 1900s, Glenora disappeared. However, the road is scenic and it ends in a turn-around with picnic tables.

On your return trip to Dease Lake, watch for the excellent views.

Arctic Pacific Divide Summit to Hyder

Arctic Pacific Divide Summit and Gnat Pass Summit

In 1.3 kilometres (0.8 miles) from the junction of the Cassiar Highway and the road to Telegraph Creek in Dease Lake, you reach the Arctic Pacific Divide Summit, at an elevation of 820 metres (2690 feet). There is a rest area and Lions Club campsite beside the Tanzilla River at kilometre 9.1 (mile 5.7) and you cross the river just after that.

Gnat Pass Summit, 1241 m (4071 feet) above sea level, is 20.2 kilometres (12.6 miles) from Dease Lake. You pass Lower Gnat Lake at kilometre 24.8 (mile 15.4) and are in the Gnat Valley. Look to your left across the valley to see the railway bed intended for BC Rail's Dease Lake extension from Prince George. Construction was halted in 1977 because of budget cutbacks.

Cassiar Highway.

To your left at kilometre 27.2 (mile 16.9) there is a rest area on Upper Gnat Lake. At kilometre 45.8 (mile 28.5) you enter the Stikine River Recreation Area and you cross the Stikine River at kilometre 51.9 (mile 32.3). The recreation area joins the Mount Edziza Provincial Park to the west with the Spatsizi Plateau Wilderness Park to the east.

Spatsizi Plateau Wilderness Park

Spatsizi Plateau Wilderness Park, popular with canoeists and hikers, is one of the largest wilderness preserves in Canada. Spatsizi means 'red goat' in the Tahltan Native language and it refers to the reddish tint that the goats' hair gets when these animals roll in the red sandstone dust at the higher levels of the mountains.

The Tahltan People have hunted in the area for centuries, but the area had few non-Native visitors before 1926. That year, the Hyland brothers set up a trading post on the Spatsizi River. Hunting and fishing camps were established at Cold Fish Lake and at the Hyland Post in 1948 by T.A. Walker. Walker was the force behind the creation of the 675,000-hectare (1.67 million-acre) park in 1975.

Because of the remoteness of the park, you have to hike, fly, canoe or ride in on horseback to enter it. Trails in this park began as game trails and some of them can be rough, or usable only during July and August, when the water levels are low. If you do decide to visit, you should be experienced in hiking and backcountry camping.

For more information, contact BC Parks in Dease Lake at 250- 771-4591.

Fortymile Flats, Iskut and Bell II

In 71.4 kilometres (44.4 miles) from Dease Lake you drive through Fortymile Flats, which has a store and cafe and offers lodging. The mountain scenery has returned and you can see glaciers on some of the peaks. Iskut, a Native village with a store and gas station along the highway, is at kilometre 12.7 (mile 7.8) from Fortymile Flats.

South of Iskut you pass three lakes, all on your right: Eddontenajon, Tatogga and Kinaskan. Only a few choices for overnighting in the area are mentioned below. Across the highway from the access road for Eddontenajon Lake is the Tenajon Motel and Cafe. The lake's name means 'little boy who drowned' in the Tahltan Native language, referring to the legend of a small boy who fell into the water while trying to imitate the cry of a loon. Tatogga Lake Resort offers camping, cabins, gas, fishing licences and boat rentals. At Kinaskan Lake there is a campground, as well as swimming, hiking trails, a boat launch and fishing (rainbow trout in July and August).

The mountain scenery is still with you as you cross Willow Creek 53.5 kilometres (33.2 miles) from Iskut. There is a rest area on Eastman Creek at kilometre 61.9 (mile 38.5). When you reach Devil Creek at kilometre 99.4 (mile 61.8), look down into the canyon that it has formed.

Between 1899 and 1901, the Yukon Telegraph line was run through this area from Quesnel, generally following the abandoned part of the Collins Overland Telegraph Route of the mid-1860s and completing the 3060-kilometre (1900-mile) connection from Vancouver to Dawson City. The line was used until about the 1930s, when radio communication became more practical.

At kilometre 121.9 (mile 75.7) you are beside the Ningunsaw River and you reach Ningunsaw Summit at kilometre 133.9 (mile 83.2). The elevation here is 466 metres (1528 feet).

Kilometre 160.2 (mile 99.5) brings you to the Bell-Irving River, and just after the bridge the community of Bell II is to your left. It offers gas, a hotel, a restaurant, a store, cabins to rent and a campground. You cross the Bell-Irving River once more before reaching Meziadin Junction at kilometre 255.3 (mile 158.6). There is a visitor information centre here, as well as a gas station and a campground. To go to Stewart and Hyder, Alaska, on Highway 37A, as described below, continue straight ahead. If you wish to bypass this section, go left and turn ahead to 'Meziadin Junction to Highway 16' section on p. 110.

The Bear Glacier

You are on good pavement as you wind through the mountains on the road to Stewart and Hyder. At kilometre 24.1 (mile 15.0) you round a curve and can see the Bear Glacier on the other side of a small lake formed by the melting of the glacial ice. There is a picnic area beside the lake and a pull-out along the highway in front of it. The Bear Glacier is one of just a few 'blue glaciers' (the ice is so compacted that it appears blue) in the world that can be reached by road. At one time the glacier reached to where the highway is today; the route of the old highway is above the present one.

At kilometre 31.7 (mile 19.6), look to your left to see what appears to be a glacier. What you are seeing, however, is actually avalanche snow that drops down the mountainside as it is warmed by the summer sun. You then drive through Bear River Canyon, with the Bear River to your left and rock walls on both sides. Then you cross the Bear River at kilometre 40.0 (mile 24.9). At kilometre 52.4 (mile 32.6) you start a 3-kilometre (2-mile) straight stretch of highway on what used to be part of the bed of the old railway that went to Stewart. In 59.5 kilometres (37.0 miles) from Meziadin Junction you enter Stewart.

The Bear Glacier from road to Stewart.

Stewart

As you enter the town, a sign proclaims Stewart to be Canada's most northerly ice-free port. The highway becomes Conway Street and then 5th Avenue as you drive through town.

The Natives who usually lived near the Nass River called this area *Skam-A-Kounst*, which means 'safe house,' because they came here not just to pick berries and hunt, but to hide from marauding Haida Natives, who were their traditional enemies.

Non-Native settlers slowly began to arrive in the late 1890s. In 1902, two brothers, Robert and John Stewart, laid out a townsite and named it after themselves. Gold-seekers arrived and, by 1910, the town was booming, with 10,000

Artifacts at Historical Society Museum in Stewart.

inhabitants. Four steamers arrived each week with passengers and supplies. But dreams of Stewart becoming a port on a transcontinental railway never materialized and, because of economic problems and the First World War, there were only 17 people living in the town by the end of the war.

Between 1919 and the early 1950s, large gold mines began operations in the area and there was a brief resurgence of the town. Another recovery happened in the late 1950s, with the opening of the Granduc Copper Mine north of Hyder.

The record annual snowfall in Stewart was 2804 centimetres (1104 inches). Movies filmed here include *Iceman*, John Carpenter's version of *The Thing*, and *Bear Island*.

Stewart's Heritage Contest

Stewart has a Heritage Walking Tour that takes you past 30 plaques located throughout the town.

To get started, park at the visitor information centre and pick up a map of the town. The first site is at the Historical Society Museum in the 1910 firehall. Continue down Columbia Street to 9th Avenue, where St. Mark's Community Church is on the corner. Its first service was in 1910. St. Felix Catholic, constructed in 1920, is at 418-8th Avenue. The goal is to locate all of the plaques in the town.

If you can locate at least 12 of the plaques, you will receive a special souvenir, which you can pick up at the visitor centre.

Stop in at Stewart's visitor information centre on 5th Avenue to pick up a pamphlet titled *Salmon Glacier Self Guided Auto Tour*—it has write-ups of about 14 sites along the road ahead. The first six sites are between Stewart and the Fish Creek Wildlife Viewing Area in Alaska. If you would like to visit the Salmon Glacier itself, bear in mind that parts of the Salmon Glacier–Granduc Road past Fish Creek are very narrow, have drop-offs and are subject to slides, so taking a motorhome or holiday trailer is not recommended. If you prefer not to drive, ask about bus tours to the glacier.

Hyder

Follow the highway from Stewart around the end of the Portland Canal to Hyder, Alaska. This salt-water fjord is the boundary between British Columbia and Alaska and, at 145 kilometres (90 miles) in length, it is said to be the fourth-longest fjord in the world. Hyder was originally called 'Portland City,' but the name was rejected by the US Post Office, because of the number of places in the United States that were already called 'Portland.'

In 2.7 kilometres (1.7 miles) you reach the Canada customs post (there is no US customs post here) and at kilometre 2.9 (mile 1.8) you are in Hyder. Immediately to your left there is a small, square stone building, Storehouse #4. Built in 1896 by the US Army Corps of Engineers, who were exploring the boundary along the Portland Canal, it is the only one of four such buildings still standing. It has been used as a cobbler's shop and a jail and it is considered to be the oldest masonry building in Alaska.

Continue on this road through Hyder. There are gift and souvenir shops all along this road and they deal strictly in Canadian money. The one place that you do need US money is the US Post Office. At kilometre 3.6 (2.2 miles) from reaching Hyder you enter the Tongass National Forest.

Bear looking for spawning salmon at Fish Creek near Hyder.

At kilometre 6.5 (mile 4.0) you cross Fish Creek and reach Fish Creek Wildlife Observation Site. There is a parking area to your left after the bridge. To your right is the creek where, if you are here in July or August, you can see salmon coming to spawn. This place is popular with photographers because of the black bears, grizzly bears and eagles that come to the creek to feed on the spawning fish. As you approach, watch out for people standing on the road with their cameras waiting for a bear to appear. The best time to see the bears is before 11 AM or after 7 PM. Although the bears are intent on eating and are not usually interested in the people, remember that they can still be dangerous: wardens patrol the area to remind visitors to stay away from the animals.

The Salmon Glacier–Granduc Road, completed in 1965, continues past the spawning area to the Salmon Glacier. However, it is very narrow, has drop-offs and is subject to slides. If you keep going, you pass site #7 in the pamphlet from the visitor centre, the start of the trail to the old Titan Mine. Then you drive through the site of the Riverside Mine and reach the border between Alaska and British Columbia. You then come to the Indian Mine and Premier Mine viewpoints and, at kilometre 17.6 (mile 10.9), you can see below you the toe of the Salmon Glacier, the fifth-largest glacier in Canada. At kilometre 24.7 (mile 15.3) you arrive at site 14, the Summit Viewpoint for the glacier. Although the road does continue from here to the site of the Granduc Mine, it is not maintained beyond this point.

Return to Meziadin Junction and turn right to head for Highway 16 and Terrace.

The Granduc Mine

Copper, a soft yet tough metal, has been used by humanity to make weapons and other articles since the Bronze Age, around 3500 BC. Non-Natives first noticed copper deposits in the Stewart Hyder area in 1931. Nothing was done about mining the ore here until 1948, when claims were staked in the Leduc area, in the mountains north of Stewart. In 1953, Granby Mines optioned the property and the next year Newmont Mining bought a half-interest in the Granduc Mine, which proved very successful.

In 1968, a 17.7-kilometre (11-mile) tunnel, constructed under mountain ridges and glaciers, was completed to take the ore from the Leduc copper ore body to the mill at Granduc Camp. The mine closed in 1978, was reopened again in 1979 under new owners, and finally shut down again in 1983.

Salmon Glacier.

Meziadin Junction to Highway 16

Meziadin River Fish Ladders and Elsworth Logging Camp

At kilometre 13.9 (mile 8.6) from Meziadin Junction there is a road to your right. To see the fish ladders and/or to fish on the Meziadin River, turn onto this road and in 0.7 kilometres (0.4 miles) you come to an abandoned airstrip. There are some roads leading into the bush on the other side of the airstrip. For the fish ladders, turn left onto the strip, go to the end and follow the rough road there 0.5 kilometres (0.3 miles) down to the river. It might be best to leave your vehicle on the airstrip and walk.

The road curves past some fishing camp cabins to a turn-around at a fence. Look at the falls on the river and notice that there are fish ladders, protected by concrete covers, on both sides of the falls. Some fish out in the middle of the river do try to jump up the falls and about 1% of them make it. The other 99% head up the ladders, where they are counted as they go through.

The first fish ladder was brought here by packhorse from Stewart in 1910. The present ladder was built in 1966. There are signs at the turn-around that tell about the spawning cycles of the sockeye, pink, coho and chinook salmon.

To fish (refer to the fishing regulations for guidelines) on the Meziadin River, return to the landing strip and take the first left off it. In 0.3 kilometres (0.2 miles) you reach a wooden bridge over the river. There are pull-outs on both sides for parking.

Return to the highway and, in 0.4 kilometres (0.2 miles) from the fish-ladder turn-off, you cross the Nass River, which has eroded a 120-metre (400-foot) wide, 40-metre (130-foot) deep gorge.

At kilometre 3.6 (mile 2.2) you reach the entrance to Elsworth Logging Camp, where you can stop for gas, propane, groceries or a fishing licence.

Man-made falls at Meziadin River fish ladders.

At kilometre 64.3 (mile 40.0) from Elsworth Logging Camp you reach Cranberry Junction. There are two routes from Cranberry Junction to Highway 16. One route (described first) keeps you on Highway 37 through Kitwancool and Kitwanga to meet Highway 16 at a point about 100 kilometres (60 miles) north of Terrace. The other takes you over the Nass Forest Service Road and through the Nisga'a Lava Bed to Highway 16 at Terrace (see p. 114).

Westward by Land: One Woman's Tale

Lillian Alling was born in Russia and, for reasons no longer known, moved to New York, where she worked as a maid. She spoke English and was well educated but her greatest desire was to return to Siberia and her homeland. Unable to save the money to buy a steamer ticket, she decided to walk across North America to the Bering Sea and then cross it to Siberia. She studied maps and books in the library and drew her route. She was about 25 when she left New York in early 1927.

How she crossed the continent no one knows, but on September 10 she arrived at Second Cabin on the Yukon Telegraph Line, which at that time ran northeast for 1600 kilometres (1000 miles) between Hazelton and Dawson City. The lineman at the cabin fed her and then telegraphed the Provincial Police in Hazelton. He told them of her quest and that she was in no condition to attempt it with winter coming on.

A police officer came after her and took her to Hazelton, where he tried to persuade her not to continue. She was adamant, so he arrested her for vagrancy but, when she was searched, she was found to have 20 dollars and an iron bar. Although she was not a vagrant (because she had money), the judge charged her with carrying an offensive weapon and fined her 25 dollars. Since she couldn't pay the fine, he sentenced her to two months in Oakalla Prison near Vancouver, BC, thus ensuring that she would not continue her trek during the winter, as well as providing food for her malnourished body.

When released from prison in November, she found work in a restaurant and in the spring she resumed her journey. She followed the telegraph line and each cabin reported her progress to the police. She arrived in Whitehorse on August 31, 1928, having travelled a distance of some 965 kilometres (600 miles) from Hazelton. She reached Dawson City on October 19.

She worked in Dawson over the winter and repaired a skiff that she had bought. When spring breakup arrived, she launched her small boat, loaded with provisions and a bedroll, on the Yukon River. She arrived at the mouth of the Yukon and headed into the Bering Sea. The last report of her journey was made by an Inuit, who said that he saw a woman beyond Teller, a post on the Seward Peninsula near the place in continental Alaska that is the shortest distance from Siberia.

In 1972, an account of Lillian's trek was written in the magazine *True West*. A reader of that article wrote the editors and told of a trip that he had taken to visit a friend in Yakutsk, Eastern Siberia, in 1965. That friend told him of a strange sight that he had seen as a boy when he had lived in Providenija, a small coastal community about 275 kilometres (170 miles) across the Bering Strait from Wales, Alaska (at the tip of the Seward Peninsula). A crowd had gathered around a white woman and three Inuit who had landed on the shore. The woman claimed to have walked a great distance across America to reach her homeland. The year was 1930.

Cranberry Junction to Highway 16 via Highway 37 and Kitwanga

There is a sign for Gitanyow Historic Village 46 kilometres (28.6 miles) from Cranberry Junction. Just past that sign, turn right onto Kitwancool Access Road to go to Totem Park in Kitwancool, a small Gitxsan (previously 'Gitksan') town. The

Row of totems at Kitwancool.

former name of the village, *Gitanyow*, meant 'place of many people.' After most of its inhabitants were killed in raids, the name was changed to *Kitwancool*, meaning 'place of reduced numbers.'

Drive 2.3 kilometres (1.4 miles) down this access road to a junction (there are no street signs). Turn left onto the road here and go 0.8 kilometres (0.5 miles) to the park. One of the 23 totems here, titled *Hole in the Ice*, represents the story of a man who chopped a hole in the ice and fished to prevent his tribe from starving to death. Inside the band administration office beside the park there is a book to sign, as well as a box for donations toward the upkeep of the park.

Continue along the road past some houses and from the edge of town it is 2.0 kilometres (1.2 miles) back to the highway. Turn right onto the highway and travel 14.7 kilometres (9.1 miles) along it to Kitwanga Road North. Turn right onto this road and drive 0.8 kilometres (0.5 miles) to a pull-out on your right at the Kitwanga Fort Historic Site, the first major Native historic site to be established in western Canada.

At the pull-out there are three interpretive signs. These signs and four more along the self-guiding trail here are in English, French and the Gitwangak Native language. They tell about the history of the Native fort that was built on nearby Battle Hill, along one of the 'grease trails' used by the Gitwangak. Grease trails were so-named because of their use in transporting eulachon oil (see the sidebar about the eulachon on p. 199), which was a trade commodity of the coast Natives.

St. Paul's Anglican Church in Gitwangak.

From these signs you go down a long set of steps and follow the path to the base of Battle Hill. Continue around the hill until you get to steps that lead to the top. Climb them and from the top of the hill you can see a bit of the Skeena River and some of the town of Kitwanga.

To get onto Highway 16 again, continue along the road, now Kitwanga Valley Road, through Kitwanga and turn right onto the highway. In 3.5 kilometres (2.2 miles) from the Kitwanga Valley Road you reach a sign that announces the upcoming junction with Highway 16 and ahead is a bridge over the Skeena River. To your left is a road into the village of Gitwangak. Once on it you can see St. Paul's Anglican Church, built in 1893, on your left. Carry on past the church to the tall totem poles of the village, which are to the right.

Return to Highway 37 and cross the Skeena River to reach the junction with Highway 16. At the junction there is a service station with a restaurant. You can turn right to go to Prince Rupert, where Chapter 6 begins, or you can turn left and pick up Chapter 6 at p. 127.

Native Totem Poles

The Native people of what we now call British Columbia have traditionally lived in separate bands or tribes. Each band evolved its own connections with spirits, mythology and legends, which centre around birds and other animals, such as bears, ravens, whales, hawks and frogs. Each clan within a tribe took one of these creatures as its crest.

As artistry developed, woodworking became a great skill. The abundance of trees helped totem poles to become an important way to recount significant events in the lives of the families of the tribes. Although totem poles were being carved for centuries before the arrival of the Europeans, carving became easier after the 1860s and the greater availability of metal tools. Redcedar is the most popular wood for several reasons, including its ease of carving, its natural resistance to rotting and the large size of redcedar trees.

Because the mythical birds and other animals were generally thought of as people, they are shown in human form on the totem poles, with a mark to indicate what animal they are.

There are a great variety of historical uses for totems. Some were used as house supports, others held the remains of the dead. Special grave markers were used to mark the grave of an important member of the tribe.

The various tribes developed different styles. The Tsimshian, who live along the Skeena and Nass rivers, are best known for their memorial poles, which stand in front of a house displaying the crests of the present or former owner. Some reached 21 metres (70 feet) in height and many still stand.

You can see some of the older poles still standing in BC, dating back to the 1840s, in the vicinity of Kitwancool, Gitwangak and Kispiox.

Totems carved these days combine the traditional with the modern, showing new influences in Native lives.

Cranberry Junction to Terrace via the Nisga'a Lava Bed

At Cranberry Junction on Highway 37, turn onto the Nass Forest Service Road, a gravel logging road. Though it is, in places, quite narrow and bumpy, it can be driven in a motorhome or a vehicle pulling a trailer if you go slow.

At kilometre 30.0 (mile 18.6) you come to an unnamed creek. Look to your right as you cross the bridge and you can see this creek flowing into the Nass River. There is a pull-out to the left after the bridge so that you can look down on the rock walls of the creek.

At kilometre 45.0 (mile 28.0), a sharp turn to your left leads to the Dragon Lake recreation site, where there is a boat launch and camping area. It is lovely to camp here among the tall trees beside the lake. If you miss the first turn-off for the campsite, there is a second one just past it.

Take the turn-off to your left at kilometre 17.4 (mile 10.8) from Dragon Lake to enter New Aiyansh, 'Home of the People of the Ponds.' As you drive into town, watch to your left at kilometre 0.8 (mile 0.5) for the community hall. It has a painting on its front that represents the four Nisga'a clans in the area: the raven, orca (killer whale), eagle and wolf. To purchase local Native art, stop in at Nass Valley Gifts at 314 Adam's Crescent.

Creek along Nass Forest Service Road.

Lava rock at Nisga'a Memorial Lava Bed Provincial Park.

Back on the main road, you cross the Tseax River (*Sii Aks* to the Nisga'a) at kilometre 0.8 (mile 0.5) from the turn into New Aiyansh and enter Nisga'a Memorial Lava Bed Provincial Park. Just after the bridge there are parking areas on both sides of the road. Behind the one to the left is the Tseax River, where Natives fish for salmon and steelhead.

Nisga'a Memorial Lava Bed Provincial Park is managed jointly by the Nisga'a Tribal Council and BC Parks. It is dedicated to the two villages that were destroyed—and the more than 2000 Nisga'a people who died—when a volcano erupted and sent lava and gases through the area in the 1700s.

As you continue into the park, you are driving over the lava bed. The vegetation on the lava in the park varies from lichen to tall trees. At kilometre 1.3 (mile 0.8) from the turn-off for New Aiyansh there is a junction with a road to Terrace, but continue ahead toward the village of Gitwinksihlkw. Shortly after the junction there is a road to your right that goes to the bank of the Nass River, which was forced from the south end of the valley to the north end by the lava flow.

The lava in the park has hardened in different ways. For example, a wrinkled effect resulted where the top layer cooled and formed a crust while the lower layer continued flowing. Watch for the Log Mould Trail at 3.0 kilometres (1.9 miles) from the turn-off for the Nass River. About five minutes' walk over the lava brings you to a 'tree mould,' which was formed where the lava hardened around a tree that later either burned or rotted, leaving a hole in the lava. Please remain on the trail so as not to disturb the area and to avoid falling through a thin layer of lava.

You pass a second road to Terrace (on returning from Gitwinksihlkw you will take this one; the two meet about 2 kilometres [1.2 miles] toward Terrace). In 2.8 kilometres (1.7 miles) from the trailhead, turn right onto Anlaw Road to go to Gitwinksihlkw, formerly Canyon City. You come to a bridge over the Nass River at kilometre 1.0 (mile 0.6). There are two totem poles at each end of the bridge and a walkway on the left side from which you can take pictures of the poles or look at the river.

At the end of the bridge, turn left and drive into the village. Continue to the end of the main street and you come to a suspension bridge. Built in 1968, it was the only way into the village until the vehicle bridge was constructed in 1995. Anyone using the old bridge does so at their own risk, as it is not being kept up.

Back at the junction with the road from New Aiyansh, turn right and to your left in 0.3 kilometres (0.2 miles) is the dedication site where the Nisga'a Memorial Lava Bed Provincial Park was officially opened in 1992.

On your way back toward New Aiyansh from Gitwinksihlkw, turn right onto (what was from the other direction) the second road to Terrace. In 1.9 kilometres (1.2 miles) from the start of this road to Terrace you come to the turn-off for the park's visitor centre and headquarters, which are in a building fashioned after a longhouse. Drive 0.7 kilometres (0.4 miles) down the access road to stop in to see—and perhaps buy—Native crafts, and to get information about the park.

The visitor centre is the meeting place for those who wish to do the 3-kilometre (2-mile) organized hike over the lava flow to the extinct volcano. Reservations are required for the hikes, which are held every day from Wednesday to Sunday between May 1 and September 31 and begin at 10 AM and 3 PM. You can phone Hayatsgum Gibuu Tours at 250-633-2150 to book your reservation.

Suspension footbridge at Canyon City or Gitwinksihlkw.

A Volcanic Eruption

The Nisga'a people have traditionally fished, hunted and gathered along *Ayns Lisims* ('murky river,' commonly known as the Nass River). Many of the Nisga'a were living in two villages beside it when the volcanic eruption of *Wil Ksi Baxhl Mihl* ('where the fire ran out') happened about 250 years ago.

For about three years they had heard rumblings. Then one day smoke appeared in the sky and a fiery lava began flowing down the mountainside. Fumes suffocated a lot of people. Some tried to escape by burying themselves in the ground. Many ran away.

After the lava stopped flowing, it was many weeks before the survivors could return and look for their family and friends. The lava had destroyed the two villages and killed about 2000 of the villagers. It was many years before fish began swimming up the new channel of the Nass River and life returned to normal.

Just after the road to the centre you meet up with, from your left, the first road to Terrace that you passed on your way to Gitwinksihlkw. After driving 3.7 kilometres (2.2 miles) from the side road to the visitor centre, you reach a turn-off to your right for Vetter Falls. The very short road into the parking lot is narrow, so park your motorhome or truck and trailer along the main road. From the parking lot you can walk over the lava rock to the top of the falls. The waterfall is not high, but it is in a pretty setting among the trees.

Vetter Falls.

You cross a bridge 3.0 kilometres (1.9 miles) from the Vetter Falls turn-off, and just after the bridge there is a wide area for you to park while you visit Beaupre Falls. A yellow sign with a black arrow shows you where to enter the forest for your five-minute walk to the falls. The waterfall is about 10 metres (33 feet) high, with the water fanning out over the rock.

At kilometre 8.3 (mile 5.1) from Vetter Falls, the Tseax River is right beside the road. In places where the lava honeycombed, some of it has collapsed, creating emerald-green pools when the river is high.

Beaupre Falls.

There is a short trail to Crater Creek at kilometre 12.4 (mile 7.7). Although it is shaped like a creek, it was formed by a flow of molten lava and there is no water in it. Kilometre 13.0 (mile 8.1) brings you to Lava Lake, or *Sii Tax*, where there is a picnic site. Thousands of years ago, during the last ice age, a small lake was formed here. When the volcano erupted, lava blocked off the outlet stream for the lake, thus raising the water level by about 30 metres (100 feet). The rock on the beach here is black, marking the end of the lava flow.

From the turn-off for the picnic site you follow the lakeshore, and at kilometre 10.2 (mile 6.3) you leave the provincial park. Kilometre 37.3 (mile 23.2) brings you to Rosswood General Store, on your right, where you can get gas, groceries, snacks, pop and coffee.

Crater Creek.

In 1.5 kilometres (0.9 miles) from the store there is a pull-out with a tall tree to your left. Pouring from a spout attached to the trunk is clear, good-tasting spring water. Somehow a hose was run up inside the trunk of the tree and this spout was attached. Stop here and fill up your water jugs.

At kilometre 40.3 (mile 25.0) from the water tree you start down a hill and can see the city of Terrace. Then you reach a stop sign at Highway 16 at kilometre 41.2 (mile 25.6). Turn right to get to Prince Rupert and begin the trip in Chapter 6.

Rosswood Water Tree.

6
Prince Rupert to Topley Landing

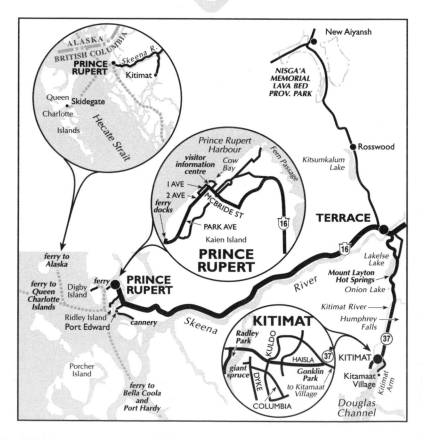

ALASKA
BRITISH COLUMBIA

PRINCE RUPERT

Skeena R.

Kitimat

Queen
Charlotte
Islands

Skidegate

Hecate Strait

New Aiyansh

NISGA'A
MEMORIAL
LAVA BED
PROV. PARK

Rosswood

Kitsumkalum
Lake

Prince Rupert
Harbour

visitor
information
centre

Cow
Bay

Fern Passage

1 AVE
2 AVE
ferry
docks

MCBRIDE ST

16

TERRACE

PARK AVE

Kaien Island

PRINCE
RUPERT

16

Lakelse
Lake

Mount Layton
Hot Springs

Onion Lake

ferry to
Alaska

ferry to
Queen
Charlotte
Islands

Digby
Island

ferry

PRINCE
RUPERT

River

Kitimat River

Humphrey
Falls

37

Ridley Island
Port Edward

cannery

Skeena

KITIMAT

37

KITIMAT

Radley
Park

Kuldo

HAISLA

Kitamaat
Village

Kitimat Arm

Porcher
Island

ferry to
Bella Coola
and
Port Hardy

giant
spruce

DYKE

Gonklin
Park
to Kitamaat
Village

Douglas
Channel

COLUMBIA

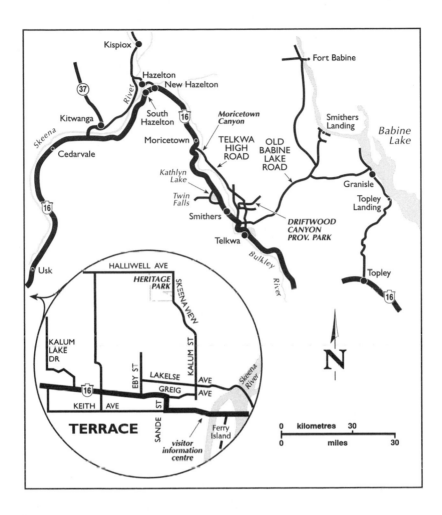

Once you have toured Prince Rupert, hiked through a stunted forest and visited a historic cannery, you will drive east through the Coast Mountains, beside the Skeena River. Expect to see beautiful mountain scenery along the Skeena River when the sun shines and wisps of clouds hanging on the mountainsides when it is overcast. Some of the history and legends of Upper Skeena are represented along this highway by the Hands of History Tour signs, the first of which is found at Cedarvale. There are 11 signs in all. Some are mentioned; see if you can find the rest.

Totem poles, tree faces, churning rivers, fossils and angels are some of the numerous sights in this chapter. And, of course, the scenery is always worth the drive.

Prince Rupert to Kitimat

Prince Rupert and Area

Prince Rupert, at the western end of the Yellowhead Highway (Highway 16) is on Kaien Island, whose name comes from the Tsimshian First Nations word for the floating foam on the reversing tidal rapids at Butze Rapids (see p. 123). Around the mid-1800s there were as many as nine Native villages on the shore of what is Prince Rupert Harbour today. The first surveyors landed at Cow Bay in 1905 to begin laying out the streets of Prince Rupert on land owned by the Grand Trunk Pacific Railway, which wanted to run a line to the coast (see sidebar on p. 161).

When the city was incorporated in 1910, it bought the land from the railway and then went bankrupt. The railway was completed in 1914 and the town slowly began to prosper, with fishing becoming a major industry. During the Second World War, American military personnel moved into the area and troops and equipment passed through here on their way to Alaska. A pulp and paper mill was set up on nearby Watson Island in 1947 and Prince Rupert was designated a national harbour in 1972.

The Museum of Northern BC and the Prince Rupert Visitor Information Centre are in the same building at 100 1st Avenue West, which is one block toward the water from where Highway 16, as McBride Street, makes a 45° turn to become 2nd Avenue West). At the museum you can take in one of the summer programs—such as an archaeological dig, a tour of archaeological sites around the harbour and a visit to a Native village, or a heritage walking tour of the city—or you can stay to watch a one-hour drama on the history of the city. Pick up the list of Prince Rupert attractions, only a few of which are referred to in this book, and decide on the ones to visit.

When you come out of the museum, a block to your left are Market Place and the courthouse. When you turn off the street into the driveway, to your right there is a steamroller. To your left you can see a totem pole in front of the archives, an old caboose and a carving shed where you can watch Native carvers at work. Walk past the courthouse and behind it is the Sunken Gardens.

Prince Rupert's original wooden courthouse burned down in 1911. Court was moved to a temporary building and excavation was begun for a new one in 1912. But the city was having financial problems and the population wasn't growing, so the provincial government in Victoria decided to halt construction, leaving the large hole sitting empty for many years. In 1921 Victoria decided a new courthouse could finally be built. Revised plans were drawn up so new excavations had to be made. When the new courthouse opened, the old diggings were turned into the beautiful Sunken Gardens.

Colourful flowers line the top part of the gardens and flower-beds are terraced down into the cavity. You can walk down to the floor of the gardens and sit in the peace and quiet. While here, look at the tunnels on each side. They were used to hide anti-aircraft ammunition during the Second World War.

Sunken Gardens in Prince Rupert.

Cow Bay is about a 10-minute walk from the museum. The bay got its name from a dairy farm that was set up here in 1909. Now shops, galleries and restaurants, some in buildings that date back to the 1930s, line Cow Bay Road. Everywhere you look you will see something that reminds you of a Holstein cow, be it the black-and-white garbage cans or names such as 'Cowpuccino's.'

When leaving Prince Rupert, begin measuring distance eastbound on Highway 16 from the corner of McBride Street and 2nd Avenue West, with the courthouse to your left. You travel through part of the city and then, at kilometre 7.9 (mile 4.9), the parking area for the Butze Rapids Trail is to your right. The trailhead is across the highway from the east end of the parking lot. Expect to take about two hours to hike this easy 4-kilometre (2.5-mile) loop trail through wetland and tall forests to the reversing rapids, which are best seen as the tide is going out.

The Queen Charlotte Islands

If you wish to visit the Queen Charlotte Islands (*Haida Gwaai* is the name preferred by the Haida First Nation), pick up information booklets and a ferry schedule at the visitor information centre in Prince Rupert. You should make reservations for the ferry ride, which takes 6–8 hours, depending on the weather. You have your choice of daytime or overnight crossings, but there is only one trip per day, and not necessarily every day of the week, so be sure to schedule enough time to cross, plus one or more days to tour the islands.

There is a basic rate one-way for two people and a vehicle up to 2.07 metres (6.8 feet) high and 6.10 metres (20 feet) in length. Discounts are given for seniors and children, and longer or higher vehicles cost more, as does an optional stateroom or dayroom.

There is an abundance of Haida history and culture—as well as lovely scenery and huge rainforest trees—to experience on the islands if you decide to visit. The islands are also popular with kayakers. Ask about guided tours of various kinds.

To get to the ferry terminal, take Highway 16 (westbound) through Prince Rupert and follow the signs.

Stunted trees at Oliver Lake.

There are two other trails that begin at this parking lot. One is for the 9.6-kilometre (6.0-mile) return hike to Mount Oldfield and the second goes to Mount Hayes, a distance of about 18 kilometres (11 miles) return. Mount Oldfield Trail is moderate to difficult, and Mount Hayes is difficult. Both climb through a forest and there are viewpoints along each for scenic pictures of the areas below.

Back on the highway, the parking lot and picnic area for Oliver Lake are to your right at kilometre 2.5 (mile 1.6) from the Butze Rapids trailhead. This small freshwater lake is surrounded by muskeg. Because the soil of the muskeg is acidic, plants cannot grow normally here. Most of those stunted trees that you see, which look like natural bonsai trees, are over 130 years old.

Three trails lead from the picnic area. One is a boardwalk, one is covered in woodchips and the third is unimproved—on a rainy day you will encounter puddles and mud on this one. They all interconnect, in case you wish to see the whole area. If you hear gunshots as you explore the area, they are probably coming from the rod and gun club's shooting range across the highway.

The right turn for Ridley Island is 0.5 kilometres (0.3 miles) from Oliver Lake. It is the site of the deep-water coal terminal that ships out coal from the Bullmoose and Quintette mines (see p. 60 and p. 62). There are no tours of the terminal but you can drive there to look at it.

At kilometre 3.2 (mile 2.0) you cross a bridge over the Galloway Rapids between Wainwright and Morse basins and leave Kaien Island. Just after the bridge you turn right to go to Port Edward and the Northern Pacific Cannery Village Museum.

Khutzeymateen/K'tzim-a-Deen Grizzly Bear Sanctuary

Located in the Western Kitimat Ranges of the Coast Mountains northeast of Prince Rupert, this sanctuary is the first in Canada specifically for the protection of the grizzly bear and its habitat. For years there had been conflict in the region between logging interests and those wanting to protect the grizzly. Finally, in 1984, a 3850-square-kilometre (1487-square-mile) area was set aside where no grizzly hunting was allowed. In 1988, logging was also discontinued. It is estimated that about 50 of the mighty bears live here today. Also within this sanctuary are old-growth rainforests, wetlands, mountains and a large variety of animal, plant and bird life. Salmon runs occur on the Khutzeymateen and Kateen rivers but fishing is not permitted.

Tours to the sanctuary last 4–10 days, but remember that you take second place to the preservation of this habitat and there are many rules that apply to your visit. See the visitor information centre in Prince Rupert for a tour outline.

Port Edward and the North Pacific Cannery

You enter Port Edward in 3.2 kilometres (2 miles) from Highway 16. Port Edward was established as a fishing village in the early 1900s. Speculation that it would be the railway terminus brought many people to the village. However, when Kaien Island was chosen for a port city instead, they moved out just as fast. It was revived for a short time when an American army camp was set up here during the Second World War and a road was built to link the village to Highway 16. Most of the buildings from the base were removed after the war, but in 1947 a pulp mill came to the area and the village's future was assured.

Stay on this road through Port Edward and, at kilometre 10.3 (mile 6.4) from the highway, you reach the parking for the North Pacific Cannery Village Museum on Inverness Passage. This salmon cannery was opened in 1889 and at its peak employed over 1000 workers. It closed in 1968. When the Canadian Fishing Company's plant in Prince Rupert burned down in 1971, BC Packers took over this site but closed it again a year later when a new plant was built. The year 1985 saw the North Coast Museum Society begin restoring the site, which opened to the public in 1989. It was also declared a National Historic Site that year because it is the oldest surviving residential cannery (at one time there were over 200 canneries including the non-residential) on Canada's West Coast.

Inside the main building you can see the workings of the cannery, photo displays and artifacts from fishing boats. The lives of the European, Japanese, Chinese and First Nations people who worked in the cannery are depicted. The restoration is ongoing and you can walk along the boardwalk and see the buildings that housed the store and the bunkhouse and see where the net boss (the person who looked after the nets) lived. The cannery buildings were set on pilings in the water so that they could be reached by land and by sea. A gift shop and a restaurant occupy the former mess house. The museum is open from 9 AM to 6 PM, seven days a week.

Northern Pacific Cannery Village Museum.

The Skeena River

Back on Highway 16, you drive through the Coast Mountains and pass a number of lakes. Most of the trees are tall through this area, but watch for areas of stunted growth, like the one at Oliver Lake. You reach Rainbow Summit, with an elevation of 160 metres (525 feet), at kilometre 17.3 (mile 10.8). At kilometre 21.6 (mile 13.4) you round a curve and the Skeena River is below on your right. You will be following it upstream as far as Kispiox and crossing many rivers and creeks that flow into it.

For those of you who wish to stop for a picnic, plenty of rest areas line the river. If fishing is what you prefer, there are a number of boat launches. If you are here while the tide is out, you will see mud-flats with the river running through them. If the tide is in, the river is so wide it looks like a lake. A rising tide can back the Skeena up all the way to Terrace.

Use caution, because in places along this stretch of the highway the pavement narrows, leaving just enough room for two vehicles to pass.

◢ River of Mists

The Skeena River was called 'River of Mists' by the Tsimshian First Nation. These coastal Natives, and Interior bands too, used the river as a trading route.

Between 1888 and 1914, sternwheelers and smaller craft pushed their way up the Skeena through the Coast Mountains to Hazelton, which was the eastern terminus of their travel. Passengers and supplies were transported upstream to the various stops along the river, while gold and furs made the trip back.

In the Kitselas Canyon (near Usk, upstream from Terrace), the river splits into three channels. To make it possible to get through the canyon, ringbolts were pounded into the canyon walls. Cables were run through the ringbolts and used to winch sternwheelers upriver. If you are interested in gold, in 1907 the steamer *Mount Royal* ran into a rock and sank in the canyon, taking five people and $70,000 in gold (in 1907 dollars) with it. Some say that the gold is still down there on the river bottom.

Skeena River, River of Mists.

Kitsumkalum Reserve and Terrace

You enter the Kitsumkalum Reserve at kilometre 129.5 (mile 80.5) from the turn-off for Port Edward. The Natives here are 'People of *Gila-quoex*' or 'Robin People,' one of the 14 tribes of the Tsimshian Nation. They were the first people in the area and their grease trails date back to prehistoric times.

To your left at kilometre 130.2 (mile 80.9) is the Kitsumkalum administration building and the House of *Sim-oi-ghets*, where you can purchase beautiful crafts made by members of the Kitsumkalum Native Band.

From the House of *Sim-oi-ghets*, it's just 0.5 kilometres (0.3 miles) until you enter Terrace, which began as a line cabin on the Dominion Telegraph Line (also known as the Yukon line) in 1901. A few years later, sternwheelers were stopping at what was then called 'Eby's,' after the brothers who owned the store, hotel and freighting business located there. Although it was also known as 'Kitsumkalum,' it was later named 'Terrace,' for the natural benches or terraces upon which it is built.

To the left at kilometre 3.0 (mile 1.9) from Sim-oi-ghets is the road up to Nisga'a Memorial Lava Bed Provincial Park. If you missed it while doing Chapter 5, take this road and refer to 'Cranberry Junction to Terrace via the Nisga'a Lava Bed' in Chapter 5 (beginning on p. 114).

As you head into Terrace, continue on Highway 16 to Sande Street, which is at a set of traffic lights. To see Heritage Park, go ahead through the lights at Sande and you are now on Greig Avenue, which you follow to Kalum Street.

Turn left onto Kalum and the road climbs and curves, becoming Skeena View Road before you reach the park, which is on your left in 2.1 kilometres (1.3 miles) from the beginning of Kalum. There is a fence around it and above the fence you can see the top of a gazebo. Open the gate, step into the gazebo and ring the bell. A guide dressed in period clothing will come to greet you.

The park's log buildings, each with its own style of construction, include the *circa* 1920 Kalum Lake Hotel, a 1912 barn, a miner's cabin and a lineman's cabin from the Dominion Telegraph Line. There are also buggies and other forms of transportation. The first guided tour begins at 10 AM and the last is at 4:30 PM, with the park closing at 6 PM.

Terrace Heritage Park.

Back at the lights at Sande, turn left onto Sande then left again onto Keith, which is also Highway 16. When you see the visitor information centre to your right, look to your left across the highway from it to see Big Bertha, the last of just four portable log spars ever built in the world. Weighing 45 tonnes (50 tons), it was brought to Terrace in 1952. Once unloaded, it sank in about 1 metre (3 feet) of mud because of its weight. This problem plus others led to it eventually being abandoned. It would have been sold for scrap if not for one of the town's councillors, who rescued it and had it set up here in 1985.

Just past Big Bertha, at kilometre 0.4 (mile 0.2), you cross the first bridge over the Skeena River and are on Ferry Island, once the site of a sternwheeler landing. Immediately after the bridge there is a turn-off to the right for the Ferry Island Municipal Campground. This lovely campground also has a day-use area with hiking trails through the park and along the river. In addition, and worth a stop even if you don't want to camp, are the faces carved in the trees by local carver Rick Goyette.

To reach the trail to the faces, drive through the entrance gate and go straight ahead toward the day-use area. On the left in 0.8 kilometres (0.5 miles) from the gates you come to a pull-out with a garbage barrel and a sign warning that motor vehicles are not allowed on the trail. Park here and take the path into the woods. You have to watch closely, because the faces are narrow and from only 10 to 25 centimetres (4 to 10 inches) high, and they are not on every tree.

When you see the first one, however, you will know what to look for and the others will be easier to find. If, however, you haven't seen any by the time you reach a bench made of two pieces of log with wood nailed to them, check the trees

The Kermode Bear

Called *Moksgm'ol*, which means 'white bear,' by the Tsimshian First Nation, the rare Kermode bear is also known as 'ghost bear' or 'spirit bear.' Kermodes are found only in the mountains and forests of BC's central and northern coast.

The first sighting of the ghostly bears by non-Natives was in the early 1900s and Francis Kermode, director of the BC Provincial Museum at the time, investigated. When he reported his findings to the New York Zoological Society, the bear was declared a distinct species and it was named in his honour. Later it was decided that the Kermode is actually a subspecies of the American black bear and it was called *Ursus americanus kermodei*.

It is a surprise to many people that, except for the colour of their coats, there is no distinction between the area's black bears and those with the famous creamy white fur (which can actually range to yellowish or reddish, or even blue-gray or brown). A double recessive gene in the normally black-furred population produces up to one in ten bears with the unusual coat colour. However, it's really not much different than dark-haired human parents giving birth to a blond-haired baby.

Kermodes have been seen in the forests by hikers and have even been spotted along the highway. If you see one of these bears, which are protected by law, remember that it is a wild animal and that the same rules apply for meeting it as for any other bear.

beside the bench and you will find two faces. As you continue on the path, you will see where some people have removed faces from the bark. Please leave those that remain for others to enjoy. The walk is a leisurely 15 to 20 minutes and you will come out at the Skeena River near the day-use area parking lot. You can return to your vehicle by walking along the road.

Just after getting back onto Highway 16, you cross the second bridge over the Skeena River and then take a right turn toward Kitimat in 0.7 kilometres (0.4 miles) from the campground road.

Mount Layton Hot Springs, Kitamaat Village and Kitimat

The road to Kitimat is paved, with plenty of mountain scenery to enjoy. At kilometre 8.8 (mile 5.5) you descend into a valley and can see Lakelse Lake ahead. Lakelse Lake Provincial Park Picnic Area is to your right at kilometre 14.1 (mile 8.8) and at kilometre 18.4 (mile 11.4) you reach Lakelse Provincial Park Campground. In the park campground you can walk through tall stands of Sitka spruce, western hemlock and western redcedar and you can fish for salmon, cutthroat or Dolly Varden. You can also swim in the lake, which is warm in summer.

The turn-off for Mount Layton Hot Springs is to your right 2.2 kilometres (1.4 miles) from the campground turn-off. You can use the hot tub, with a temperature of about 41°C (105°F) or, if you prefer it a little cooler, the main pool, the turtle pool for children and the waterslides, all with a temperature of 32°C (90°F). The development also has a hotel and a play area for children. Inside the hotel is a picture of the log bathhouse that was built in 1930. At that time, the water travelled some 1525 metres (5000 feet) down a wire-bound pipe to the pool.

Log bathhouse and water pipe at Mount Layton Hot Springs.

You pass Onion Lake, which is rumoured to be bottomless, and cross the Kitimat River 12.8 kilometres (8.0 miles) from the hot springs. To the right after the bridge there is a camping area from which you can fish for coho, chinook and steelhead.

Kilometre 20.8 (mile 12.9) brings you to the left turn for the road to Humphrey Falls. There is no sign to watch for, but you will know that you have gone too far if you cross Humphrey Creek at kilometre 22.0 (mile 13.7); just turn around and go back to the first road to the right. Just after you turn off the highway there is an area to the left where you can leave your holiday trailer or motorhome, or even your car if you prefer to hike in.

The road is very bad in places and it is recommended for four-wheel-drive vehicles or pick-up trucks only. It is only one lane wide, with bush growing right to the edge. Just after getting onto the road you reach a T intersection where you turn right. You pass one road to your right and at kilometre 2.3 (mile 1.4) you turn right onto the second one. At kilometre 2.5 (mile 1.6) from the highway there is a parking area. Take the highest of the two paths that begin here.

Humphrey Falls.

When you reach the end of the path, you can see water gush out between the rock walls and down the canyon in front of you, but you cannot actually see the falls unless you climb up and over some steep rock. From there you can look down as the water pours over the edge. Below you (which you cannot see) the water makes a right angle turn and flows through the above-mentioned canyon.

If you decide to hike in to the falls, take the second road to the right after turning right at the T intersection.

To see some of BC's wildlife up close without worrying about safety, turn right onto Oolichan Road at kilometre 11.8 (mile 7.3) from the Humphrey Falls road. Mike's Taxidermy, with over 83 square metres (900 square feet) of stuffed-animal display area, is on your left just down the road. Stop in to ask about his work or to strike a deal to buy, sell or trade.

At kilometre 5.0 (mile 3.1) from Oolichan Road there is a sign that says 'Welcome to Kitimat' to your right and the visitor information centre is to your left. At the visitor information centre you can book a variety of tours: the Alcan smelter, where they turn bauxite into aluminum; the Eurocan Pulp and Paper Company; the Kitimat River Fish Hatchery; and the Methanex Corporation, where they produce methanol (the locations of these sites are listed later in this chapter). Note that none of these tours are available on weekends.

Kitimat was established in the early 1950s after the BC government invited the Aluminium Company of Canada (Alcan) to set up a smelter in the province. The name of the city is a variation of *Kitamaat*, which is the name of the nearby Native village in the language of the Tsimshian. It means 'People of the Snow,' a comment on the fact that the area usually gets over 380 centimetres (150 inches) of snow each winter. The people who actually live in the village, the Haisla, call their village *Tsee-Motsa*, meaning 'Snag Beach.'

You drive into Kitimat on Haisla Road and in 0.5 kilometres (0.3 miles) from the welcome sign turn left onto Kitamaat Village Road to see the village and visit a Native carver.

Although you are following the shoreline of Minette Bay on the Kitimat Arm of Douglas Channel, it is hidden by trees most of the way. At kilometre 8.4 (mile 5.2) there is a pull-out to your right that overlooks the waters. In 10.1 kilometres (6.3 miles) there is a marina to your right and you are at Kitamaat Village. Follow the road through the village and turn right at kilometre 11.3 (mile 7.0). Soon afterward, turn left onto Haisla Avenue, which is just past Haisla Community School. At kilometre 12.1 (mile 7.5) the road curves right and you reach another marina, where there is also a boat launch. To your left, a totem pole marks Sammy's Carving Shop.

Sam Robinson has been carving for most of his life and his pieces have been displayed and sold around the world. He welcomes visitors to stop in and see exhibits of his carvings.

Back on Haisla Road in Kitimat, in 0.7 kilometres (0.4 miles) from Kitamaat Village Road, you can sit on a bench and look out over a wide stretch of land and the Kitimat Arm of Douglas Channel at lovely Gonklin Park, which is to your left.

Carry on through the town and you will reach the traffic lights on Kuldo at kilometre 3.0 (mile 1.9) from the park. If you want to see the largest Sitka spruce tree in the province, turn left onto Kuldo and drive one block to Columbia, where you turn right. Continue along Columbia to the T intersection on Dyke Road. Turn right onto Dyke Road and then left onto the gravel road. Drive 0.5 kilometres (0.3 miles) to a sign for 'the Giant Spruce' and turn left into the parking area. A sign at the beginning of the path warns you not to walk through here on a windy day.

It is a short path to this huge tree, which is more than 500 years old. According to the sign, the spruce is 50.32 metres (165 feet) tall, 11.2 metres (36.7 feet) in circumference and

BC's largest Sitka spruce, at Kitimat.

3.35 metres (11.0 feet) in diameter. It was registered as the largest living Sitka spruce in the province in 1983. Sitka, by the way, is a Tlingit word that means 'by the sea.'

Since the time of registration of this tree, a taller Sitka spruce—95.0 metres (312 feet) in 1988—has been found in the Carmanah Valley on Vancouver Island (see Chapter 2 in my *Backroads of Vancouver Island*). However, it does not have the circumference this one has. Also, a tree with a larger diameter of 13.7 metres (45.0 feet)—but much shorter—was found on Meares Island in 1985.

After you complete your stroll through the tall forest, retrace your drive to Haisla Road and turn left to camp, to visit the three plants and the fish hatchery for the tours mentioned earlier, or to see Moore Falls. In 0.7 kilometres (0.4 miles)

you cross the Kitimat River on the Haisla Bridge. The road curves to your left and you drive through an industrial park. At kilometre 1.6 (mile 1.0) is the left turn into Radley Park, where you can camp along the Kitimat River.

To your left in 1.6 kilometres (1.0 mile) from Radley Park is the Kitimat Fish Hatchery, which offers wheelchair-accessible fishing and a viewpoint overlooking the river.

The road to Eurocan Pulp and Paper Company is to your right at kilometre 0.4 (mile 0.2) from the fish hatchery, and at kilometre 0.9 (mile 0.6) is the road to the left for Methanex Corporation. You cross Anderson Creek and can see Alcan to the left just past the bridge. You reach the 'Smelter Tour' sign at kilometre 4.6 (mile 2.9); turn left into the parking lot for your tour.

After your tour, continue along the road and, in 0.3 kilometres (0.2 miles) from the turn-off for Alcan, there is a pull-out to your right at which you can see steps leading uphill through the trees. You have to duck under overhanging branches to climb the steps and you are in a tall, dimly lit forest. Follow the short path to a fence and turn right to get to the viewpoint for Moore Falls.

Moore Falls.

Usk, Cedarvale and Skeena Crossing Road

Back on Highway 16, in 19.6 kilometres (12.2 miles) from the turn-off for Kitimat, the Usk Chapel is to your right. This chapel was built in 1967 to celebrate Canada's centennial. Inside there are four pews and a guest book to sign. A picture of the Marsh Memorial Church, after which the chapel was designed, hangs on a wall.

In 11.4 kilometres (7.1 miles) from the chapel, there is a rest area to your

Usk Chapel.

left along the Skeena River. At kilometre 20.8 (mile 12.9) you cross Little Oliver Creek and then you cross Big Oliver Creek at kilometre 22.5 (mile 14.0).

At kilometre 39.6 (mile 24.6), turn left onto Cedarvale Road. In 1888, a mission was set up at Cedarvale and the parishioners abstained from working on Sunday, the day of rest. This move earned the hamlet the nickname 'the Holy City.'

As you drive along Cedarvale Road, you follow the Skeena River and then travel past residences, acreages and farms to reach the highway again at kilometre 2.1 (mile 1.3). At this junction there is a Hands of History Tour sign about the hamlet of Cedarvale, which is divided by the Skeena River.

The Undamaged Bible

In May 1936, melting snow and days of pouring rain caused so much water to enter the Skeena River that it could not flow fast enough through narrow Kitselas Canyon, about 3 kilometres (2 miles) downstream from Usk. And so, on May 30, the river at Usk rose to record heights, about 3 metres (10 feet) above normal, and overflowed its banks.

The residents of Usk moved to the school, which was on higher ground, leaving their homes and possessions behind. Also abandoned to the flood was the Marsh Memorial Church, built to honour a late canon, T.J. Marsh, who had spent his life administering to the needs of the people in the wilderness of Canada.

After a few days, the waters receded and the people returned to their homes. When they checked on the church, they found that the swirling water had done considerable damage, tipping over the organ and knocking the chairs around. The table that held the church bible was water-soaked and damaged from bumping into other objects and the walls but, miraculously, the bible itself was untouched.

In 9.1 kilometres (5.7 miles) from the east end of Cedarvale Road there is a rest area to your left with a write-up about the Kispiox Forest District that describes both the trees and the communities of the district. Another panel shows the Seven Sisters Mountains to the south and a third depicts the fish in the Skeena River.

At kilometre 18.3 (mile 11.4) you pass the junction with Highway 37, which goes to Kitwanga, Stewart, Dease Lake and Upper Liard (see Chapter 5). In 36.6 kilometres (22.7 miles) from Cedarvale Road you reach Skeena Crossing Road. Turn left onto it and drive 0.5 kilometres (0.3 miles) to the railway bridge. If you look up on the wall of the concrete pillar beside the road you can see '1911' carved into it. This 283-metre (930-foot) bridge was constructed as part of the Grand Trunk Pacific Railway (incorporated into Canadian National Railways in 1923; see sidebar on p. 161) that was built to link the towns along here with the coast.

Back on the highway, in 15.6 kilometres (9.7 miles) you reach the turn-off to the right for Seeley Lake Provincial Park campsite and picnic area. In the parking lot there is a Hands of History tour sign about Medeek, a large mythical water grizzly slain here.

Three Mile

During the construction of the railway, red-light districts were set up in the towns that sprang up along the tracks. The residents and businesses of Hazelton, wanting to bring respectability to their town, decided to pass a law restricting its 'ladies of the evening' to 5 kilometres (3 miles) outside the town limits.

The ladies moved outside the limits and set up their business at a place they called 'Three Mile.' Because the construction workers went out there to spend their money, other businesses soon followed and eventually the name of the settlement was changed to 'New Hazelton.' The several Hazeltons in the area, which are named for the hazelnut (filbert) bushes of the area, vied to be the area's stop on the railway when it was built, with New Hazelton eventually winning.

Railway bridge built in 1911 at Skeena Crossing.

South Hazelton, New Hazelton and Hazelton

You pass the road to South Hazelton on the left and enter New Hazelton, reaching the turn to Hazelton and Kispiox at kilometre 9.5 (mile 5.9) from Seeley Lake. On your left after the turn is the visitor information centre, where a sign explains the Hands of History Tour. Inside the centre you can pick up a map that shows where all the signs are. Next to the building there are two statues: one of a prospector and one of Cataline (see sidebar on p. 143), said to be the best packer in the province and possibly the continent.

Statue of Cataline at New Hazelton.

You pass through the Native village of Hagwilget and, to your left 1.3 kilometres (0.8 miles) north of the junction, there is a pull-out where you can look down on Hagwilget Canyon about 80 metres (260 feet) below. From here you can see an arched suspension bridge over the Bulkley River and canyon. The Natives called the river *Watsonqual*, but the non-Natives renamed it for Colonel Charles S. Bulkley, who was the chief engineer for the building of the Collins Overland Telegraph (see sidebar on p. 23).

The arched bridge is one lane wide, so you have to yield to traffic already on it. There are walkways on both sides of the bridge and a parking area to the left on the other end of the bridge, where you can park if you want to walk out on it for a better view of the canyon.

Hagwilget Bridge.

Hagwilget Canyon from Hagwilget Bridge.

Bridging Hagwilget Canyon

Since the early 1800s, four bridges have spanned Hagwilget Canyon, which was carved by the Bulkley River. To build the first footbridge over the canyon, local Natives pushed a pair of long poles from each side out over the river until the ends overlapped. The trunk ends were weighed down by huge rocks on the cliff top while the smaller top ends were tied together using rope made from the inner bark of cedar trees. The poles were positioned to make a bridge about 1.8 metres (6 feet) wide. A floor and sides made of bark rope were added to complete it.

This bridge was used for years. When it began to fall apart, the Natives built a second one, using telegraph wire left behind after the Collins Overland Telegraph Line was abandoned in 1866. The wire replaced the cedar bark rope, making the bridge stronger, to withstand the weight of packhorses.

In 1913, the government constructed a low-level bridge further down the Bulkley River. However, it was so narrow that a team of horses could barely cross and its steep approaches prevented the hauling of heavy freight. Late in 1913, Robert Douglas of New Hazelton decided to build a bridge where the Native bridge stood. He hoped that it would bring prosperity to his town. Working with a wire and cable firm, he constructed his bridge and then the road to it. Although it was used for years, the bridge's drastic sway in the strong winds made it unpopular with drivers.

Finally, in 1931, the government moved Douglas's bridge further up the Bulkley and turned it into a footbridge. The government then built the fourth and current bridge over the Bulkley River.

You pass the Native villages of Two Mile and Gitanmaax along the road and then reach the turn-off for Kispiox, which is to your right 4.0 kilometres (2.5 miles) from the bridge. Continue ahead (instead of taking the turn-off) and at kilometre 5.5 (mile 3.4) the road curves to the right and you are on River Road. As soon as you come out of the curve, turn left to go to the 'Ksan Historical Village and a campground. Shortly after turning off, you can go left between two totem poles to enter the village or go right to reach the campground.

'Ksan Village is a replica of the type of Gitxsan and Wet'suwet'en village that has been here for hundreds of years. In the village there are traditional houses, one of which is the House of Wood Carving, where you may see jewellery, masks or wall panels being made. Or you can watch the 'Ksan Performing Arts Group act out events from their history and culture. You can also explore the burial house, smokehouse and other buildings. Visit the Gift House of Arts and Crafts to learn about the style and designs of the Gitxsan people, or tour the Skeena Treasure House, a museum that displays Native artifacts. There is also a trail that leads from the parking lot to a viewpoint overlooking the Skeena River, which flows past the village.

'Ksan Indian Village and Museum.

Replica of a riverboat at Old Hazelton.

From the village, return to River Road and turn left to get to Hazelton, also called 'Old Hazelton' to differentiate it from the other, newer Hazeltons. Hazelton was founded in 1866 and, until the railway came through in 1914, was the terminus for riverboats plying the Skeena River.

Park your vehicle and walk through the village to see the old-style buildings from the 1890s, with verandas out front. There is also a replica of sternwheeler on display. Next to the sternwheeler is the Hazelton Pioneer Museum, where you can see displays about the history of the area. Self-guided walking-tour routes are available at the town office.

Kispiox

Return to the road to Kispiox, turn left onto it and you will be following the Skeena River. To your right at kilometre 4.7 (mile 2.9) there is a Hands of History Tour sign about Peter Gunanoot. He hid from the Mounties (RCMP) in these mountains for 13 years, while living as his ancestors had done. When he finally surrendered, he was tried and found innocent of the shooting that he had been charged with.

At kilometre 5.8 (mile 3.6) the highway curves to the right. The road that goes straight ahead, along the north side of the Skeena River to Kitwanga (see Chapter 5), has two more Hands of History Tour signs along it.

If you wish to pick your own vegetables for lunch, to your left at kilometre 10.5 (mile 6.5) there is a market garden with many kinds of pesticide-free, organically grown vegetables. At kilometre 13.3 (mile 8.3) you cross a one-lane bridge over the Kispiox River and arrive in Kispiox. Shortly after the bridge, turn right onto Sim-gii-gyat Avenue and follow the signs that lead to the totem poles. Look right for the Hands of History Tour sign about Fort Stager, the farthest-north point that the Collins Overland Telegraph Line reached before the plan was abandoned.

Just past the sign, the road curves left and you reach two long lines of totems. It's worth spending the time to look at the many different carvings on these poles.

Go back to Highway 16 and turn left onto it so that you drive through New Hazelton.

Totem at Kispiox.

The Biggest Gunfight

In 1913, seven outlaws robbed the bank at New Hazelton of $17,000 in payroll money. They were not caught and, it is believed, because of their earlier success, the same seven men returned to New Hazelton on April 7, 1914 and attempted to rob the bank again.

However, the townspeople were wiser this time and, when they realized what was happening, they set up an ambush. Over 200 shots were fired in the resulting battle, in which three outlaws were killed and three wounded. The seventh man, however, escaped with the money, $1400.

This gunfight is said to have been the biggest ever in western Canada.

Moricetown to Topley Landing

Moricetown and Twin Falls

After New Hazelton, you drive beside the Bulkley River, with occasional viewpoints overlooking it. At kilometre 36.2 (mile 22.5) you reach a flashing amber light as you drive through Moricetown.

In 0.5 kilometres (0.3 miles) from the flashing light, the Telkwa High Road, which follows part of the original Collins Overland Telegraph Line route, goes left. Turn onto it and drive across the bridge over the Moricetown Canyon. Here the broad Bulkley River squeezes through a 15-metre (49-foot) wide gorge. After the bridge there is a picnic site on your right where you can park if you want to see the river churn through the canyon or, in August and September, watch the Wet'suwet'en people stand on ledges on the canyon walls as they spear or net spawning salmon, just as their ancestors have done for centuries.

Bulkley River at Moricetown Canyon.

On the highway just past Telkwa High Road there is a pull-out to your left where you can take another look at the river and the canyon.

You can get groceries and tackle or camp on your right at kilometre 9.4 (mile 5.8) at Two Creeks and a River Store. Then you cross Trout Creek at kilometre 9.6 (mile 6.0) and Toboggan Creek at kilometre 9.8 (mile 6.1); these two creeks and the Bulkley River give the store its name.

Adam's Igloo, which has a wide range of stuffed animals plus jewellery and Native crafts, is to the right at kilometre 22.6 (mile 14.0). To go to Twin Falls and Glacier Gulch, turn right onto Lake Kathlyn Road at kilometre 24.2 (mile 15.0).

The road passes Kathlyn Lake (previously called 'Chicken Lake' because it is drained by the Chicken River) and crosses a railway track. In 1.7 kilometres (1.1 miles), turn right onto Glacier Gulch Road and, at kilometre 3.4 (mile 2.1) from the highway, you pass Davidson Road. The pavement is replaced by rough gravel—any type of vehicle can make it if you go slow—and you begin to climb uphill past tall trees. At kilometre 4.9 (mile 3.0), look up through the tree branches to see one of the waterfalls. At kilometre 6.0 (mile 3.7) you reach a picnic area and the trail to the gulch and falls.

You begin the trip to either Twin Falls or Glacier Gulch on a single-wide trail covered in loose rock, but you soon come to the junction where the trails part. To the left, a sign at the beginning of the gulch trail warns that it is steep, with an elevation gain of 355 metres (1165 feet) and that the marked trail ends after 1260 metres (4135 feet). On the way you have views of Twin Falls and you get close to the Kathlyn Glacier but not to the toe. If you decide to hike this trail, you should plan on about four hours for the round trip.

Go to the right for Twin Falls. You can see the two separate 150-metre (500-foot) high waterfalls ahead of you and soon the path narrows and goes uphill. When you reach the first bench, you are at the best place to get a photo of the two falls together, unless you have a wide-angle lens. The waterfall to your right is lighter and whispier, and the one of the left is fuller and stronger. If you look at the rock wall around you, you can see many more smaller falls.

Continue past other benches to the viewpoint for a closer view of the falls and, if you wish, to the base of the left waterfall. The hike will take about three-quarters of an hour.

Twin Falls.

Smithers

Back on the highway, you reach the town of Smithers 6.4 kilometres (4.0 miles) from Kathlyn Lake Road. The Bulkley Valley Museum and Visitor Information Centre is on your left at kilometre 7.8 (mile 4.8). In the yard of the museum is the *Quesnel*, a railcar bought by the Lions Club of Smithers in 1974. It was restored and is now used for local meetings. Across the side street from the museum there is a replica of the world's largest goat, which was shot by hunters in the area in 1949.

Inside the museum you can see fossils from Driftwood Canyon Provincial Park that date back 50 million years. At one time, members of the public could hunt for fossils in the canyon, with the request that they turn over anything they found to the museum. But soon the fossil beds were being wrecked and fossils stolen, so as many fossils as could be found were dug up and moved to the museum. After looking at the fossils in the museum, you can head out to Driftwood Canyon Provincial Park to see where they came from.

To reach the park, once you are finished visiting Smithers, head eastward out of town on

Replica of record mountain goat shot near Smithers.

Little Switzerland

Smithers is known as 'Little Switzerland' because of its surrounding mountains and Bavarian-style buildings. Across the highway from the museum is the statue of 'Alpine Al,' a 2.1-metre (7-foot) tall Swiss herdsman blowing a 3-metre (10-foot) long alpenhorn.

Al previously stood in front of the Edelweiss Hotel in Little Rock, until the hotel burned down in 1973. Because Smithers had decided on the Bavarian theme the year before, it was decided to purchase the statue (which had been moved to Christina Lake, BC) and bring it to the town.

Highway 16. Just after you cross the Bulkley River at kilometre 2.7 (mile 1.7) from the museum, turn left onto the Old Babine Lake Road. This paved road curves past residences and then farms. At kilometre 7.2 (mile 4.5) from the highway, turn left onto Telkwa High Road, which is gravel. Kilometre 9.2 (mile 5.7) brings you to Driftwood Road, where you turn right. At kilometre 11.2 (mile 7.0) you cross a Bailey bridge over Driftwood Creek and at kilometre 13.4 (mile 8.3) you reach the parking area for Driftwood Canyon Provincial Park.

This park was established in 1967 to protect the fossil beds. Part of the land was donated by Gordon Harvey, an area pioneer. The shale outcroppings through which Driftwood Creek carved Driftwood Canyon suggest to geologists that at one time there was probably a long, narrow lake here.

Go to the footbridge over Driftwood Creek, which marks the beginning of a 300-metre (980-foot) trail. Along the trail there is a write-up that tells how the fly, twig and trout in the display ended up as fossils. You can continue walking, through the woods, until you reach a viewing platform. From here you can look up the cliff face, but there is not much to see, except marks where fossils were removed from the rock.

The Best Packer in BC

Born near the Spanish border in France, John Jacques Caux came to Canada in the 1850s. He headed to Yale, BC, where he gained his nickname, 'Cataline.' One explanation for the nickname goes as follows. He could not speak English so, when asked if he came from Catalonia, he nodded his head and was thereafter known as Cataline. While in Yale he formed a partnership with another man from his home area and began leading a pack train between Yale and Barkerville, and eventually all over the north of the province. After a few years, Cataline set up his own packing business.

Because of his determination to succeed, he always got his pack train through to its destination—even if it was a remote settlement or a placer claim—and he became known as a man you could trust to get your supplies to you.

There are many legends surrounding this man. It is said that he had such good blood circulation that he would sleep in the snow with just a canvas pack between him and the ground, and no cover. He never wore socks but, on one occasion, when the streets of Hazelton were slippery after a thaw followed by freezing weather, he went into the Hudson's Bay Company store and bought a pair of socks. Everyone in the store was shocked until they saw him pull the socks over his boots. He was using them for better traction on the ice.

His favourite liquor was cognac, and after every drink he would pour a small amount into his hand and rub it into his hair. He'd say 'A little on the inside, a little on the outside,' as he was doing it. Some people claim that he thought it was a cure for baldness, and others say that it was to prevent a hangover.

In 1913, when Cataline could no longer make the packing trips, he sold his business to George Beirnes and settled into a small cabin on Beirnes's ranch, across the Bulkley River from Hazelton. He later moved into Hazelton, where he died in 1922.

There are write-ups at the platform about the formation of fossils, as well as pictures of some of the discoveries made at Driftwood Canyon Provincial Park. A fossil discovered here is of a species of fish, *Eosalmo driftwoodensis*, that is considered to be the missing link between salmon and trout.

Smithers Landing, Granisle and Topley Landing

Drive the 4.2 kilometres (2.6 miles) back to Telkwa High Road and turn left. Go 2.0 kilometres (1.2 miles) to the junction with Old Babine Lake Road. (If you want to head straight for the highway and skip the rest of this chapter, turn right. When you reach the highway, go left to go to Telkwa, where Chapter 7 begins.) To go to Smithers Landing, Granisle and Topley Landing, turn left onto Old Babine Lake Road. This road is suitable for any vehicle, but the driving will be slow.

There are residences along the beginning of this road. At kilometre 18.4 (mile 11.4) you reach a T intersection. Burnt Cabin Road, to the right, will take you to the highway. Turn left to continue on Old Babine Lake Road.

This piece of road takes you through valleys with great mountain scenery. There are several hiking trails that are also used for skiing and snowmobiling in winter. One, Dome Mountain Trail, is at kilometre 19.7 (mile 12.2) from the junction of Old Babine Lake Road and Telkwa High Road.

You are on a logging road; the side roads leading off it just go into logging areas. Explore them if you wish, but watch for logging trucks. If a road has an 'Active' sign on it, it is best to stay away.

There are also 'deactivated' roads along here that are being left to return to nature. You shouldn't drive on them, but you may want to hike up one or two that rise above a valley to enjoy the view.

At kilometre 40 (mile 24.9) you cross a bridge over a marsh. There is a pull-out to the left if you want to overlook the wetland and watch for birds and animals. Look way across the marsh to see Chapman Lake.

To your right at kilometre 47.0 (mile 29.2) is the Granisle Connector Road. Continue ahead to go to Smithers Landing. Doris Lake is to your left at kilometre 49.1 (mile 30.5) and at kilometre 49.7 (mile 30.8) you cross a bridge over a creek between Doris Lake and Tanglechain Lake, which is hidden by trees. If you would like to camp along the shore of Doris Lake, watch for a sharp left turn for Doris Lake Forest Recreation Site at kilometre 50.8 (mile 31.6).

Kilometre 52.3 (mile 32.5) brings you to a Y junction in the road. Take the road to the left if you want to head for the campground at the old site of Fort Babine, 41.5 kilometres (25.8 miles) from this Y.

Go right at the Y junction for Smithers Landing Provincial Park. This very winding road is mainly downhill. Suskwa Lodge, with guides and cabins and boats to rent, is to your right at kilometre 10.9 (mile 6.8). Kilometre 11.5 (mile 7.1) brings you to a second Y junction, where you go right to pass a resort area and Tukii Lodge with a store, marina, boat gas, and boats and cabin rentals.

You arrive at Smithers Landing Provincial Park on Babine Lake. There are picnic tables, a campground and a boat launch.

At 177 kilometres (110 miles) in length, Babine Lake is the longest natural lake in British Columbia. You can fish for whitefish, kokanee and burbot, or try for a trophy rainbow trout or lake trout (char).

Fishing Babine Lake at Smithers Landing.

Bear Island on Babine Lake.

Return the 18.3 kilometres (11.4 miles) to Granisle Connector Road and turn left. This road is rougher than Old Babine Lake Road. There are other roads off it but just stick to the main one and watch for small 'Granisle' signs. At 24.5 kilometres (15.2 miles) from the beginning of the connector road you join a road from your left and 0.5 kilometres (0.3 miles) from this junction is the turn-off to the left for the Bear Island campsite and viewpoint.

It is a short but steep descent off the road into the Bear Island Recreation Site, where you can picnic or camp on Babine Lake. As you look out from the campsite, you can see two islands. The larger one on the left is called Bear Island, but if you look at the smaller one, it seems to have the snout of a bear at one end—so could it be 'Cub Island'?

In 3.8 kilometres (2.4 miles) from the turn-off for Bear Island you reach pavement and the village of Granisle. Granisle Museum and the visitor information centre are in the large log building to your left at kilometre 4.8 (mile 3.0).

The first copper mine in the area opened in the 1920s, but soon failed. In 1967 a second attempt at mining was made and a small village, Granisle, was established. A third mine began operation in the early 1970s and the village expanded from 300 residents to over 2000. When this mine finally closed in 1992, the population declined to 300 again. Recently, though, Granisle has become a retirement community and its population is growing again.

During excavation at one of the copper mines, the remains of a 34,000-year-old mammoth were found. People in the village hope to rebuild the skeleton some day, but for now you can see some of the bones at the museum.

Take the left turn for Topley Landing at kilometre 10.0 (mile 6.2) from the museum.

In 1.6 kilometres (1.0 mile) you reach the Topley Landing Heritage Building. From 1948 to 1988 it was Our Lady of Fatima Mission. It was restored in 1995 and is now called 'the Church of Angels,' because of the number of angel statues inside it. It is not used as a church anymore.

Besides the angels, you can also look at lanterns, a wood stove, a pump organ, a bell rope, a write-up on Topley Landing, and other exhibits. If the building is locked, there is a number on the door for you to call.

The 39.6 kilometres (24.6 miles) of road from Topley Landing to Highway 16 and Topley is paved. Chapter 7 begins up the highway to your right about 90 kilometres (55 miles) away at Telkwa, but if you are in a hurry, you can turn left onto the highway and pick up Chapter 7 at Topley (p. 152).

The Church of Angels

If you have a family member or friend who has passed away and is now an angel, bring an angel statue of any shape or size with his or her name on it to the Church of Angels. The statue will be hung on the wall or placed on a shelf. Also bring a brief history and picture of the person, which will be placed in the angel registry, along with the angel's name. Although the angel statue becomes part of the church and will be looked after, it still belongs to the donor and may be reclaimed at any time. Financial donations by visitors help pay for the upkeep of the Church of Angels.

The Church of Angels at Topley Landing.

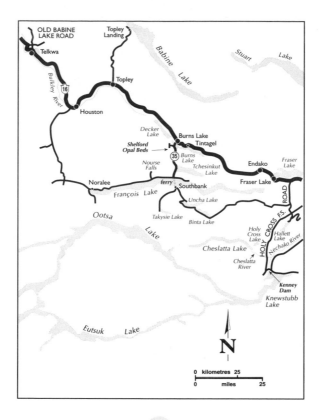

7

Telkwa to Quesnel

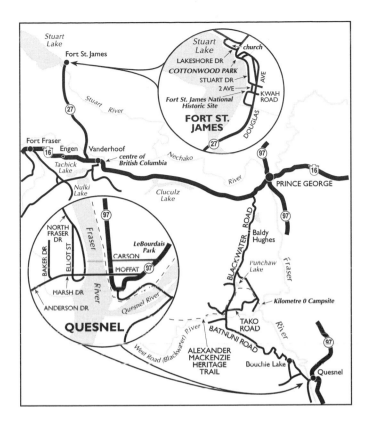

Driving across a dam, standing in the geographical centre of the province, and visiting the historic Fort St. James, the capital of the colony called New Caledonia, are just some of the highlights in this chapter. You will also pass through the Lakes District, where there are over 4800 kilometres (3000 miles) of shoreline from which to fish, and you can compare your fishing rod to the world's largest when you reach Houston.

But some of the best features of this trip are left almost to the last. On the route southeast of Prince George towards Quesnel, you can camp beside the Fraser River near the spot where Alexander Mackenzie put his canoe ashore over 200 years ago. As you continue towards Quesnel, you can hike on some of the trail he used to cross this part of British Columbia and reach the Pacific Ocean.

Telkwa to Fraser Lake

Telkwa

Telkwa is at the junction of the Telkwa and Bulkley rivers. It is the oldest village on the route that pioneers travelled between Prince Rupert and Fraser Lake in the early 1900s. Many of its original buildings are still standing. You can take a walking tour of the town's heritage sites by starting with a tour brochure from the Telkwa Museum in the old Telkwa Elementary School on Fourth Street (Highway 16), halfway between Hill and Hankin Avenues.

Telkwa Museum.

To see the rock bluff that appeared in *Ripley's Believe It Or Not* as the only bluff in the world with three attached bridges, turn west onto Hankin Avenue just before the highway begins to climb out of town towards Houston. Go to where Hankin curves left and becomes Riverside Street. There is parking along here for you to stop and look at the one-lane vehicle bridge over the Bulkley River, the railway bridge across the Telkwa River and the piers of the third bridge that also crossed the Telkwa River. This bridge was removed in the 1930s.

Bluff and bridges at Telkwa.

If you continue driving, you can cross the vehicle bridge (into another residential section of Telkwa). Or you can walk across the bridge and stroll on the screened walkway beside the tracks, at your own risk of course. You can see the piers of the third bridge better from the railway bridge.

As you leave Telkwa, stop at the Bulkley View Rest Area, to your right 4.2 kilometres (2.6 miles) from Hankin Avenue, for a great view of the Bulkley River and the Telkwa Mountain Range beyond it. The highway curves left at kilometre 14.9 (mile 9.3) and you begin the climb up Hungry Hill. You reach the summit, with an elevation of 844 metres (2769 feet), at kilometre 23.7 (mile 14.7). At kilometre 35.7 (mile 22.2) you cross the Bulkley River on the Pleasant Valley Bridge and kilometre 40.7 (mile 25.3) brings you to Buck Creek in Houston.

Bulkley Valley.

The History of the Bulkley Valley

The Bulkley Valley was left untouched by non-Natives until the building of the Collins Overland Telegraph Line in the 1860s. The fur traders didn't come farther west than Fraser Lake and up the Skeena River to Hazelton to the east. There was no gold to lure the prospectors and settlers. When the Collins line went through the area, men and supplies came with it and, when it was abandoned, those men were left without work.

Most of the new arrivals tried prospecting, but with little luck. For the next 30 odd years, not much happened in the valley. Then gold was discovered in the Yukon and many gold-seekers passed through the area on the old telegraph trail as they headed north. Finally, in 1899, the federal government decided to run a telegraph line to the Yukon, in part following the old Collins route. It was completed in 1901, with a line cabin and lineman every 50 kilometres (30 miles) from Quesnel up through the Bulkley Valley to Hazelton and onward to Dawson City. Homesteaders began to work the land and, with the arrival of the railway in 1913, settlements appeared.

Although the valley was called 'Pleasant Valley' in 1904 by one of the settlers, it is officially named after the Bulkley River.

Houston and Topley

Houston bills itself as 'the World Steelhead Capital.' As you drive through Houston, Steelhead Park and the visitor information centre are to your left just after you pass Buck Creek.

The parking lot for the visitor centre is the site of the world's largest fly-fishing rod. Made of aluminum and put up in 1990, it is 18.3 metres (60 feet) long and weighs over 360 kilograms (800 pounds). The fluorescent orange 'Skyomish Sunrise' fly tied to the end of the line, according to the plaque, is 53 centimetres (21 inches) in length.

If you wish to take a sawmill or mine tour, registration for both is at the visitor information centre. The Northwood Pulp and Timber sawmill tour starts at 1:30 PM and you have to supply your own vehicle. The Equity Mine tour begins at 9 AM and lasts most of the day. A bus is supplied for transportation.

Across the parking lot from the visitor centre is Steelhead Park. An asphalt sidewalk takes you through a picnic area, lush lawn and flowerbeds to a fountain with a large sculpture of steelhead salmon in a fountain.

World's largest fishing rod at Houston.

On your way out of Houston you cross the Bulkley River and then pass through farmland and the community of Perow. At kilometre 29.2 (mile 18.1) from the bridge you reach Topley Landing Road (see end of Chapter 6) in Topley. Topley has a service station, a grocery store and a few businesses along the highway.

At kilometre 10.5 (mile 6.5) from Topley Landing Road you reach Sixmile Summit, elevation 1423 metres (4669 feet). After passing through the community of Decker Lake, a sign welcomes you to Burns Lake at kilometre 49.4 (mile 30.7).

 The Mexican Grinding Stone

In the corner of Steelhead Park is a cairn and grinding stone. During the 1500s rich deposits of gold and silver in what is now Mexico attracted Spanish explorers from Europe. They used this ancient 3-tonne (3.3-ton) grinding stone, along with hundreds of others, to grind the ore for the extraction of the silver.

One of the mining companies in New Spain, as Mexico was then called, was Real de Angeles. Today mining continues there and miners from the Minera Real de Angeles at Zacatecas, Mexico, visited the Equity Silver Mines Limited here to learn new and different ways of mining. As a thank you, the Minera Real de Angeles presented the Equity Silver Mine with this grinding stone on July 21, 1985.

Mexico and British Columbia are two of eight major places in the world where pure silver is mined.

Burns Lake and Area

At kilometre 1.7 (mile 1.1) from the welcome sign there is a white building to your left that contains the Burns Lake (or Lakes District) Museum, along with an art gallery and the Chamber of Commerce. The structure is the original Ministry of Forests building and inside it are rooms depicting life in the 1930s and 1940s.

Behind the white building there is a small log one. Around 1917 it was a gambling hall that was nicknamed 'the Bucket of Blood' after a shooting over a card game. Go inside to see an old table and chairs, a bed, a Hudson's Bay Company beaver trap and a washing machine. Next to the white building is the visitor information centre.

'Bucket of Blood' at Burns Lake Museum.

If you wish to take a side trip to taste fresh spring water, hike through the bush, or look for opals, turn south on Highway 35 in Burns Lake. You begin by crossing a bridge over the lake. To go to the Shelford Opal Beds or sample the spring water, turn right onto Eagle Creek Road at kilometre 1.0 (mile 0.6). This road begins paved and in 0.4 kilometres (0.2 mile) there is a Y junction. Go right onto the gravel and you will come to a sharp curve and then another Y junction. This time go left. At kilometre 3.1 (mile 1.9) from Highway 35 turn left onto Eagle Creek Forest Service Road.

To your right at kilometre 0.3 (mile 0.2) from the last junction, there is a pullout with a rock cairn. Stop here to try some of the spring water, which runs through a clear hose. It is cool and refreshing and you might want to fill your water containers.

At kilometre 1.3 (mile 0.8) from the last Y junction there is another Y where you go right. At kilometre 2.6 (mile 1.6) there is a parking area with trailheads for the 1.4-kilometre (0.9-mile) Eagle Creek Trail and the 0.8-kilometre (0.5-mile) Beaver Pond Trail, which ends at a forest service recreation site. Continue driving along this road for less than 1.0 kilometre (0.6 miles) to the recreation site.

From the recreation site you can take the 1.8-kilometre (1.1-mile) Lookout Trail or the 1.9-kilometre (1.2-mile) Opal Beds Trail. The Opal Beds Trail takes you to a ridge overlooking the valley of Eagle Creek and then you will reach a point where it follows above a small creek. The opal beds are between the trail and the creek.

The opal beds were discovered and staked in 1980 by John Shelford. In 1984 he reached an agreement with the Ministry of Forests, the Village of Burns Lake and the Chamber of Commerce, whereby he gave up his claim and the area was set aside as a reserve where no staking is allowed and anyone can search for the gemstones.

François Lake Ferry.

Go back to Highway 35. Turn right if you would like to fish or camp at François Lake or explore this area further. You pass roads to Guyishton Lake and Tchesinkut Lake, said by the local people to be the purest lake in the province. At kilometre 22 (mile 13.7) you reach a flashing red light. Turn right and in 0.8 kilometres (0.5 miles) the François Lake Ferry is to your left.

The MV *Omenica Princess* leaves here on the half hour and it is about a 20-minute ride across the lake to Southbank. A map at the ferry shows the lakes on the south side of François Lake, where you may want to fish. (Note that it is also possible to drive around the lake.)

If you would like to camp along François Lake or see Nourse Falls, continue past the ferry and follow the road as it curves between the lakeshore and farmland. McLure Pit Forest Service Recreation Site is at kilometre 10.1 (mile 6.3) and 0.5 kilometres (0.3 miles) farther you pass Government Point Recreation Site, where there is a boat launch.

To get to Nourse Falls on Allin (Nourse) Creek, continue along the road and in 3.8 kilometres (2.4 miles) from Government Point Recreation Site you reach Henkel Forest Service Road, which is to your right. Turn onto it and you immediately cross a cattleguard (an arrangement of bars with gaps between them) set into the roadbed to limit the movement of cattle. At kilometre 5.2 (mile 3.2) there is another road to your right. Turn onto this one and very soon you come to the parking area for the trail to the falls viewpoint. The waterfall is across the canyon and hard to see but the canyon itself, which you walk beside most of the way, is well worth the hike.

As you walk, you can catch a glimpse of the falls across the canyon and you have good views of François Lake. In about 15 minutes you reach a picnic table from where you can see how deep the canyon really is. The trail continues past the table; when you arrive at the Y junction, go right. After about 10 minutes you arrive at the viewpoint. The falls tumble in layers and the rock wall of the canyon is spectacular. If you want to take photographs, you should come in the afternoon.

You can continue on the road along the north shore of François Lake, passing through Colleymount and Noralee, and then either head north to Houston or south to visit more lakes of the Lakes District.

The Lakes District is also known as 'the Land of a Thousand Lakes.' This 1.2-million-hectare (4630-square-mile) region is bounded on the south by the northern part of Tweedsmuir Park, on the west by Topley, on the east by Endako and on the north by Babine Lake. Four of the major lakes are Babine, François, Tetachuck and Ootsa.

Babine Lake is reached by going north of Topley (see Chapter 6) or by heading north to Donald Landing on Babine Road just west of Burns Lake. To get to François Lake and the heart of the Lakes District you go south of Burns Lake on Highway 35. By crossing François Lake on the ferry you can reach great fishing lakes, but you could also tour through the 'South Country,' as it is called by the locals.

Besides swimming, camping and boating on the lakes in the South Country, fishing for some of the largest char and rainbow trout in the province is very popular. You can pick up a copy of the *Lakes District Visitor's Map* at the visitor information centre in Burns Lake.

Tintagel, Endako and Fraser Lake

Back on Highway 16 and heading eastward, you have Burns Lake to your right. In 12.0 kilometres (7.5 miles) from the junction with Highway 35, look to your right for the Tintagel Rest Area, which has a cairn. The community of Tintagel, once a stop on the railway, was named after Tintagel, Cornwall, England in 1913. The 45-kilogram (100-pound) central stone of this cairn was sent here in 1967 at the request of the local residents. It once was part of the walls of Tintagel Castle, the supposed birthplace of King Arthur. Inside the cairn there is a time capsule to be opened in 2067, Canada's Bicentennial.

In 52.5 kilometres (32.6 miles) you cross the Endako River and you enter the town of Endako at kilometre 55.9 (mile 34.7). Many of the residents here are employed by the Endako Mine, Canada's largest molybdenum mine. Molybdenum is a hard, heavy chemical element used to strengthen and harden steel alloys. The Endako Mine Road is to the right at kilometre 57.8 (mile 35.9) and the mine is 11.2 kilometres (7.0 miles) along that road. If you wish to tour the mine, phone 250-699-6211 to check on tour times.

In 11.6 kilometres (mile 7.2) from the side road to the mine, a sign welcomes you to Fraser Lake, established when the railway was built. The visitor information centre and Fraser Lake Museum are to the left at kilometre 13.2 (mile 8.2). Just as you enter the museum, look to your right to see the carved bear, then spend some time viewing the rest of the displays.

Tintagel cairn.

The Kenney Dam to Vanderhoof

The Kenney Dam

Look to your left 5.7 kilometres (3.5 miles) from the Fraser Lake Museum for a sign put up by Fraser Lake Sawmills. Opposite the sign, turn right off the highway onto Holy Cross Forest Service Road to go to the Kenney Dam. (If you are in a hurry, flip ahead to 'The Highway Route to Vanderhoof and Fort St. James,' on p. 161.) This road is also called 100 Road, because the distances (in kilometres) marked on signs along this road begin at 100 and so, for example, 5 kilometres (3.1 miles) will actually be 105 on the sign. You can relax and not have to worry about keeping track of your odometer, just watch for the posted kilometre signs.

There is a self-guiding forestry tour along this forest service road and the first of the 14 sites, each with a safe pull-out, is at the corner where you turn off the highway. You can pick up a brochure from the box on the sign to your right (if there are no brochures, you can return to the Fraser Lake visitor information centre to get one). The sites are marked by oval signs along the road that correspond to the numbered information in the brochure; only a few of the sites are mentioned in this book.

The best time to travel this road, which has a speed limit of 70 kilometres per hour (43 miles per hour), is on weekends. If you are on it during the week, drive with your headlights on and, if possible, follow one of the radio-equipped logging trucks. The driver will advise others of your approach. Do not pass the logging truck unless the driver signals for you to do so. If the logging truck pulls over and stops, do the same, because the driver is probably making room for a truck coming the other way.

The road is wide, with the usual curves and hills. At the 102-kilometre mark (2.0 kilometres from the highway) is site #2. Here you can see an immature forest of mixed trees, with lodgepole pine as the dominant species. Site #3, where you can see flooding caused by a beaver dam, is at kilometre 107.5.

Kilometre 112 brings you to the Holy Cross–Binta Forest Service Road. A right turn and a 70-kilometre (43-mile) drive would take you to Southbank on the south shore of François Lake, but continue straight ahead instead to continue the tour.

Trees line the road and, when you reach a logged area, a sign tells when it was logged, treated, replanted, weeded and pruned. At kilometre 117.5 (mile 10.9) you get to the junction with Holy Cross–Smith Creek Road, which goes to Fort Fraser, and Holy Cross–Tahultzu Forest Service Road, which goes to a recreation site on Hallet Lake. The road to Mary Jane Lake Recreation Site is to your left at kilometre 126.5 (mile 16.5). You need a boat to try your luck at this local trout-fishing spot, because the trees reach right to the lakeshore. It is about a 1-kilometre (0.6-mile) drive and then a short walk from the road.

Cabin Creek seedling cache on Holy Cross Forest Service Road to Kenney Dam.

Site #11, at the kilometre 130.5 sign, is the Cabin Creek Seedling Cache. You can drive into a large parking area to see the gravel-covered log building where tree seedlings are kept cool during planting season.

Kilometre 155.5 brings you to site #14 and the end of the tour. Here a new type of logging, called 'roadside' or 'landingless,' is being tried. By not having landings, which are places where logs are taken before going to the sawmill, more area is available for regeneration of new plants.

Natural Refrigeration

The Cabin Creek Seedling Cache is used by Fraser Lake Sawmills as cold storage for seedlings during the spring and summer planting season. It has a mesh floor built over water reservoirs. These reservoirs freeze during the winter and remain frozen into the summer. Air circulated through the vents, along with the dirt and gravel insulation covering the cache, keep the temperature inside low so that the seedlings remain in maximum health until it's time to plant them.

This storage area is large enough to hold 1,000,000 seedlings awaiting planting.

Cheslatta River at campsite.

The kilometre markers continue and you cross the Cheslatta River at kilometre 159. To your right just past the river is the Cheslatta River Recreation Site. A hiking trail to Cheslatta Falls begins across the road from the site's lower campground. The trail is part of the route that was used by the Dakelh-ne (Carrier People) for centuries and you can see evidence of their winter lodges on the return loop.

There are some very steep climbs at the beginning of the trail. After about 10 minutes you reach a Y intersection in the path where the return loop joins the main trail. Keep right. It is a very pleasant hike through the trees and then you reach the edge of a cliff, where a sign warns of a steep drop-off.

You are above the falls and can't see much because of trees. If you want a good view, you have to work your way down a steep hillside and through the trees to get to a ledge where you are level with the top of the second section of the waterfall and at the base of the first part. There are no fences, so don't take any risks. It seems that in spring and early summer the water plunges hard and heavy over the 18-metre (60-foot) waterfall, creating mists that rise high into the air. Watch for the rainbows.

Cheslatta Falls.

On the return loop of the trail you climb and descend along the Cheslatta River. When you reach the sign marked 'House Pits,' walk through the area off the trail and watch for indentations in the ground. They mark where the Dakelh-ne winter lodges, which were partly dug into the ground, once stood. Nearby, on a point at the edge of the river, there is a place for tenters to camp. When you can see the road bridge over the Cheslatta River, you have a steep climb just ahead before you rejoin the beginning of the trail.

The kilometre signs continue from the Cheslatta River. At the kilometre 167 marker there is a junction. Turn left here for the Kenney Dam, which you reach immediately afterward. As you drive the 400-metre (1300-foot) dam-top roadway, the Nechako Canyon is far below you to your left and the reservoir, Knewstubb Lake, where you may see loons on the water, is to your right.

Kenney Dam.

This dam was constructed in the early 1950s to provide power to the Alcan smelter at Kitimat (see p. 131) and was the largest rock-fill dam in the world at that time. It is 96.6 metres (317 feet) high and 12.2 metres (40 feet) thick at its top. At the far end of the dam there is a wall with a rock high up on it and a plaque stating that the rock was placed there on May 10, 1952 by the Honourable E.T. Kenney, Minister of Lands and Forests, and Minister of Public Works, in the BC government.

If you climb to where the rock sits, you have a great view of the dam, the reservoir and the canyon. Because of submerged trees and fluctuating water levels, you are warned not to swim or boat in this lake. Turn left at the wall to continue to Vanderhoof. The kilometre signs along this road are going backwards to Vanderhoof so keep track of distances on your odometer.

There are replicas of old-style log fences along here. Watch out for cattle on the road, because you will be driving through several large ranches. In some places the road goes through a gap in a fence where, instead of a gate, there is a cattleguard. At kilometre 66.0 (mile 41.0) from Kenney Dam you reach the junction with Kluskus Forest Service Road. A self-guided tour follows this road as it goes south for 73.2 kilometres (45.5 miles) and then continues westward for 26.2 kilometres (16.3 miles) along 500 Road, ending back at the Kenney Dam. Brochures are available from the box at the sign at the junction.

Cairn at Kenney Dam.

Continue ahead to Vanderhoof and in 10.2 kilometres (6.3 miles) from the junction with Kluskus Forest Service Road you reach pavement. *Sai'Kuz* Park, sponsored by the Department of Indian Affairs, is at kilometre 10.9 (mile 6.8). Within the log-and-wire fence surrounding the park stands a potlatch house, where potlatches are demonstrated, and there are also cabins, picnic tables and camping sites open to the public.

You go through the community of Stony Creek at kilometre 12.8 (mile 8.0). At kilometre 18.3 (mile 11.4) the road curves left and at kilometre 25.6 (mile 15.9) you start down a hill into Vanderhoof. You reach Highway 16, which is First Street in Vanderhoof, at kilometre 26.8 (mile 16.7).

Turn left onto First Street and drive to Burrard Avenue, at the set of traffic lights, and turn left onto it. You cross a set of railway tracks and then the visitor information centre is to your left in a grey building. Continue along Burrard to Riverside Park, which is on your left 1.0 kilometre (0.6 miles) from the lights. Here you can camp or picnic, or climb to the viewing stand to look out over the Nechako River Migratory Bird Sanctuary situated along about 5 kilometres (3 miles) of the Nechako River. Although it is lovely here any time of the year, the best time to visit is during the birds' spring and fall migrations.

Return to First Street, turn left and drive along it for less than 1.0 kilometre (0.6 miles) to Pine Avenue, where the Vanderhoof Heritage Village Museum is located. The gift shop is in the Murray House, which was the first jail. There is also a cafe, as well as some old buildings and farm equipment. The hours are 10 AM to 5 PM, seven days a week.

Settlement at Vanderhoof was begun during the agriculture boom of the early 1900s. It was originally called 'Nechako City.' When the railway went through, an employee of the railway, a Mr. Vanderhoof, wanted to turn the town into a place for retired and burnt-out writers. His plan failed, but his name stayed.

It is 6.4 kilometres (3.9 miles) west from the Heritage Site to the junction with Highway 27, which goes to Fort St. James (see the next section).

Vanderhoof Heritage Village Museum.

The Highway Route to Vanderhoof and Fort St. James

Coming along the highway from where Holy Cross Forest Service Road meets it, you follow Fraser Lake, which is to your left. You then cross the Nechako River and, in 1.5 kilometres (0.9 miles) from the crossing, you reach Fort Fraser.

This community was named for Simon Fraser, who established a fur-trading post for the North West Company here in 1806, with the first canoe-load of furs being sent out in 1807. As the fur trade west of the Rockies grew, so did Fort Fraser, until it had 225 residents in 1844. When the Grand Trunk Pacific Railway was completed in 1914, the last spike was driven here on April 7.

You pass through the village of Engen and, at kilometre 31 (mile 19.3) from Fort Fraser, you reach the junction with Highway 27, where you turn left to go to Fort St. James. The highway is paved the 52.9 kilometres (32.9 miles) to Fort St. James. At kilometre 54.3 (mile 33.7), go left on Kwah Road to reach Fort St. James National Historic Site, which you get to in two blocks.

The Grand Trunk Railway

The Grand Trunk Railway was incorporated in 1852 to build a track from Toronto to Montreal. Its routes expanded over the next 40 or so years, and in 1895, Charles Melville Hays took over as general manager. When it was decided to run a line out to the West Coast as competition for the Canadian Pacific Railway, a subsidiary, the Grand Trunk Pacific, was set up. Hays was named president in 1905 and it was his dream to have Prince Rupert as the western terminus for the track. Work was begun and, after some setbacks, the Grand Trunk Pacific line was completed to Prince Rupert in 1914. But Hays didn't live to see it: he had perished during the *Titanic* disaster on April 15, 1912.

The Grand Trunk Pacific did not make money and the parent company, the Grand Trunk Railway, declared bankruptcy in 1919, with the federal government taking over ownership later that year. In 1923 its assets became part of the Canadian National Railways.

Fort St. James National Historic Park.

Simon Fraser established Fort St. James, for the North West Company, in 1806. It became known as the capital of New Caledonia, the name that Fraser gave to the central area of what is now BC, because it reminded him of the homeland of his Scottish ancestors. When the North West Company and the Hudson's Bay Company merged in 1821, the fort became a Hudson's Bay Company post.

At the reception centre at the fort you can read about the history of the fort, see a fur-trade canoe and look at a map of the area. The original buildings here date back to the 1880s and the fort has been restored to its 1896 appearance. In the Tradestore, boots, coats and frying pans hang from the ceiling, and bottles, blankets and dishes sit on the shelves. In the Fur Warehouse you can see the pelts of various animals. The staff, dressed in historic costumes, guide you through the buildings and tell you of the fort's fur-trading history.

From the park, turn left to go back up Kwah Road and then take the first left, onto 2nd Avenue. Drive along it until you reach Stuart Drive. Turn left onto Stuart Drive and follow it as it curves through the main section of town. Cottonwood Park is to your left at 1.0 kilometre (0.6 miles) from the turn onto Stuart. The small silver replica of an airplane, which honours the bush pilots of the area, was dedicated on July 13, 1991.

You might want to have a picnic here at the park, which is on the shore of Stuart Lake. This lake was once called 'Sturgeon Lake,' but its name was changed to recognize John Stuart, a Hudson's Bay Company clerk. As you look toward the water, you can see Our Lady of Good Hope Catholic Church to your right.

Stuart Lake at Fort St. James.

To go take a closer look at the church, turn left onto Lakeshore Drive immediately after getting back onto Stuart Drive and go only a short distance. The church was constructed in 1873 by the Dakelh-ne (Carrier People) and the Oblate Missionaries. Behind the church there is a log cabin where Father Morice, who moved here in 1885 and stayed for 19 years, printed Native prayer books, hymn books and a newspaper in a syllabic alphabet that the Dakelh-ne could read.

North of Fort St. James, the road continues to Manson Creek and Germansen Landing in Omineca Country, where a gold rush took place in 1871.

Return to the junction of Highways 16 and 27. As you continue eastward, it is 6.4 kilometres (4.0 miles) from the junction to Pine Avenue, where the Vanderhoof Heritage Village Museum (see p. 160) is located.

Our Lady of Good Hope Church in Fort St. James.

Cabin behind Our Lady of Good Hope Church.

Long-Ago Massacres

Prior to 1745, a large village of Dakelh-ne (Carrier People) was situated on the banks of the Stuart River near its confluence with the Nechako River. For years its chief, Khadintel, had been marked for death by the Ts'ilhqot'in (Chilcotin) First Nation to the south in revenge for the slaying of one of their chiefs. One day in 1745, Khadintel and two companions were returning by water to the village when they saw a party of Chilcotins coming downstream.

Khadintel urged the others to run because it was he whom the warriors were after. They headed to shore and were bombarded by arrows. Khadintel managed to dodge the arrows and the Ts'ilhqot'ins, thinking that he possessed magical powers, stopped firing and told him to dance to show that he was a man. He did so and they turned and left.

Wondering why they had spared him, Khadintel returned to his village to find that it had been destroyed, leaving few survivors.

Three years later, Khadintel and a group of men—some survivors of his village and some from other villages—headed south. They travelled some 240 kilometres (150 miles) to the Ts'ilhqot'in village near where Anahim Lake is today. There they took revenge by killing the people and burning the village.

But the Dakelh-ne village was never rebuilt and the few remaining residents moved to other villages.

The Centre of BC to Quesnel

The Centre of BC

As you head eastward from Vanderhoof, watch for Grants Frontage Road to your left in 6.2 kilometres (3.8 miles) from Burrard Street. Turn onto it and there will be a trailer park to your right. In the front yard of the park there is a short cairn with a BC flag flying over it, marking the exact centre of BC.

In 50.9 kilometres (31.6 miles) from the cairn there is a sign that says 'Welcome to Prince George.' To go to the beginning of the Mackenzie Heritage Trail, watch for Blackwater Road to your right 3.3 kilometres (2.1 miles) from that sign.

Centre of BC cairn.

Blackwater Road and Baldy Hughes

Blackwater Road is paved as it curves past urban residences, then rural acreages and farms, until kilometre 28.0 (mile 17.4), when you reach Baldy Hughes. Baldy Hughes used to be the Baldy Hughes Air Force Base, which was built by the US government. Later, the Canadian government took it over and now it has been bought by private citizens who are turning it into a community.

As you leave Baldy Hughes, the pavement ends and Blackwater Road becomes gravel. In 1.7 kilometres (1.1 miles) from leaving Baldy Hughes there is a Y junction. Go left and, when you reach the second Y, at kilometre 6.5 (mile 4.0), go right.

When you reach another Y, at kilometre 20.5 (mile 12.7), you have a choice. The road to the left can be very bad in places and if you are driving a motorhome or pulling a trailer, continue to the right on the Blackwater Road to reach the Blackwater Forest Service Recreation Site on the Alexander Mackenzie Heritage Trail. (This road continues toward Quesnel and you will be rejoining it after the following side trip.) If you have a half-ton truck or a car with high clearance and want to go to the actual beginning of the Alexander Mackenzie Heritage Trail on the Fraser River, go left. If your vehicle does not meet these specs, you can continue along until Tako Road.

Alexander Mackenzie's Journey to the Pacific

In 1793, Alexander Mackenzie became the first European to cross the North American continent. He had travelled from Montreal to Athabasca Lake in northern Alberta in the late 1780s and early 1790s and from there he started out in his quest for a route to the Pacific. He and his companions paddled down the Fraser River to a point (now the Kilometre 0 Campsite) where they were met by the Dakelh-ne (Carrier People) and guided across country on a 'grease trail' to Burnt Bridge Creek (see p. 201).

From here they were taken by canoe to the site of Bella Coola. He canoed out into North Bentinck Arm of Burke Channel, where he mixed vermilion and melted grease and wrote on a rock: 'Alex Mackenzie from Canada by Land July 22, 1793,' on what is now known as 'Mackenzie Rock' (see p. 203).

The trail is looked after by the Alexander Mackenzie Heritage Trail Association. If you wish to do the approximately three-week hike along this historic trail, contact the association at Box 425, Station. A, Kelowna, BC V1Y 7P1 for more information and brochures.

The Alexander Mackenzie Heritage Trail

After taking the left fork at the Y junction, you reach a road to your right in 9.9 kilometres (6.2 miles) from the Y. When Alexander Mackenzie and his men landed, they were guided this way from the river by the Dakelh-ne (Carrier People), then taken into the forest to the right, to a fishing camp on Punchaw Lake. Continue left to reach the beginning of the trail.

To your right at kilometre 12.2 (mile 7.6) there is a sign about Alexander Mackenzie and a map showing the trail. The road winds through tall, tall trees and you get occasional glimpses of valleys. At kilometre 13.4 (mile 8.3) there is a junction with two signs. One says 'Alexander Mackenzie Heritage Trail Lookout' and has an arrow that points right, along Tako Road. Follow the other sign, which says 'Alexander Mackenzie Heritage Trail Campsite' and has an arrow to the left.

The road gets progressively narrower and rougher as you work your way down to the Fraser River. In 2.0 kilometres (1.2 miles) from Tako Road you begin a steep descent. At kilometre 2.6 (mile 1.6) there is a road to your right. If you don't want to continue, you can turn right here and join up with Tako Road.

If you stay on this road, you come to another steep downhill at kilometre 3.4 (mile 2.1) and at kilometre 4.9 (mile 3.0) you reach the Kilometre 0 BC Forest Recreation Site, which is to your right. A sign warns that the road ahead is dangerous to travel on.

Fraser River at Kilometre 0 BC Forest Service Recreation Site.

At the campsite a map shows the portion of the Alexander Mackenzie Heritage Trail in this area and an overview of the trail going to Burnt Bridge Creek on the road to Bella Coola (see p. 200). A sign here quotes from Alexander Mackenzie's journal, telling how the party had followed the Natives' directions to this spot on the river, cached some of their supplies and the single 7.6-metre (25-foot) canoe that they had been travelling in, and began their overland journey.

This campsite is unserviced, with grass and weeds growing in the camping areas. There are no garbage cans, so take your garbage out with you. On the other side of the road from the campsite is the Fraser River. In the early morning, if it is overcast or cool, a mist rises from the water.

Part of Alexander Mackenzie Heritage Trail.

From the Kilometre 0 Recreation Site, retrace your drive, uphill all the way until kilometre 2.3 (mile 1.4) from the site. Take the road to your left here and shortly afterward you join Tako Road on the left. In 4.3 kilometres (2.7 miles), take the road to your left, which goes to the Alexander Mackenzie Heritage Trail Lookout. At kilometre 1.3 (mile 0.8) from the beginning of this road, it ends in a parking area. An easy 2-kilometre (1.2-mile) long trail, which leads to the lookout—where there is a picnic area overlooking the confluence of the Fraser and Blackwater rivers—begins here.

After your picnic, go back to Tako Road. In 5.8 kilometres (3.6 miles) from the road to the lookout you cross Tako Creek. At kilometre 16.6 (mile 10.3) you reach a stop sign, where you turn left onto Blackwater Road. Notice the little yellow signs with hikers on them to mark the heritage trail along here. (If you stayed on Blackwater Road instead of taking the side trip, you would have been seeing them since south of Punchaw Lake.)

To your left at kilometre 1.1 (mile 0.7) from where you rejoined Blackwater Road is the Alexander Mackenzie Heritage Trail Forest Service Recreation Site. You can park here and cross the road if you want to walk on the historic trail.

In 1.9 kilometres (1.2 miles) from this recreation site you cross the West Road (Blackwater) River. Look down at the water and you will understand why it was called 'Blackwater.' You climb uphill after the river crossing and at kilometre 5.4 (mile 3.4) you reach a T intersection and a stop sign. Turn left onto Batnuni Road and continue toward Quesnel.

You cross Pantage Creek just after getting onto Batnuni Road and begin driving through ranchland. To your right at kilometre 47.3 (mile 29.4) there is a rock with a plaque commemorating the Collins Overland Telegraph (see sidebar on p. 23). A map here shows where the old telegraph trail goes back to the West Road (Blackwater) River.

At kilometre 47.8 (mile 29.7) you reach pavement and pass through the community of Bouchie Lake. When you reach the stop sign at kilometre 57.6 (mile 35.8), turn left to carry on to Quesnel.

The Largest Canoe in BC's Interior

In November 1911, eight surveyors stationed at Fort St. James wanted to return to Quesnel before freeze-up. However, there wasn't a scow or boat big enough to hold them along with their equipment and belongings. Finally they heard about an old Native dugout canoe nearby that had been used by the Hudson's Bay Company on Tatla Lake. When they all went to look at it, they found a canoe 17 metres (55.8 feet) long and 1.2 metres (4 feet) wide that had been carved from a cottonwood tree—instead of the usual redcedar. They inspected it and, though its sides were very thin in places, they decided to use it.

The men, along with a guide, left Fort St. James in December, using six oars instead of paddles because of the great width as compared to other canoes. Their route took them on the St. James, Nechako and Fraser rivers. In some sections they had to stop many times a day because even thin ice would cut a hole in the side, and it would need patching. Sitting on a platform at the back they had a wood stove that they kept burning and when one of the party was overcome by cold, he would go back to have a cup of soup and warm up.

They arrived in Quesnel on the seventh day and left the canoe on the shore of Fraser River. The residents of Quesnel put a roof over it to protect it from the elements. It remained there for about 30 years before it had decayed so badly that residents pushed into the river to get rid of it.

Quesnel

You go downhill most the way to Quesnel and come into the town on North Fraser Drive, which becomes Marsh Drive. At kilometre 9.8 (mile 6.1) you cross the Fraser River on the Moffat Bridge, sometimes called the 'New Fraser Bridge.' Look to your left while on the bridge to see the old Fraser River footbridge. Follow the signs for the visitor information centre to LeBourdais Park (on Carson Avenue, opposite the BC Rail Station) where the visitor centre shares a building with the Quesnel Museum and the Chamber of Commerce. Inside the museum the artifacts include an old wood-burning cookstove and late 1800s period clothes, and there are displays about the Chinese and First Nations peoples.

If you would enjoy a quiet, peaceful walk through Riverfront Park, beside the Fraser and Quesnel rivers, turn right onto Carson Avenue when you come out of LeBourdais Park and drive to the end of Carson. The footbridge that you saw from the Moffat Bridge is ahead of you. Turn left onto Front Street, where there are some parking areas along the street. You can begin the 5-kilometre (3-mile)

Old Fraser River footbridge in Quesnel.

asphalt trail by following the path between Front Street and the Fraser River until it loops back beside the Quesnel River to where you started.

At the footbridge there is a large waterwheel. It, and many others like it, were brought to the gold-fields when the surface gold had been depleted and the miners had to dig deeper into the bedrock. Water from a nearby river or stream was run to the wheel, which then operated pumps to keep water out of the diggings and powered the winches that were used to haul the buckets of ore out of the mine. The water from the buckets on the wheel was then directed to sluice boxes into which crushed ore had been put, to wash away the lighter material, leaving the gold in the riffles.

Beside the waterwheel are some parts from the SS *Enterprise* (see p. 177), the first sternwheeler-steamer to ply the Fraser River between Soda Creek and Quesnel during the Cariboo Gold Rush.

Because of the gold rush and the number of people in the area, in the 1870s it was thought that Quesnel would become the capital of British Columbia because Victoria was too far from Barkerville.

The next chapter, Chapter 8, begins in Quesnel.

Waterwheel in Riverfront Park in Quesnel.

8
Quesnel to Williams Lake

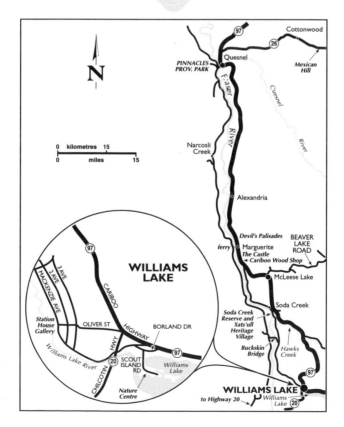

This chapter encompasses much more than the title implies, for you will be travelling much like a sidewinder snake. You will go from Quesnel to Williams Lake by the gravelled West Fraser Road, make the return trip via Highway 97 (which in part follows the old Cariboo Wagon Road) and finally another jaunt from Quesnel to Williams Lake on another section of the Cariboo Road and on some of the original Cariboo Gold Rush Trail. Cariboo Gold Rush history is the main theme of this chapter and you will see roadhouses, stagecoaches and towns that date from that era.

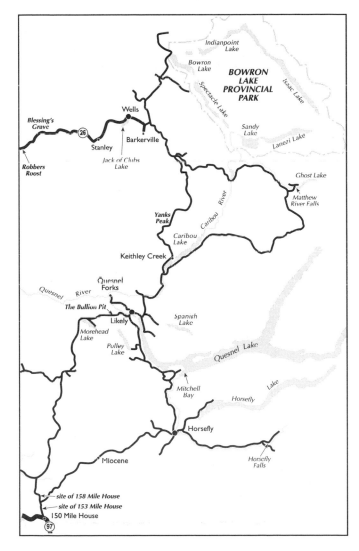

Quesnel, Pinnacles Provincial Park and West Fraser Road

Quesnel and Pinnacles Provincial Park

To begin this chapter, return over the Moffat Bridge, the same bridge that you entered Quesnel on in Chapter 7, and you are on Marsh Drive. Turn right onto Baker Drive 0.3 kilometres (0.2 miles) from the bridge. After 3.6 kilometres (2.2 miles) continue straight ahead on Pinnacles Drive where Baker Drive goes to the right. The parking area for Pinnacles Provincial Park is to your left at kilometre 5.7 (mile 3.5) from Marsh Drive.

The path from the parking lot is wide and it is a pleasant walk through the trees to a Y intersection, where you go left. You quickly reach a chain-link fence that stands between you and a deep gorge. Follow the fence to the viewpoints to look down on the tan-and-cream pinnacles. The last 0.8 kilometres (0.5 miles) of the walk, to the end of the fence, is also enjoyable.

Pinnacle Formation

Millions of years ago, successive layers of volcanic ash fell over the dirt and rock in the Quesnel area. Then molten lava flowed and cooled in basalt layers. The glaciers advanced and then melted during the ice ages, the last of which ended 10,000 years ago. As the glaciers receded, a stream laden with rock particles eroded away the softer basalt.

The ash layer was harder but had areas of different composition that were softer. When the rushing water reached the ash, the erosion varied because of the weaker material, leaving pinnacles, or hoodoos. Although the stream formed the pinnacles and the valley below, now it is the wind and rain that are continuing the erosion process.

West Fraser Road

Return on Pinnacles Road and then Baker Drive to Marsh Drive and turn right to head down the west side of the Fraser River. Follow Marsh Drive as it becomes Anderson Drive and then West Fraser Road. The Fraser River is to your left, so watch for glimpses of it. You drive past acreages and farms and at kilometre 14 (mile 8.7) you round a curve and can see the high, steep river banks across the valley. At kilometre 20.5 (mile 12.7) you cross Deserters Creek. After the bridge, pavement alternates with gravel for the next 5 kilometres (3 miles).

Narcosli Creek School is to your left at kilometre 29.6 (mile 18.4) and you then drive through the associated farming community. Look to your left at kilometre

45.4 (mile 28.2) and you can see Highway 97 across the valley. At kilometre 50.6 (mile 31.4) you enter the Alexandria Indian Reserve. Keep watching to your left for views of the river, its valley and the highway.

You reach the junction with the road to the Marguerite Ferry at kilometre 57.5 (mile 35.7). If you wish to get off the gravel road and finish the trip to Williams Lake on the highway, drive 1.6 kilometres (1.0 mile) downhill to the ferry. Or go there if you just wish to watch the reaction ferry cross the river. (You will pass the other end of this ferry crossing later in this chapter; see p. 178.)

After the turn-off for the ferry, you drive over many cattleguards as you pass through several ranches, where you have to watch for cattle on the road. At kilometre 28.8 (mile 17.9) from the ferry access road you come to a T intersection. Turn left here to continue to Williams Lake.

Look to your left at the junction to see the long, silver-coloured railway bridge over the river. At kilometre 4.3 (mile 2.7) from the T there is a Y junction in the road. The West Fraser Road carries on to your right and ends at Highway 20 to the west of Williams Lake. Take Buckskin Road to your left instead.

Buckskin Road curves at kilometre 5.9 (mile 3.7) from the T intersection and the orange-painted Buckskin Bridge is now just ahead of you. The maximum height for this one-lane bridge is 4.9 metres (16 feet), which shouldn't be a problem even for most RVs. As you cross the river, look at the beautiful canyon wall ahead.

Buckskin Bridge over the Fraser River.

The Buckskin Bridge

At one time the Buckskin Bridge was the only privately owned toll bridge in BC. It was installed here by Rudy Johnson of the Buckskin Ranch. He purchased it second-hand in 1968 and, by the time that he had paid for transportation and assembly, the bridge had cost him over $200,000. Before there was a bridge, though, he had had to make a slow, dusty, 60-kilometre (37-mile) drive from his ranch to Williams Lake, going by way of Meldrum Creek. This bridge cut his drive to about 25 kilometres (15 miles), saving him valuable time and gas.

Other people used his bridge too and he charged commercial vehicles a toll to off-set his costs. The government eventually purchased the bridge and now it is part of the provincial highway system.

After the bridge, the road climbs and you have beautiful views of the Fraser River to your right. At kilometre 7.7 (mile 4.8) you come to a Y intersection, where you go left. Just after the Y you round a curve and a road goes to the right. You stay left again. At kilometre 9.2 (mile 5.7) you reach the top, cross a cattle-guard and come to a stop sign for a railway. Williams Lake Cut-Off Road is to your left at kilometre 9.7 (mile 6.0), but you continue straight ahead.

At kilometre 19.2 (mile 11.9) you round a curve and can see Williams Lake ahead and just after the curve you reach pavement. At kilometre 23 (mile 14) you then enter the town of Williams Lake.

Williams Lake

In its early days, Williams Lake had a roadhouse, a courthouse and a jail to serve the first prospectors in the area. When the gold rush occurred, it also became the headquarters for the Gold Commissioner for the area. During the construction of the Cariboo Wagon Road, 1862–63, when the contractor, G.B. Wright, reached 140 Mile House, he didn't have the cash available to pay his workers' wages. He contacted the owner of the roadhouse at William's Lake and asked for a loan. The owner refused and so Wright approached landowners at 150 Mile House. They agreed, if the road went through their property. Therefore, 150 Mile House became a stop on the new road before it continued northward to 153 Mile House (part of Patenaude Ranch today) and 158 Mile House. It then turned west and followed Deep Creek (now Hawks Creek) to Soda Creek.

Williams Lake languished, but William Pinchbeck and William Lyne stayed and established a farm that supplied the gold camps and towns with fresh vegetables, meat, flour and their own whiskey. Though you might expect that the lake and town had been named after these two men, it is believed to have been named after a Secwepemc (Shuswap) First Nation chief named Williams.

In 1919 the Pacific Great Eastern Railway line from Squamish to Quesnel arrived in Williams Lake, and the community flourished as people moved to the area and farm products could be shipped out.

The BX Company

With the number of miners heading for the Cariboo in the late 1850s, there was a need for transportation to bring in supplies and equipment, as well as mail and passengers. A safe way of taking the gold out of the area to buyers was also required. One such transportation company was formed in June 1858 and remained in operation until February 1859. Another, begun in July 1858, ended business after just two months.

On April 1, 1859, the Jeffray & Company's Fraser River Express began hauling freight. The company operated under this name until December 1861, when it was bought by Francis Jones Barnard. In June 1862, Barnard's company merged with the British Columbia and Victoria Express Company. The new company then joined forces with another one, Deitz & Nelson, to form a single transportation company that covered the route all the way from Victoria to Yale and onward to Lillooet.

In July 1862, Barnard and his associates got a contract to service the northern Cariboo. Over the next few years, the company at first ran wagons from Lillooet to Alexandria, and then stagecoaches from Yale to Soda Creek. Coach routes from Quesnel to Barkerville were also added.

In 1878, the company put together by Barnard and his associates became the British Columbia Express Company—'the BX Company' for short. The company grew until it was second only to Wells-Fargo in the transportation business. Eventually, changing times and the motor vehicle led to the BX Company's decline and it went out of business in 1911.

At kilometre 25.3 (mile 15.7) from the T intersection on the other side of the Fraser River—or 2.1 kilometres (1.3 miles) from entering Williams Lake—you reach a stop sign, where you turn right onto Mackenzie Avenue.

As you drive along this road about 2.5 kilometres (1.5 miles), watch to your right for the Station House Gallery in the historic BC Rail Station (across from the end of Oliver Street). The gallery is run by the non-profit Station House Studio and Gallery Society, which was organized in 1981 to restore the station and, at the same time, provide a setting for local, regional and touring artists. Some of what you can see here includes pottery, photography, paintings, weaving and Native art.

Follow Mackenzie Avenue across Highway 20 until you come to a Y junction. If you continue straight ahead, you would come out on Highway 97. Instead, go right on Borland Drive and then turn right onto Scout Island Road. You cross a causeway and reach Scout Island, where the Scout Island Nature Centre and Recreation Area is located.

Scout Island Nature Centre and Recreation Area in Williams Lake.

In addition to a nature house, there is plenty of grass with picnic tables, as well as walking trails and access to Williams Lake for swimming, boating, canoeing and sailing.

At the nature house there is an explanation of the wetland environment along with a map showing you the trails that lead around the island. Inside the building there are stuffed specimens of the animals and birds that live in the marsh. The gates to the island open at 8 AM and close at dusk, and the nature house is open Monday to Saturday from 9 AM to 4 PM and on Sunday from 1 PM to 4 PM.

Williams Lake to Quesnel on Highway 97

Soda Creek Reserve and Soda Creek

Begin this section at the junction of Highways 97 and 20 in Williams Lake and head northward through the town. The highway then climbs as you pass ski trails, gas stations, resorts and campgrounds. To your left at kilometre 30.1 (mile 18.7) from the highway junction you can see the same silver-coloured railway bridge that you saw from the West Fraser Road.

When you get to kilometre 33.7 (mile 20.9), at a corner marked by a large log building, turn left onto Williams Lake Cut-Off Road to go to the Soda Creek (Xats'uall) Reserve and the Xats'uall Native Heritage Site.

In 1.1 kilometres (0.7 miles) you drive under a railway bridge and the road into Xats'uall Native Heritage Site is to your right at kilometre 1.7 (mile 1). Just ahead past the turn-off there is a viewpoint that overlooks the heritage village, which is set on the banks of the Fraser River.

Heritage Village.

This heritage site was developed to educate the children of the village—as well as visitors—about traditional Native culture. You can see winter houses, as well as the tanning of hides and the making of baskets and drums. If you want to stay overnight in one of the teepees you can listen to an elder relating a story or see a powwow.

Tours can be arranged if you call the band office at 250-297-6323 between 9 AM and 4:30 PM.

Back at the highway, turn left and go 2.7 kilometres (1.7 miles) to Soda Creek Townsite Road and turn left. In 3.9 kilometres (2.4 miles) from the highway you come to a stop sign at the Soda Creek-McAllister Road. Turn left and the road soon passes through the Soda Creek cemetery. Kilometre 1.4 (mile 0.9) from the turn brings you to the Soda Creek cairn, to your right, which is dedicated to all the people who travelled through or settled in the area during the 100 years between 1858 and 1958.

Soda Creek cairn.

Look at the Fraser River here: it is wide, slow and smooth. The river conditions here are much better for water travel than those downriver and that's why Soda Creek was made the terminus of the Cariboo Wagon Road and the starting point for the sternwheeler trip upriver to Quesnel. G.B. Wright had the SS *Enterprise* built to take miners and freight up the Fraser River from Soda Creek to Quesnel, where the overland journey to Barkerville would begin. The upstream trip took a full 24 hours, but the return voyage was completed in just three hours.

As you come into the village of Soda Creek at 0.3 kilometres (0.2 miles) from the cairn, you can see the old jail on the right. A large log building, with bars still on the windows in the back wall, it is supposedly the oldest jail still standing in BC. After its time as a jail, it was used as a residence until the 1960s. Nowadays it is on private land and not open to the public.

Soda Creek jail.

When the Fraser River Gold Rush in the Yale area ended, prospectors began looking for gold along the upper parts of the Fraser and its tributaries. Gold had been discovered on the Horsefly and Quesnel rivers in 1859, but it wasn't until the precious metal was found on Williams Creek (a tributary of the Fraser River) in 1861 that the Cariboo Gold Rush began. With the number of miners heading northward to the quickly established mining towns, a new and better route than the existing narrow trail had to be built into the area. At first a water route beginning at Harrison Lake was used (see sidebar, Chapter 10, p. 206), but it was superseded by the Cariboo Wagon Road, which was begun in 1862 and completed through from Yale to Soda Creek by the end of 1863.

Sternwheelers took the miners from Soda Creek up the Fraser to Quesnel, and then they followed a trail to Barkerville. Stagecoach service began in 1864 and road-houses were established along the road from Lillooet (Mile 0) to Barkerville. Each roadhouse was a day's stagecoach drive from the next and they had names such as '70 Mile House,' '83 Mile House,' '93 Mile House,' '100 Mile House,' etc.

Continue past the jail to the end of the road and look to your right to see the Soda Creek Social Club building. It dates from the gold-rush days and is now boarded up.

After the gold rush ended, Soda Creek remained as the start of navigation upriver to Prince George. It prospered, with a school, mills, stores and hotels, until the Pacific Great Eastern Railway was built. Now only a few families call Soda Creek home.

McLeese Lake and Alexandria

Back on Highway 97 and headed north, in 7.2 kilometres (4.5 miles) from the road to Soda Creek you enter McLeese Lake, a resort town. A general store, a motel, a cafe and a campground are situated along the highway. Beaver Lake Road is to your right at kilometre 8.4 (mile 5.2). It goes to Likely and Horsefly (see p. 187 and 190).

The Cariboo Wood Shop—where you can get handmade cedar chests, tables, bunk-beds and kitchen accessories—is to your left at kilometre 20.7 (mile 12.9). If you like chocolate, visit the Fudge Factory, which is operated by the same owners as the wood shop. The hours for both are from 9:30 AM to 5:30 PM daily.

The Castle, to your left at kilometre 24.1 (mile 15.0), does look just like a castle. Stop in and watch a demonstration of glass-blowing, tour the glass museum or visit the gift shop to purchase a glass gift or gold jewellery. The Castle opens at 9 AM and stays open until 9 PM.

You soon pass the Marguerite Ferry (you passed the other end of it early on in this chapter) and, if you look to your right at kilometre 29.4 (mile 18.3), you can see a group of basalt columns called 'the Devil's Palisades.' Kilometre 31 (mile 19.3) brings you to the cairn, on the left, for Fort Alexandria. This fort was built by the North West Company in 1821 and was the last one constructed by the company before its amalgamation with the Hudson's Bay Company later that year. It was named in honour of Sir Alexander Mackenzie, who had reached the Pacific Ocean by land in 1793 while working for the company (see the sidebar on p. 165).

Beside the cairn there is a 'trading post' where you can get hot corn on the cob in season or a large ice-cream cone on a hot day. It is a nice, scenic drive from Fort Alexandria to Quesnel, which you reach in 52.7 kilometres (32.7 miles).

The Cariboo Wagon Road to Horsefly

The Cariboo Wagon Road

Head northward on Highway 97 through Quesnel 5.6 kilometres (3.5 miles) from the visitor information centre until you reach the junction with Highway 26 to Barkerville. Turn right onto Highway 26 and in 26.1 kilometres (16.2 miles) from the junction you reach Sorum Road. It goes to Cottonwood House, which you can see from the highway. Park in the lot (if this one is full, there is a second parking area just down the highway) and cross the little bridge. Go to your left and you are walking on the path of the actual Cariboo Wagon Road to reach Cottonwood House.

Cottonwood House was constructed in 1864-65 and, after changing hands a few times, was bought by John Boyd in 1874. It provided stagecoach passengers with a hot meal and a room for the night. The store on the premises sold provisions, fresh vegetables and mining equipment. John Boyd died in 1909, but his family continued to operate Cottonwood House until 1951.

Stagecoach in front of Cottonwood House.

Cottonwood House Interpretive Centre.

When you have toured the house, barn and root cellar, and fed the chickens, you can follow the Cariboo Road back past the parking lot for a walk beside the Cottonwood River. Before you leave, you can buy crafts, baked goods, homemade fudge and fresh produce here as well. Cottonwood House is open daily from 8 AM to 5 PM.

Between Cottonwood House and Barkerville there are a number of pullouts with signs that explain a tragedy or success story of the area. Some of these stories are mentioned here.

At kilometre 8.6 (mile 5.3) from Sorum Road you are at Lover's Leap and, a little later, Mexican Hill. Both of these names arose during the Cariboo Gold Rush. Lover's Leap got its name because stagecoach driver Cassy Shaw loved a beautiful school teacher. While he was taking her to Quesnel one day, he demanded that she marry him or he would drive over the edge of the cliff into Lightning Creek. She refused. After some thought, Cassy decided to keep the horses on the road after all and they safely reached their destination.

Mexican Hill was named for Antone Parade, one of a number of Mexicans who came to the area to haul freight to the gold-fields. On the first wagon road, this section was a particularly steep, winding hill and one winter day Antone lost control of his sleigh which overturned and killed him.

Even though it has been improved since those days, Mexican Hill still has the steepest grade on the Barkerville Road.

Cottonwood House site.

You go downhill from the viewpoint for Lover's Leap and Mexican Hill and at kilometre 8.1 (mile 5.0) you pass by Robber's Roost. The colourful name was given to this section of road because it was deemed to be the perfect place to rob a passing stagecoach but there is no record that an actual robbery ever took place.

At kilometre 8.9 (mile 5.5) you reach Blessing's Grave. There is a parking area to your left. Walk into the woods to find the grave, which is surrounded by a picket fence. The original cedar grave marker still stands.

In spring 1866 Charles Morgan Blessing and a man whom he had recently met, James Barry, were travelling along this part of the Cariboo Road when Barry shot Blessing in the head and stole 60 dollars and a gold clasp pin. When Blessing never arrived at Van Winkle (a small town that stood just upstream from Stanley) to meet his friend, W.D. Moses, as arranged, Moses became worried. When Blessing's body was found, Moses suspected Barry. The evidence implicated Barry and so he was arrested, convicted of murder and hanged in front of the Richfield Courthouse (near Barkerville) on August 9, 1867. Charles Blessing was buried here in 1868.

Charles Blessing's grave.

Stanley Road

At kilometre 16.6 (mile 10.3) from Blessing's Grave you arrive at Stanley Road. Turn right to go to the ghost town of Stanley, which was established when gold was found on Lightning Creek in 1861. This gold rush lasted only a few years, but renewed interest beginning in 1870 resulted in mining that continued for more than three decades, after which Stanley all but disappeared.

The Stanley cemetery is to your left at kilometre 0.7 (mile 0.4). In the cemetery there are 36 indentations that mark the former graves of Chinese miners. The bones of the men buried in them were disinterred and sent home to family plots in China.

At kilometre 1.2 (mile 0.7) the old Lightning Hotel still stands on your right. There are remains of other building throughout the area, many overgrown by bush. By kilometre 2.8 (mile 1.7) you are back on the highway.

Old Lightning Hotel on Stanley Road.

The most popular story about how the Cariboo, in south-central BC between Lytton and Bowron Lakes, came by its name suggest that it was named after a North American reindeer, the woodland caribou, and that the miners simply spelled misspelled the word. A more elaborate version says that 'Cariboo' is a mangling of the Algonquin word *Xalibu*, which means 'a pawer or scratcher of the ground.' Yet another variation is that it comes from the French Canadian word *'cariboeuf'* for either 'reindeer' or 'elk.'

A different version claims that the Dakelh-ne (Carrier People) had a tradition that a widow must carry her dead husband's remains until the six ritual-feasts for the dead are over. It goes on to say that the word used for this custom was cari and that caribouef comes from that word.

Wells

At kilometre 10.6 (mile 6.6) from Stanley Road, Jack of Clubs Lake is to your right. It got its name from a nearby creek of the same name that was named after William Giles, a prospector whose nickname was 'Jack of Clubs.' If you look toward the northeastern end of the lake, you can see a pile of tailings that was dumped into it by the Cariboo Gold Quartz Mining Company, filling in that part of the lake.

The Cariboo Gold Quartz Mining Company began operations in 1933, when Fred Marshall Wells put together the necessary financing and attracted a work force. Wells was a prospector who had searched for 10 years before discovering what he thought was 'the mother lode' in 1932. The town of Wells was established to support the company's activities. The Island Mountain Mine also opened and the town grew to 4500 people, with many places staying open 24 hours a day to accommodate the three shifts at the mines. When both mines closed in 1967, the town's population dropped to 500.

Turn left onto Pooley Street at kilometre 12.6 (mile 7.8) to drive into Wells. A cairn with Fred Wells' ashes is in a small park across Pooley Street from the newly renovated Wells Hotel. Some of the old buildings in Wells are being

Newly renovated Wells Hotel.

The most famous Cariboo character is Billy Barker, for whom Barkerville is named. After gold was discovered on Williams Creek, which flows past present-day Barkerville, Billy Barker, as well as thousands of other prospectors, headed to the Cariboo. All the claims on Williams Creek at the time were above its canyon and, since there was no room left there, Barker and his partners decided to try below the canyon, where Williams Creek flowed through a valley. They set up a shaft house and began digging into the creek bank. By the time that they had reached the 10.6-metre (35-foot) mark in their shaft, they had run out of money.

Judge Begbie, who travelled the north administering justice and who had been authorized by the government to give destitute miners $100 for a return trip home, gave Barker and his partners $700, but pointed out that he could not force them to leave.

They bought supplies and continued their work. After digging another 5.2 metres (17 feet), they found pay gravel that yielded about $5 per pan and $3300 per metre ($1000 per foot) of ground.

Word quickly spread, and soon the rest of the creek was staked. A shanty town, Barkerville, was set up, complete with bakeries, hotels and saloons. Billy Barker spent the winter in Victoria, where he married, and then returned to Barkerville with his wife in the spring. They enjoyed a good time and, although Barker helped many down-and-out miners, he spent most of his money in saloons, gaming-houses and dancehalls. When the money was gone, his wife left him.

In 1866, a public subscription in Barkerville raised enough money to send Barker to the coast and for the next 28 years little was heard of him. He died of cancer on July 11, 1894, at the age of 75. He was buried in an unmarked pauper's grave in Victoria's Ross Bay Cemetery.

In July 1962, 68 years after Barker's death, a headstone was finally set on his grave.

restored. You can pick up a street map of the town at the visitor information centre. The map shows you the historic buildings, many of which house artists who have studios that are open to visitors.

'The Meadows,' one of the unsuccessful Cariboo claims, is at kilometre 2.7 (mile 1.7) from Wells along the highway. In 1870, the owners, Kurz and Lane, dug some 73 metres (240 feet) into the ground but found only about 70 grams (2.5 ounces) of gold. In contrast, just east of this site, at the Ballerat Claim, $2 million in gold was taken out in the 22 years following its staking in 1875, and it is still being worked today.

At kilometre 5.0 (mile 3.1) from Wells you pass the left turn for Likely and Bowron Lakes Provincial Park, (described later in this chapter). Just past that road is the former site of Cameronton, another gold-rush town, this one built around John A. Cameron's claim. It was staked by seven prospectors and it yielded $350,000 worth of gold in less than a year.

Just past Cameronton you arrive at the parking area for Barkerville, which is immediately ahead of you.

Barkerville

As you turn into the Barkerville parking lot, there is a road to your right that goes to the Barkerville Cemetery, where the first grave was dug for Peter Gibson, who died on July 24, 1863, at the age of 31. Past the cemetery there is a provincial campground.

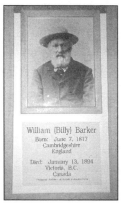

William (Billy) Barker
Born: June 7, 1817
Cambridgeshire
England

Died: January 13, 1894
Victoria, B.C.
Canada

Billy Barker picture hanging at Barkerville.

Barkerville was founded in 1862, soon after Billy Barker struck his rich gold claim on Williams Creek. The creek was named after William 'Dutch Bill' Dietz, who first discovered gold along the creek in 1861. Soon claims were staked up and down Williams Creek and most of the other creeks in the area and, for the next eight years, thousands of people travelled the Cariboo Wagon Road in search of riches.

In 1866, Madame Bendixon, owner of the Hotel de France, brought some girls from poor but respectable families in Victoria to Barkerville. They were taught the Hurdy Gurdy style of dance, which involved jumping, their feet swinging and sliding between the legs of the miners and possibly even being flung into the air by their partners. The girls charged a dollar a dance and they were very popular. One miner, breaking Madame Bendixon's rule about the girls not associating with the men outside of dancing, attempted to steal a kiss from

The Cariboo Poet

Just as the Klondike had Robert Service to write about its gold rush, the Cariboo had James Anderson. Anderson came from Scotland in 1863 and tried for the first few years to earn a living as a miner. Eventually, though, he had to seek employment as a mine labourer at 10 dollars a day. Although that amount may seem like a lot for those days, sugar in Barkerville was $2.20 per kilogram ($1 per pound) and butter was $6.60 per kilogram ($3 per pound).

Although his attempts at mining were fruitless, he was a success at writing poems and songs about the everyday trials of the honest miner and the social and economic life of the town of Barkerville. Through poems published in the *Cariboo Sentinel*, he told of the hard-luck miner working 18 hours a day and of the lucky miner who entered the unstable good life where everyone was his friend until the gold ran out. He wrote about claim-jumpers who took over unprotected claims and about mine-salters who sprinkled some nuggets around their claim and sold it to a newcomer for a high price. He penned poems about professional gamblers and prostitutes and even about the clergy who closed their churches in the fall so that they could spend the winter in a warmer climate.

He also sang his songs and read his poetry at the many concerts held in the community hall.

But, because of his lack of success at finding gold, Anderson left Barkerville in 1871 and returned to Scotland. He later moved to England and died in 1923 at the age of 85.

His writings were collected into a book and published in 1895.

one of them in the back of the hotel. She tried to avoid him and in her manoeuvers she knocked out the stove pipe. A fire immediately started and, when it was over an hour and 20 minutes later, only one building in the town remained standing. But the next day the townspeople began rebuilding.

Barkerville reached its peak in the early 1870s, but remained a supply centre for this part of the Cariboo until the 1940s. In 1958, restoration work was begun, and there are now over 125 restored or reconstructed buildings on this site, including churches, cabins, stables, and shops. Some of the activities that you can indulge in include taking a stagecoach ride, dining in one of the restaurants, making a purchase at the bakery and dry goods store, and watching a demonstration at the blacksmith shop. At the far end of the site is the beginning of a 1.6-kilometre (1-mile) trail to the Richfield Courthouse where you can listen to 'Judge Begbie' tell stories about the criminals that he tried.

Bowron Lake Provincial Park

Return to the road to Bowron Lake Provincial Park and Likely and turn right onto it. In 0.6 kilometres (0.4 miles) you reach a T intersection. Go left for the park, which you reach in 28.0 kilometres (17.4 miles). The lake and park were named after John Bowron, who was one of the Overlanders (see sidebar on p. 33). He worked as a mining recorder and Gold Commissioner in Barkerville.

This provincial park is most famous for its canoeing circuit on a chain of six larger lakes (Bowron, Indianpoint, Isaac, Lanezi, Sandy and Spectacle), two rivers (Bowron and Cariboo) and some smaller lakes and streams. There are seven portages and the trip begins with a 2.4-kilometre (1.4-mile) portage from the registration centre to Kibbee Creek. Because canoes travel nearly silently, you can expect to see moose, bear, deer, caribou and other wildlife along the shores of the lakes and rivers.

You should be properly equipped and in good shape to do this wilderness circuit. Expect to take up to 10 days for the 116-kilometre (72-mile) paddle. For more information or to make reservations, phone 250-992-3111 after March 1. As many as 3000 canoeists visit the park each year, though not all make the whole circuit.

Likely and Quesnelle Forks

Back at the T intersection, continue straight ahead on the Likely Road for Yanks Peak and the town of Likely. You are now on a rough logging road with sharp curves and blind corners. Up ahead you will have great views of valleys and mountains and drive beside canyon walls. The road to Yanks Peak is to your right at kilometre 14.8 (mile 9.2) from the T. If you have a rugged four-wheel-drive vehicle, you have the option to take this road over the Cariboo Mountains to Likely.

At kilometre 21.0 (mile 13.0) you start a 1-kilometre (0.6-mile) narrow downhill stretch into a gorge, with a drop-off to your right and a rock wall to left. There are pull-outs along this stretch in case you happen to meet a logging truck or other vehicle.

At kilometre 27.2 (mile 16.9) you can see the road snaking across a valley ahead through the trees, then you cross a creek and travel up the other side of the valley, accompanied by the Cariboo Mountain scenery as you go. At kilometre 39.8 (mile 24.7) you cross the Cariboo River. Just after the bridge you pass Cariboo River Provincial Park, with camping on both sides of the road. Kilometre 60.8 (mile 37.8) brings you to a Y junction, where you go to the left for Ghost Lake and Matthew River Falls (the other fork goes toward Likely).

Lower falls on Matthew River.

In 2.9 kilometres (1.8 miles) there is another Y, where you again bear left. At kilometre 4.3 (mile 2.7) you cross a bridge over the Matthew River. Look to your right to see the lower falls and to your left to see the top of another short waterfall. Just after the bridge, turn right to go to Cariboo Mountains Provincial Park Campground, which overlooks Ghost Lake and Matthew River Falls. The road is steep, but you reach the campground just 1.5 kilometres (0.9 miles) from the bridge.

Matthew River Falls at Ghost Lake.

At the picnic site at the campground you can see the deep emerald green waters of Ghost Lake. Follow the path from the higher picnic site for a great view of the beginning of the Matthew River as it roars out of the lake over Matthew Falls.

Back on the way to Likely, past the Y intersection, the road narrows, with a drop-off to your left at kilometre 11.0 (mile 6.8) from the turn-off for Ghost Lake. At kilometre 22.4 (mile 13.9) you round a corner to find a big, bald mountain ahead of you before you drive along its base for a few minutes. At kilometre 52.3 (mile 32.5) you start a sharp downhill and can see Cariboo Lake ahead.

At kilometre 66.5 (mile 41.3) you reach a T intersection. To the right about 8 kilometres (5 miles) is Keithley Creek, another gold-rush town that has since almost completely disappeared. Turn left to go to Likely, which you reach at kilometre 20.5 (mile 12.7). To camp on the shore of the Quesnel River, or to see some equipment from the gold-mining era, turn left for Cedar Point Park at kilometre 21.4 (mile 13.3).

In 4.1 kilometres (2.5 miles) you come to the entrance to the park. Drive down the entrance road to the bulletin board, where you turn right to reach the beach and play area and to see several pieces of equipment, including a steam shovel that was brought to the area to dig a ditch from Spanish Lake to the Bullion Pit (see sidebar on p. 188) and a 'monitor' (a water cannon used to wash down the bank of a creek or stream in hydraulic mining).

Steam shovel at Cedar Point Park in Likely.

Turn right in 0.9 kilometres (0.6 miles) from the entrance to Cedar Point Park to go to the historic town of Quesnelle Forks (the spelling of which reflects its historic roots; somewhere along the line other places of the same name have been spelled without the final 'le'). Go left at the yield sign and at kilometre 1.7 (mile 1.1) from the turn-off the pavement changes to gravel. At kilometre 9.8 (mile 6.1) you enter a 3-kilometre (2-mile) section of narrow, winding, descending road along which are viewpoints that overlook the Quesnel River. At kilometre 11.8 (mile 7.3) you reach the bottom of the hill and Quesnelle Forks.

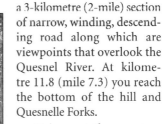

Tong House at Quesnelle Forks.

Drive past the cemetery on your left to the Quesnel Forks BC Forest Recreation Site on the river. Turn right at the recreation site, and the old buildings of Quesnelle Forks are sitting by the water ahead of you. Most of them are falling down, but repairs have been started on some. The intact one beside the river is the Chee King Tong House (a Chinese society clubhouse). It is thought to be the oldest tong house in Canada.

When the town was established in the early 1860s, the visionaries of Quesnelle Forks figured that it would eventually have a population of 10,000 people. However, it was almost deserted as soon as Barkerville was founded. Just past the buildings you can see where the Quesnel and Cariboo rivers join. If you stay at the recreation site, help to protect these heritage buildings by not building any fires near them.

Go back to where you turned right off the road to Likely to go to Quesnelle Forks and turn right to continue along it. In 0.4 kilometres (0.2 miles) from the junction, turn right to get to the cluster of Likely businesses section. Stop beside the park to the right and take a quiet peaceful walk beside the river.

Just after you turn onto the road from Barkerville again, you drive over the Quesnel River. It was near here, in 1898, that Joseph Hunter and his crew of 500 men built a dam to keep back the waters of the Quesnel River so that they could remove the gold from the downriver areas. However, the attempt was only partially successful.

As you leave Likely, the road climbs. To see the 'Bullion Pit,' turn onto the Sharpe Pit Road, to your right at kilometre 5.4 (mile 3.4), and then take the first right. At kilometre 0.3 (mile 0.2) from the main road you reach a Y junction, where you go left. At the next Y go to your right. In 1.1 kilometres (0.7 miles) from the road from Likely, the road curves to the right and you reach a place to park. It is tough to turn around, so you should leave larger vehicles at the main road and walk in.

The Bullion Pit

The Cariboo Hydraulic Mining Company was formed in 1892 to retrieve gold from 'Dancing Bill's Gulch.' The gulch was named after Thomas 'Dancing Bill' Latham, who had found gold on the Quesnel River in 1859. Mining was done by 'hydraulicking,' in which an exposed wall of dirt and/or gravel is washed away by a stream of water under pressure. Morehead Lake was created by damming a creek and some 35 kilometres (22 miles) of ditches were built to bring water from Morehead Lake to the gulch, as well as from Bootjack and Polley lakes. As the banks were washed away, the gulch widened.

In 1901, in an effort to attract attention to the mine, the gold from one 'clean-up' was melted and poured into the shape of a large naval gun shell. It had handles on it so that four men could carry it, and it sat on display in a Toronto bank without guards. Though the shell was worth $178,000, the bank officials didn't have to worry about someone walking away with it, for it weighed about 295 kilograms (650 pounds).

More water was needed, so plans were formulated to dig a ditch from Spanish Lake. However, in 1906 the mining stopped—only to begin again in 1935, when the largest 'monitor' (water cannon) ever used in North America was installed here. After 10 years, heavy mining ceased and the giant hole or pit was left behind. Further attempts at finding gold here, on a smaller scale, have continued off and on ever since.

From the parking area you can walk, at your own risk, to the edge of the Bullion Pit, where there is no fence or railing. Go to your right, where there is a bench, if you would like to sit and look at the pit, which is long, narrow and deep (approximately 3 kilometres [1.8 miles] long and 100 metres [330 feet] deep) and looks like an artificial canyon.

Return to the road from Likely and, if you are tired of gravel roads, you can continue on this paved road to 150 Mile House on Highway 97 south of Williams Lake. However, to finish the chapter, return toward Likely for 2.9 kilometres (1.8 miles) and turn right onto Polley Lake Road. You won't see the sign for this road until after you have made the turn, but you can see the road going uphill parallel to the highway beforehand.

Bullion Pit.

This rough gravel road through the trees is a lovely shady drive on a sunny day. Watch for the small pull-outs from which you can see the town of Likely and the Quesnel River below.

Then the road follows Quesnel Lake, the deepest lake in BC and said to be the deepest 'fjord lake' in the world. (A fjord lake is formed when a glacier scrapes out the bottom of a valley during its advance and then fills the depression as it melts. Most of the lakes in BC are fjord lakes.)

At kilometre 16.7 (mile 10.4) you reach a T intersection. Go left and in 7.1 kilometres (4.4 miles) from the T you can go left again to Mitchell Bay Forest Service Recreation Site, where there is a boat launch, as well as a nice campsite on Quesnel Lake. If you want something a little more fancy, at kilometre 9.6 (mile 6.0) there is a sharp turn to the left to Mitchell Bay Landing, where there are cabins to rent, a camping area, boat launch and boat rentals.

The Gold Rush Trail

Gold was discovered in the Horsefly River in June 1859, and on the Quesnel River in July. Upon hearing the news, miners from Yale on the played-out lower Fraser River headed to where the town of Williams Lake is today. They set out over a slippery, root-and-rock-strewn, swampy trail that went to where the Quesnel River meets the Cariboo and onward to Quesnel Lake. Eventually they continued up the Cariboo River to Keithley Creek and over the Snowshoe Plateau to Williams and Antler creeks.

Towns such Quesnelle Forks, Keithley, Camerontown and finally Barkerville sprang up to accommodate the inrushing miners. In the 1860s a wagon road was surveyed and built along this trail, making travel easier.

After the road to Mitchell Bay Landing, you turn away from the lake and the Horsefly River is now to your left. At kilometre 27.6 (mile 17.2) from the T you reach pavement and the town of Horsefly.

Horsefly

Gold was discovered in 1859 some 16 kilometres (10 miles) upstream from where the Horsefly River flows into Quesnel Lake. When the gold petered out, miners moved northward along Keithley and Antler creeks and onward to Williams Creek, where the gold discovery by Billy Barker resulted in the Cariboo Gold Rush. In 1884, a hydraulic mine began operating on the Horsefly River and, in 1897, a second gold rush occurred. Two villages were established, Harper's Camp and Horsefly, but Horsefly was deserted by 1908. In 1930, the people of Harper's Camp voted to call their village Horsefly.

Follow the main road a short distance until you reach the Jack Lynn Memorial Museum and a mini-mall to your left. At the museum there is a yard full of machinery and there are two buildings with artifacts from the mining history that you can tour. Jack Lynn, whom the museum's name commemorates, helped found Horsefly, but was killed when a log fell on him.

To reach Horsefly Falls, drive past the mini-mall, after which the road curves to the right. Turn left at the general store and cross the bridge over the Horsefly River. To your right in 0.4 kilometres (0.2 miles) from the bridge is the Horsefly River Spawning Channel. In the parking area there is a write-up that tells about the life

Horsefly Falls.

Quesnel Lake.

cycles of the sockeye, chinook, coho and pink salmon and when they come upstream to spawn. From here you can walk beside the river to view the returning salmon.

Just past the parking area you cross the channel. You pass the road to Horsefly Lake and Quesnel Lake at kilometre 1.3 (mile 0.8) and just after that junction you are on a gravel logging road with the Horsefly River to your right. You drive over cattleguards as you pass through ranches and hayfields, with plenty of opportunity to enjoy the mountain scenery. You pass the Black Creek Ranch in 26.9 kilometres (16.7 miles) from the junction and, when you reach the Y intersection at kilometre 28.6 (mile 17.8), go left onto Horsefly River Forest Road. At kilometre 3.1 (mile 1.9) from the Y there is a sharp right turn and drive to a small parking area. Or you can park in the pull-out just past the turn and walk into the parking area. A short, steep path leads to the rugged-looking falls from the parking area. The waterfall is not very high, and the trees and bushes make it difficult to take a good picture.

Return to Horsefly. Turn left after crossing the bridge over the Horsefly River to head back to Highway 97 along a road that is paved all the way. Along the way, you pass the Miocene Ranch and then the Miocene Community Centre at kilometre 35.3 (mile 21.9). At kilometre 53.5 (mile 33.2) you come to Highway 97, where you turn right to go to Williams Lake.

In 8.3 kilometres (5.2 miles) from the junction you arrive at the outskirts of Williams Lake. Kilometre 14.5 (mile 9.0) brings you to Highway 20, which goes west to Bella Coola and is described in Chapter 9.

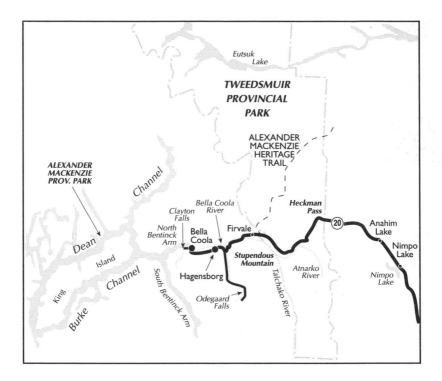

9
Williams Lake to Bella Coola

In the past, many travellers avoided Highway 20 westward to Bella Coola because of its reputation for being a long drive on gravel that was hard on both nerves and vehicles. Most of this highway is now paved and the rest is being improved. There are just two sections where the road is steep and has drop-offs: the first is where you cross the Fraser River near the beginning and the other is as you head down into the Atnarko River valley in Tweedsmuir Provincial Park (make sure that your vehicle can handle 18% grades up and down if you plan to go that far west). The rest of the road is fairly level.

With its many lakes, lodges, bed-and-breakfast operations, craft shops, resorts, tour businesses, rest areas and campgrounds, this area of the province has been a well-kept secret. All of the villages along this highway have a store and a restaurant and a place to buy gas, and they serve as convenient jumping-off points for the lakes in the area.

If you would like to do a bit of fishing at some of the many lakes between Williams Lake and Bella Coola, but don't yet have a BC fishing licence, you can get one and a copy of the current regulations in Williams Lake before you leave town.

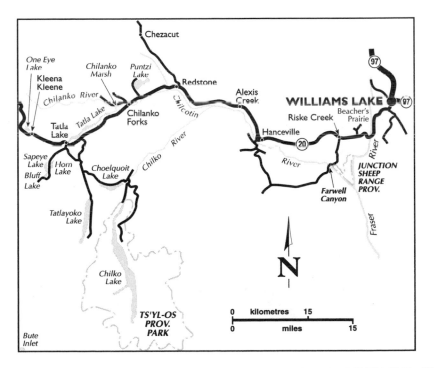

Williams Lake to Nimpo Lake

Williams Lake, Riske Creek and Farwell Canyon

To begin this trip, head west on Highway 20 from its junction with Highway 97 in Williams Lake. In 2.5 kilometres (1.6 miles), the road to Dog Creek (see p. 208) is to your left. Highway 20 climbs for a ways out of Williams Lake and then you have the Chimney Valley to your left. Look ahead at kilometre 23.0 (mile 14.3) to see the Chilcotin Bridge, on which you will cross the Fraser River. Some people call it 'Sheep Creek Bridge,' but the original Sheep Creek Bridge, built in the same place in 1904, was replaced by this one in 1961. Just before the bridge there is a pull-out to your right if you wish to take a photo. Once you cross the river at kilometre 24.7 (mile 15.3), you are entering Chilcotin Country.

As the highway climbs after the bridge, the hills beside you have an arid, desert-like look to them. When you reach the top of the incline, you are in Beacher's Prairie, part of the Chilcotin Plateau. This natural grassland

Chilcotin Bridge over the Fraser River.

habitat—which contains sagebrush, rabbitbrush, wheatgrass, bluegrass, spear grass and prickly-pear cactus—is home to many wild mammals and birds,

Beacher's Prairie.

including bighorn sheep and eagles. Though Beacher's Prairie runs from here to the community of Riske Creek, you will still be travelling through the grasslands for a ways west of there.

You can see the tall Williams Lake Loran C Canadian Coast Guard tower long before you reach the road to it at kilometre 35.6 (mile 22.1). This tower, with its 4000-kilometre (2500-mile) range, is part of a marine navigation system that tracks ocean-going vessels, such as tankers, travelling along the BC coast from Alaska to Washington so that their positions can be pinpointed in case of mishap.

Riske Creek General Store is to your right at kilometre 47.5 (mile 29.5) and just past it is where you turn left onto Chilcotin South Forest Service Road to head for Farwell Canyon on the Chilcotin River. This dusty gravel logging road goes through grassland and you can see for a great distance as you drive.

At kilometre 15.0 (mile 9.3) you slow down for a sharp curve to begin zigzagging down the hill. Look to your right to see Farwell Canyon below. At kilometre 15.3 (mile 9.5) there is a pull-out to your left from which you can look out over the canyon. Here also is the start of the one-hour drive to Junction Sheep Range Park. In the park, which covers 6700 hectares (16,600 acres) immediately north of the junction of the Fraser and Chilcotin rivers, you might see bands of California bighorn sheep. The road, however, is not maintained and can be driven only with a four-wheel-drive vehicle.

The view of the hills, canyon and prairie is spectacular as you continue downhill through hairpin curves. At kilometre 6.0 (mile 3.7) from the pull-out you reach the canyon itself and the one-lane bridge over the Chilcotin River. Just before the bridge there is a pull-out to your left where you can park to take pictures of the river, the canyon walls and the surrounding prairie. Remember that logging trucks use this one-lane bridge, so don't stop or walk on it.

Bridge over Chilcotin River at Farwell Canyon.

Chilcotin River churning through Farwell Canyon.

The Chilcotin River is a milky green colour because of the glacial till that it carries. If you have your tackle and licence, try fishing for Dolly Varden, rainbow, steelhead and salmon here. Although it is possible to continue to Hanceville via logging roads from here, the route described below involves returning to Riske Creek and following Highway 20.

Hanceville and Alexis Creek

As you continue to travel westward, the grasslands slowly give way to trees. The Hanceville Rest Area, to your left at kilometre 35.9 (mile 22.3), overlooks the lovely Chilcotin River valley. Then you go downhill to Hanceville, which is also called 'Lee's Corner' because Norman Lee started one of the first ranches in the area. Lee's Corner Store is to your left at kilometre 40.9 (mile 25.4).

You then drive through Tl'etinqox-t'in Native Territory, with glimpses of the Chilcotin River to your left. In 35.5 kilometres (22.1 miles) from Hanceville you reach Alexis Creek.

Settlers arrived in the area in the early 1890s. They built along the Chilcotin and ranching soon became the main industry. The village of Alexis Creek evolved there over time as people saw opportunities to supply goods and services to the ranchers. Most of the original buildings are gone now, and some of the remaining ones have been renovated to keep with the times.

To see the old Red Cross Outpost Hospital, drive through the town past the Alexis General Store until you reach the 'Medical Clinic' sign at Morton Street. The hospital is the pink-and-white building to your right. Built between 1912 and 1914, it still serves the people of the area today.

At White Pelican Provincial Park, about 10 kilometres (6 miles) northeast of Alexis Creek by gravel road, endangered white pelicans come to breed and raise their young. Though the area is closed to the public between March 1 and August 31 to protect the nesting birds, you may see some white pelicans on other lakes mentioned in this chapter.

A Cattle Drive to the Klondike

Norman Lee was born in England. He came to British Columbia to build a new life for himself and his family. He started ranching and, when the Klondike Gold Rush began, decided that the miners there would love some fresh meat. The next year, in 1898, he picked 200 head of cattle from his herd and began a cattle drive to the Klondike, following the old Collins Overland Telegraph Line to Telegraph Creek.

He made it to Hazelton with little mishap, but was plagued by high supply costs, men quitting, mud, no grass and lame horses from Hazelton to Telegraph Creek. When he reached Telegraph Creek on September 7, he was ready to quit but, upon receiving a loan of supplies decided, to continue with the now-skinny cattle. He took a trail to Teslin, which he reached on October 3. Here food prices were even higher than at Hazelton and Telegraph Creek but beef prices were low, because of the cattle and oxen being sold by prospectors who decided to turn back home.

Lee butchered his cattle and tried floating the meat to Dawson City on scows, but a storm forced them on shore, where the scows broke up and the meat fell in the water. What was saved was dragged through the dirt as it was pulled ashore. Lee divided the remaining supplies among his men and, while they continued to the Klondike, he returned to his ranch empty-handed.

Bull Canyon Provincial Park, Redstone and Chilanko Marsh

Bull Canyon Provincial Park is to your right 8.0 kilometres (5 miles) from Alexis Creek. It was named for the cattle that at one time were allowed to roam the area. In the canyon there is a rock cliff known as 'Battle Bluff.' Here members of the Nuxalk (Bella Coola) and Ts'ilhqot'in (Chilcotin) First Nations had a battle in which the Ts'ilhqot'in rolled huge boulders over the cliff onto the approaching Nuxalk, scaring them off.

At kilometre 33.0 (mile 20.5) there is a gravel road to the right that goes to the village of Chezacut, which is about 38 kilometres (24 miles) to the northwest.

Coming up are some roads that lead off the highway to lakes with resorts, lodges and camping areas on them, but not all of them are mentioned here. Fishing on these lakes is the most popular sport in the area. If you wish to try your luck fishing and don't yet have a BC fishing licence and regulations, you can pick them up at one of the stores along the way.

You pass the community of Redstone at kilometre 33.4 (mile 20.8) and enter the Redstone Indian Reserve at kilometre 52.3 (mile 32.5). As you drive through the reserve, look ahead to see the Coast Mountains. The road to Puntzi Lake is to your right at kilometre 61.1 (mile 38.0). It is popular for camping, swimming, boating and fishing (for kokanee). Watch for the white pelicans that come to feed and swim on the lake.

Chilanko Forks Road is to the right at kilometre 62.1 (mile 38.6). To see the Chilanko Marsh Wildlife Management Area, turn right onto Puntzi Airport Road, which is 1.2 kilometres (0.7 miles) past Chilanko Forks Road. Drive along the airport road for 1.6 kilometres (1.0 mile) then make a left. This road curves right and you are on gravel. When you come to the Cariboo Initial Fire Attack Crew station, to your right in 5.2 kilometres (3.2 miles), you can see the marsh to the left but continue ahead until you reach a parking area for the marsh, at kilometre 6.1 (mile 3.8) from the highway.

This 900-hectare (2200-acre) reserve of wetland and surrounding land was designated a wildlife management area in 1987. It is on the Pacific Flyway and over 800 species of birds either live on the marsh or visit it on their migrations. Deer, moose, mink, coyote and beaver are just some of the larger mammals found in the region.

There is a map showing the marsh and a trail through it, which starts from the parking area.

Go back to the highway and, at kilometre 46.2 (mile 28.7) from Puntzi Airport Road, the highway curves right and there is a road to the left with signs for Buffalo, Horn, Sapeye, Bluff, Chilko and Tatlayoko lakes, to name just a few in that area. They are all good fishing lakes.

Chilko Lake is mostly surrounded by Ts'yl-os (also spelled Ts'il-os) Provincial Wilderness Park. This 233,240-hectare (576,300-acre) park was established in 1994 and is jointly managed by the provincial government and the Nemaiah Native people. Exploration of the park is only allowed on foot, by horseback or by boat.

Tatla Lake and Nimpo Lake

The highway curves left after the junction and you reach the community of Tatla Lake, at the western edge of the Chilcotin Plateau. For a treat, stop in at the inn for fresh-baked bread.

At kilometre 15.2 (mile 9.4) from Tatla Lake you cross the Klinaklini River. Some sources say that Kleena Kleene, the name of the settlement, means 'eulachon grease' in the Kwakwala Native language; other sources say it means 'shining place.'

If you would like to camp beside a lovely clear-blue lake, turn right onto Holm Road at kilometre 25.9 (mile 16.1). In 0.2 kilometres (0.1 miles) you turn right and, at kilometre 1.1 (mile 0.7) from highway, you reach One Eye Lake BC Recreation Site. It is a dusty drive to the lake but the serenity there is worth it.

Shortly after Holm Road the highway swings northward and you temporarily lose your mountain scenery. You reach the village of Nimpo Lake 51.2 kilometres (31.8 miles) from Holm Road. Called 'the Float Plane Capital of BC,' it has a bakery, a lodge, a cafe, a post office, a motel and a general store—with beautifully carved doors—as well as tours and charters to fly you to remote areas for hiking, fishing or camping.

The Eulachon

The eulachon (also spelled 'ulichan,' 'oulachen,' 'ooligan,' 'hooligan,' 'hollikan' and 'oolichan') is a member of the smelt family of fish. To the First Nations people of the West Coast, they were called the 'saviour' or 'salvation' fish because they were the first to come up the rivers and streams at the end of winter. 'Grease trails' were established, along which the Interior Natives would come to trade goods for the fish and its oil, which was considered to have medicinal properties.

The eulachon is about 20 centimetres (8 inches) long and 4 centimetres (1.5 inches) from belly to backbone. It has silver sides and a brown or black back. Early settlers dubbed this slender fish 'candlefish' because they used to light dried ones and burn them like candles.

Anahim Lake to Bella Coola

Anahim Lake and Tweedsmuir Provincial Park

You reach the turn-off for the hamlet of Anahim Lake 17.0 kilometres (10.6 miles) from Nimpo Lake, at a junction marked by a restaurant. At the junction there is a sign that warns of 18% grades at Heckman Pass on the highway ahead just after you enter Tweedsmuir Provincial Park. You will also have the climb back up, so if you don't think that your vehicle will make it, now is the time to turn around.

From Anahim Lake you head towards the Coast Mountains and you enter Tweedsmuir Provincial Park in 36.1 kilometres (22.4 miles). Across the highway from the sign at the entrance to the park there is a map that shows the park, the road to Bella Coola and the hiking trails in the park. With an area of 994,246 hectares (2,456,748 acres), Tweedsmuir is the largest provincial park in British Columbia.

After entering the park, you climb up to Heckman Pass (elevation 1524 metres [500 feet]), reaching it at kilometre 7.2 (mile 4.5). From here you begin a very scenic, winding descent with grades up to 18% for about the next 6 kilometres (4 miles), so gear down at the top, especially if you are driving a motorhome or pulling a trailer. Even if you are driving a car or a truck with a camper you might want to gear down at the top, just to save wear and tear on your brakes and your nerves if you start going too fast.

After you cross Young Creek at kilometre 12.8 (mile 8.0) the road climbs again before beginning another descent, again at up to 18% for about 9 kilometres (5.5 miles) more. You have a rock wall on one side and a drop-off on the other, and there are no guard-rails. Use the pull-outs located here and there to stop and look down into the gorge, to let your brakes cool or to give someone coming uphill room to pass.

The road is narrow and there are hairpin curves at kilometres 21.4 and 22.4 (miles 13.3 and 13.9). At kilometre 25.8 (mile 16.0) you cross Camera Channel and are on flat pavement as you drive among the tall trees of the Atnarko River valley. The highway follows the Atnarko River to where it joins with the Talchako to form the Bella Coola River.

Atnarko Campground, the first of two campgrounds in Tweedsmuir Park, is to your left at kilometre 27.3 (mile 17.0). If you want to camp under old-growth Douglas-firs, this is the place to stop. The park headquarters is on the right, just past the campground.

At kilometre 38.0 (mile 23.6) you are at the Big Rock/Kettle Pond picnic area. Look to your right to see the big rock, which is split down the middle. Across the highway from this picnic site you can take a 1-kilometre (0.6-mile) hike through old-growth fir forest to a kettle pond, formed when a huge piece of glacial ice was left buried under glacial till. When the ice melted, it created a lake in the depression left behind by the ice.

The road begins to climb and then Tweedsmuir Fisheries Pool Campground is to your left at kilometre 43.7 (mile 27.2). Just past the campground is the confluence where the Bella Coola River begins and at kilometre 48.4 (mile 30.1) there is a boat launch.

Kilometre 53.6 (mile 33.3) brings you to the Alexander Mackenzie/Grease Trail parking area, to your left. Ahead is the bridge over Burnt Bridge Creek. There are two trailheads across from the parking area on the north side of the highway. The trail to your left begins on the other side of the bridge over Burnt Bridge Creek. This path is part of the Alexander Mackenzie Heritage Trail and the Valleyview Loop Trail until they divide, with the Mackenzie going left and the loop trail going right. The trailhead to the right of the parking area is for the other end of the Valleyview Loop Trail. A side trip that branches off it goes to a viewpoint from which you can see Stupendous Mountain (the one on the left as you face the highway or the viewpoint, which was named by Mackenzie) and the valley of the Bella Coola River. The Mackenzie/Grease Trail is rugged—and steep in places—and you have to watch for bears.

Stupendous Mountain mainly hidden by cloud.

Highway 20 from Williams Lake to Bella Coola is known as 'the Chilcotin Highway,' 'the Route to the Valley of the Thunderbird' and 'the Freedom Highway.' Between Vancouver and Prince Rupert, this highway is the only one that comes out to the coast from the BC Interior, and it wasn't easily built.

By the early 1950s, a road went from the Interior as far west as Heckman Pass. Although the people of the Bella Coola area wanted the road continued through the Coast Mountains, the provincial government said that it couldn't be done.

The frustrated residents finally got tired of fighting for the road, which would have given them the freedom to drive to other points in the province. In summer 1953 they decided to take matters into their own hands and build it themselves. One bulldozer headed west from Heckman Pass and the other headed east from the end of the road in the Atnarko valley. They met on September 26 and the Freedom Highway was complete.

Alexander Mackenzie and his crew were guided along this trail from the Fraser River (see sidebar on p. 165) to Burnt Bridge Creek. From here they were taken to the village of Nutteax, which Mackenzie named 'Friendly Village' because of the friendliness of the Natives. He was then transported down the Bella Coola River to the coast. Alexander Mackenzie was the first non-Native to cross the full North American continent and the first recorded non-Native to walk on the 4000-year-old grease trail.

When you get back on the highway, immediately after the parking area you cross Burnt Bridge Creek and leave the park.

Firvale and Hagensborg

You pass through the village of Firvale in 7.7 kilometres (4.8 miles) from the park and cross the Bella Coola River, designated a BC Heritage River in 1997, at kilometre 15.4 (mile 9.6).

At kilometre 25.4 (mile 15.8) you cross the Nusatsum River (there is no sign). Just after the bridge is the left turn for Nusatsum Forest Service Road. Odegaard Recreation Site and Odegaard Falls are 25.0 kilometres (15.5 miles) along this gravel logging road. There is a short trail from the recreation site parking area to see the falls or you can continue on the road for 1.0 kilometre (0.6 miles) more to the Nusatsum River Recreation Site and take the 2-kilometre (1.2-mile) Odegaard Trail to a spot near the base of this narrow, but very high, waterfall. These two primitive recreation sites are very popular in the summer, so camping space is limited.

You reach the village of Hagensborg at 5.6 kilometres (3.5 miles) along the highway from the forest service road. The Hagensborg Heritage House is on your left as you drive through the village. This house was built in the early 1900s by Andrew Svisdahl and has been restored and furnished to represent the lifestyle of the early Norwegian settlers. Hours are from 10 AM to 4 PM Monday and Tuesday, and from 10 AM to 5 PM Wednesday to Saturday.

Hagensborg has all the amenities, including a swimming pool. Walker Island Regional Park is to your right at kilometre 4.4 (mile 2.7) from Hagensborg. This regional park has a baseball diamond, a playground and a picnic area. Snootli Creek Park, which is also on the island, has hiking trails through tall cedars. You reach the town of Bella Coola in 14.5 kilometres (9.0 miles) from Hagensborg.

The 'Chilcotin War'

Gold was discovered in Williams Creek in the Cariboo in 1861 and the Cariboo Gold Rush began. However, the route to the gold-fields was long and consisted of some 640 kilometres (400 miles) of trails and portages from the mouth of the Fraser River at Vancouver to Williams Creek.

One of the many entrepreneurs of the Victoria and Vancouver area, Alfred Waddington, decided that the construction of a road from the British Columbia coastline to the gold-fields would shorten the trip by one-third. After a team of surveyors sent by Governor Douglas reported that no such route could be found, Waddington set out to find the route himself.

His men surveyed eastward from Bute Inlet (north of Campbell River, on the mainland) until late in the fall of 1861 and were assured by Natives that open country was just beyond where they turned back. Work was begun on a wagon road from the inlet to the Fraser River by way of the Homothko River, Puntzi Lake and the Chilcotin River in March of 1862. As work progressed, a survey was done all the way to the Fraser near Fort Alexandria. The route would be about 260 kilometres (160 miles) long. After delays and difficulties, by spring 1864, it looked as if the road would be opened by summer.

By then the Ts'ilhqot'in (Chilcotin) decided that they didn't want the road through their land. Reports of the events leading up to the 'war' vary but they include smallpox being spread among the Natives and other offences committed against them by the roadbuilders. The upshot was that the Natives killed a ferry operator and then attacked two work camps, killing the men there.

A ship sailed from Vancouver up Bute Inlet with police and volunteers and another ship came from Bentinck Arm with marines, all of whom headed inland. Native scouts and a group of men headed across country from the Fraser River at Fort Alexandria. The murderers were either shot during a gunfight or later hanged, and the roadwork was terminated.

Bella Coola

The town of Bella Coola is about 100 kilometres (60 miles) inland by boat from Fitz Hugh Sound, at the head of North Bentinck Arm of Burke Channel. The Bella Coola Valley is home to the Coast Salish Nuxalk First Nation. It is also said to be the dwelling place of the Thunderbird, a large and powerful eagle-like bird featured in Native legends.

Just stay on this highway as you come into the village of Bella Coola. The Bella Coola Museum, consisting of two log buildings, is to your left. The larger building was built in 1898 and was once a school. The smaller one was constructed in 1892 as a house for one of the first surveyors in the area. Inside there are artifacts from the history of Bella Coola, the Norwegian settlers in the area and the Heritage Road.

If you would like to see Mackenzie Rock, where Alexander Mackenzie signed his name in 1793, you can ask for advice at the Dream Factory Adventures Limited (in the Cedar Inn), or at Tweedsmuir Travel on Cliff Street (one block north of the highway). You will need to charter a boat or a plane, since there is no regular boat excursion out to Mackenzie Rock Provincial Park, where it is located.

If you would like to dine and sleep in a restored cannery built in the early 1900s, phone 250-982-2344 for a reservation at the Tallheo Cannery, across the arm from Bella Coola on the north shore of North Bentinck Arm. You will be picked up by boat at the Bella Coola ferry dock and taken to the cannery. The restaurant is in a separate structure beside the huge cannery building. Sleeping accommodations are in a restored bunkhouse. You can tour the cannery, stroll through the historic site and visit the local artists' gift shop.

To see Clayton Falls, continue on the highway past the museum toward North Bentinck Arm. At kilometre 1.0 (mile 0.6) from the museum you come to a large rock with two plaques on it. One honours the pioneers and one is for Alexander Mackenzie.

Further along this road is the Bella Coola Harbour, and at kilometre 2.8 (mile 1.7) the road becomes North Bentinck Forest Service Road, an active logging road on which you should be alert for logging trucks. At kilometre 4.2 (mile 2.6), go right at the Y junction. Just after that Y there is another Y, where you go left. Immediately after the turn you round a curve and can see a blue building (BC Hydro's Clayton Falls Hydro Generating Station) with a fence around it and

a parking area in front. Just past the row of trees is the parking lot for falls visitors. Across the road from it there is a picnic area over-looking the North Bentinck Arm, where you might want to sit for a while after you see the falls.

To find the path to Clayton Falls, return on foot to the earlier parking area at the fence and go to its left corner. You reach the first viewpoint in just a few steps. There are a lot of branches here that obstruct your view of the falls, so go to the second viewpoint, just steps away, for a better look. The water has smoothed out the rocks, giving them a shiny look.

From Bella Coola you can return to Williams Lake, where you began this chapter, and start on Chapter 10.

Clayton Falls.

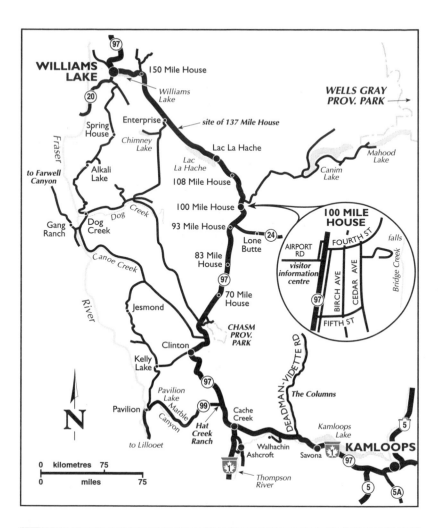

WILLIAMS LAKE

150 Mile House

Williams Lake

site of 137 Mile House

WELLS GRAY PROV. PARK →

Enterprise

Spring House

Chimney Lake

Lac La Hache

Mahood Lake

Fraser

Alkali Lake

Lac La Hache

Canim Lake

to Farwell Canyon

108 Mile House

Gang Ranch

Dog Creek

Dog Creek

100 Mile House

93 Mile House

Lone Butte

24

100 MILE HOUSE

falls

Canoe Creek

83 Mile House

AIRPORT RD

FOURTH ST

97

97

visitor information centre

BIRCH AVE

CEDAR AVE

Bridge Creek

River

Jesmond

70 Mile House

FIFTH ST

CHASM PROV. PARK

Clinton

Kelly Lake

97

N

Pavilion Lake

Marble Canyon

99

The Columns

DEADMAN-VIDETTE RD

Pavilion

Hat Creek Ranch

Cache Creek

Kamloops Lake

5

to Lillooet

0   kilometres   75

0   miles   75

Walhachin
Ashcroft

Savona

KAMLOOPS

97

Thompson River

5

5A

10
Williams Lake to Kamloops

Like Chapter 8, the theme of this chapter is the Cariboo Gold Rush. Many of the towns you will visit were named for the number of miles that they were from Lillooet, the beginning of the Cariboo Wagon Road built in the early 1860s. Roadhouses from that era still stand, although they have been added to or renovated over the years. And you can have your picture taken beside one of the original stagecoaches to operate on the Cariboo Road.

But there is more to this chapter than just the gold rush. The largest ranch in the province, the oldest ranch in the province, the world's largest cross-county skis and the site of an ill-timed orchard are just some of the other attractions you will see.

Williams Lake and the River Road

Williams Lake, Springhouse and Alkali

If you wish to avoid the gravel roads that are described in this first section of the chapter, skip to the beginning of the next section (p. 209). Otherwise, begin at the junction of Highways 97 and 20 in Williams Lake. Head west out of Williams Lake on Highway 20 and in 2.5 kilometres (1.5 miles) you reach Dog Creek Road. Turn left onto it and set your odometer at zero. Before the Cariboo Gold Rush, this road was known as 'the River Road.'

As you drive this paved road, residences give way to acreages. You reach Springhouse Trail Ranch at kilometre 20.2 (mile 12.6). Spring House (often 'Springhouse') is a ranching community and you will be travelling through ranchland for the rest of this section of the chapter. Look left at kilometre 22.9 (mile 14.2) to see the different types of airplanes at the Williams Lake Flying Club. At kilometre 24.0 (mile 14.9) the road turns to gravel. Watch out for cattleguards, and cattle, on the road.

By kilometre 36.4 (mile 22.6) you have a beautiful view of ranches at the bottom of the Alkali Valley and then you drive down to the valley floor. To your left at kilometre 37.8 (mile 23.5), on bluffs above the road, is the village of Alkali Lake, occupied largely by the Esketemc First Nation (formerly Alkali Lake Indian Band).

After the village, the bluffs rise higher, and you soon come to the Alkali Lake Ranch, site of a former River Road roadhouse. The ranch itself was established in 1861 and is considered to be the oldest ranch in the province. Old buildings line the road and all along the driveway up to the office and house.

⬧ The First Route to the Cariboo

In 1858, there was no way for prospectors to get through the Fraser River Canyon, north of Yale, to look for gold further up the river. Governor James Douglas enlisted the help of 500 miners, who were divided into groups so that they could work on several parts of the trail simultaneously. They slashed a trail from Port Douglas on Harrison Lake to the south end of Lillooet Lake and from the north end of Lillooet Lake to Anderson Lake and then to Seton Lake. The finished Douglas Trail went from Port Douglas to Lillooet, with the road portions being driven by wagon or packhorse and the lakes traversed at first by row-boats and later by steamers.

Once in Lillooet, the miners headed north on the River Road, which ran on the east side of the Fraser River from Pavilion to Williams Lake. When the Cariboo Wagon Road (see Chapter 8) was completed in 1863, both the Douglas Trail and the River Road were abandoned. (For more information about following the Douglas Trail, see Chapters 6 and 7 of *Backroads of Southwestern British Columbia*. The River Road is described further in a sidebar on p. 208.)

After the ranch, wide-open valleys and rolling hills with yellows, greens, tans and browns keep you looking in all directions at the semi-arid landscape. To your right at kilometre 40.7 (mile 25.2) there is a pull-out for the Reidemann Wildlife Sanctuary on Alkali Lake. A sign here explains about the birds and other animals that call the sanctuary home year-round or stop in on their migrations. The land around the sanctuary is private, so use binoculars to watch the wildlife.

You follow Alkali Lake until kilometre 42.4 (mile 26.3) and, when you reach kilometre 46.8 (mile 29.1), there is a huge rock in the field to your right. You are climbing and kilometre 48.6 (mile 30.2) gives you a beautiful view of the valley to your right and you can see the huge rock again. At kilometre 49.3 (mile 30.6) you can see a long way ahead and then the road curves and you are on the benchland of the Fraser River, with more panoramic views of hills and mountains.

The road continues to climb and, by kilometre 56.8 (mile 35.3), you turn away from the views and come out of the valley onto a flat hilltop. At kilometre 62.8 (mile 39.0) you start down into the semi-arid Fraser River canyon. You won't see much of the river, so watch to your right at kilometre 67.8 (mile 42.1) for a glimpse of it.

You begin a 1-kilometre (0.6-mile) drive through an old landslide area at kilometre 68.8 (mile 42.8), then turn away from the Fraser River canyon. Kilometre 73.4 (mile 45.6) brings you to a junction. To your right is the road to the Gang Ranch; to your left is the road to Dog Creek.

The Gang Ranch, Dog Creek and Enterprise

Although there are no tours of the Gang Ranch and the drive to it is on very steep, narrow roads with drop-offs, go there if you just want to say that you have set foot on the largest ranch in BC, and for the views along the way. You will be using your brakes a lot, so they should be in good condition and you may have to stop and let them cool. Use caution, considering the type of vehicle you are driving. After you turn right at the junction, for the first 2.0 kilometres (1.2 miles) you are into a very steep and winding climb. You then reach a plateau and are looking down on the Fraser River canyon to your right. At kilometre 5.0 (mile 3.1) you begin a descent on a switchbacked washboard road. Then you drive over a hill and are rewarded with a spectacular view of the Fraser River below, with sagebrush-covered hills around it. At kilometre 8.8 (mile 5.5) you reach a junction, where you go right to continue to the Gang Ranch.

You continue descending to the river on the narrow road and in 1.1 kilometres (0.7 miles) from the junction you cross the Churn Creek Bridge, a single-lane wooden suspension bridge over the Fraser River. Just after the bridge you enter the land of the Gang Ranch.

The Gang Ranch is one of the oldest ranches in the province and consists of over 12,000 hectares (29,700 acres) of deeded land and 380,000 hectares (939,000 acres) of crown land. It was begun in 1888 by brothers Jerome and Thadeus Harper who, some people claim, were outlaws from West Virginia. The ranch was the first in the Cariboo to use the double-furrowed gang plow and was named after it. You can see a gang plow at the Clinton Historic Museum, described later in this chapter.

The First Flour Mill

In the late 1850s, a French noble-man named Comte de Versepuche (or Versepeuch) came to the area. Deciding to set up a ranch near Dog Creek, he built a waterwheel to power a whipsaw to saw lumber for a large house. 'Gaspar,' as he was called, then traded his blue satin jacket and tri-cornered hat to Chief Alexis for a band of horses.

He constructed a flour mill, the first on the BC mainland begun by pri-vate enterprise, which ground its first wheat in 1866.

The road continues through the ranch to Farwell Canyon and Highway 20 west of Williams Lake (see p. 195).

Back at the junction where you first turned right to go to the Gang Ranch, take the other road and continue toward Dog Creek. Dog Creek Elementary School is to your left in 0.5 kilometres (0.3 miles) and at kilometre 2.0 (mile 1.2) there is an old, bright blue church with a black roof to your left. A hotel was built in Dog Creek in 1856 to service the miners passing through. The Dog Creek Stagelines, with headquarters in the hotel, was the first such company to be licensed in BC and it operated until the 1980s, when it was using a bus to transport travellers from Dog Creek and area to Williams Lake. When the general store and bus service went out of business, the population dwindled.

By kilometre 3.0 (mile 1.9) from the junction you are out of Dog Creek and the road curves left. The semi-arid land is slowly replaced by trees. You are following Dog Creek and at kilometre 13.2 (mile 8.2) you are in the Dog Creek canyon, with tall trees creating almost total shade.

Look to your left as you drive through the canyon to see a wooden flume on the canyon wall. The flume ends at kilometre 14.0 (mile 8.7) as you leave the

The River Road

The River Road was built in 1858 to take gold-seekers from Lillooet to Williams Lake. What was open land at the time of the road's use by prospectors is now ranches, many of which were begun by former Cariboo miners. The road passed through the Native village of Pavilion, went over Pavilion Mountain and headed northward to what is now Kelly Lake, where Edward Kelly established the Kelly Lake Ranch in 1866. Further northwest is Jesmond, where the former store and post office is now a private residence.

Just past Jesmond is the turn west to the Big Bar Ferry on Big Bar Creek. The ferry began operation in 1894. The River Road passes the Native village of Canoe Creek, follows the benchlands of the Fraser River for a ways, passes the road to Gang Ranch, goes beside Dog Creek, Alkali and Spring House and reaches Williams Lake.

From Williams Lake the miners followed the fur-brigade trails north to look for gold along the Fraser River and its tributaries.

canyon. In 18.2 kilometres (11.3 miles) from the beginning of the road to Dog Creek, you reach the junction with Chimney Lake Forest Service Road. If you went right, you would be headed for the town of Clinton on Highway 97. Turn left instead onto the fairly good gravel road and it is a mainly straight 49.5-kilometre (30.8-mile) drive to the community of Enterprise, which is also on Highway 97.

At the highway you can turn right to go to Lac La Hache (see p. 210) or go left to 150 Mile House to begin the next section.

150 Mile House to 100 Mile House

150 Mile House and 137 Mile House

If you didn't drive the Dog Creek Road, then head south on Highway 97 from the junction with Highway 20 in Williams Lake and you will enter 150 Mile House at kilometre 14.5 (mile 9.0). Watch for the little red schoolhouse beside the highway. The school was built in the 1890s and, after restoration, opened as a heritage building on September 19, 1984.

To your right after the school is the 150 Mile Roadhouse, part of which is still the original roadhouse from the gold-rush era. From this point southward, many of the places along the highway are named for the distance in miles that they were from Mile 0 in Lillooet. You pass through the community of 140 Mile House and, at kilometre 16.8 (mile 10.4) from 150 Mile House, look to your left for 137 Mile House. There is no sign, but watch for a large, weathered log house in a yard. As you look at the house, the section closest to the highway was the gold-rush roadhouse. The building is now private property.

The sign that says 'Welcome to Lac La Hache' is at kilometre 33.6 (mile 20.9).

The Last BC Express Robbery

The last robbery of a BC Express (BX) stagecoach took place on November 1, 1909. A man and a woman dressed as a man held up the stage between 144 Mile House and 141 Mile House. She hid behind a tree and he behind a boulder, both stepping out when the stage reached them.

The driver was partially deaf and pretended that he didn't understand their demands for the registered mail sacks. In the confusion he managed to give them some empty ones along with full ones. When they had the bags, the robbers sent the coach on its way and went into the bush, where they evidently opened the sacks and took out about $2000.

The police scoured the area and finally decided that the culprits were a woman and her brother-in-law who had been in the area only a few weeks. Although the police couldn't prove anything—the coach driver apparently not being a sufficiently reliable witness—they took the couple to Ashcroft and put them on the train, telling them to get out of Canada and stay out.

Lac La Hache and 100 Mile House

Lac La Hache bills itself as 'the Longest Town in the Cariboo.' As you drive through it, you will see why. The long lake itself—with homes, resorts, campgrounds, picnic areas, public boat-launches and cabins to rent—is to your right. You finally reach the business section at about kilometre 15 (mile 9) from the welcome sign.

After leaving Lac La Hache, you re-enter semi-arid terrain. After crossing 111 Mile Creek at kilometre 7.6 (mile 4.7), you then turn right off the highway at kilometre 11.0 (mile 6.8) for the 108 Mile House Heritage Site. Once you are off the highway, 108 Mile Lake is in front of you. Turn left into the parking area for the historic ranch.

The buildings here, such as the bunkhouse and the telegraph office, have plaques on them that give a brief history, including the year that they were built and when they were moved to this site. Inside the house, pick up a pamphlet with a more detailed write-up on the buildings, as well as a brochure that explains about the rooms of the house and the items in them. You can visit the parlour, which has a wooden carpet sweeper and a wind-up phonograph, or see the hand-woven bedspread from 1820 in the upstairs bedroom, or look in the kitchen for the hand pump, icebox and old cook stove.

The heritage site is operated by the 100 Mile District Historical Society, which is a non-profit organization, so donations are appreciated. After your tour you can have lunch in the tea house or picnic in the rest area beside the site.

You pass 105 Mile Lake and then, at kilometre 9.1 (mile 5.7) from the heritage site, 103 Mile Lake. The road to the resort area, which includes Canim Lake, Mahood Lake and many smaller lakes, is to your left at kilometre 11.6 (mile 7.2). Besides fishing the lakes for rainbow, whitefish, kokanee or lake trout, there are resorts, lodges, campgrounds, picnic sites and waterfalls. For a detailed description of the area, first stop in at the visitor information centre in 100 Mile House, which you reach in 1.8 kilometres (1.1 miles) from the junction.

105 Mile Ranch House at 108 Mile House Heritage Site.

Just after coming into town, watch to your right for the Red Coach Inn. Turn into its parking lot to see an original BX stagecoach. 'The Red Coach,' which was BC Express #14, sits beside the inn, covered by a roof. The Red Coach Inn is on the site of the original roadhouse, destroyed by fire in 1937, which served the miners who stopped here during the gold rush.

Continue along the highway to the visitor information centre, which is to your right. In front of it are the world's largest cross-country skis—11-metre (36-foot)

Express Service

long replicas of a pair of Karhu racers. Since 100 Mile House calls itself 'the International Nordic Ski Capital'—there are about 200 kilometres (125 miles) of cross country-ski trails in the area—the community decided that these skis were a fitting symbol. They were dedicated on April 7, 1987, by Rick Hansen, who

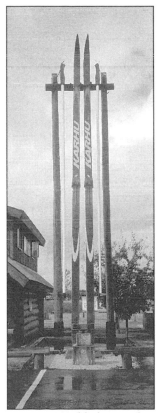

World's largest skis, 100 Mile House.

stopped in on his Man In Motion World Tour to raise money for spinal cord research.

The town hosts the annual 50-kilometre (31-mile) Cariboo Ski Marathon, which attracts Nordic skiers from across Canada and also from Australia, England and the US. The event, with its various levels, is held the first weekend in February and has over 1000 participants, ranging from preschoolers to octogenarians.

At the Lumber Industry Display set up by the Rotary Club of 100 Mile House, beside the centre, you can see equipment used by the lumber industry. Behind the display is the 8-hectare (20-acre) 100 Mile Marsh, which has an easy walking trail around it.

When you come out of the centre back onto the highway, if you want to walk beside a gurgling creek and see a small (but pretty) waterfall, immediately turn right onto Fourth Street and then right again onto Cedar. Look to your left for the entrance to a park once you are on Cedar.

The trail to Bridge Creek Falls (100 Mile House was originally called 'Bridge Creek') begins from the parking lot and follows the creek, which is to your left. There are benches along the path and in about five minutes you reach a bridge to a small island formed by the splitting of the creek. When you cross the second bridge to get off the island, look to your left to see the falls.

Head southward out of 100 Mile House and in 9.0 kilometres (5.6 miles) you reach the junction with Highway 24, which goes to Lone Butte.

Bridge Creek Falls at 100 Mile House.

The First BC Express Robbery

The BX Company operated in the Cariboo for many decades without a problem. That changed, however, on September 16, 1890, when a lone gunman held up the stage at 99 Mile Hill, which involved a 6.4-kilometre (4-mile) long climb. The bandit, a miner from Barkerville, picked this place because the stage usually stopped at the base of the hill to rest the horses before beginning the climb, and the driver would not be able to urge the tired horses to gallop away.

The stagecoach driver knew that the gold shipment had been put in two separate containers: the safe and the treasure bag. He convinced the robber that all the gold dust was in the safe, so the gunman made off with it, leaving the bag behind.

Instead of hightailing it out of the country with his loot, the bandit, whose name is believed to have been Martin Van Buren Rowland, went to Ashcroft. After spending a few weeks supposedly working a claim on a creek, he sent some gold dust to Barkerville to be made into bullion. What Martin didn't know was that gold dust can be identified. Its texture, size and colour can tell a good Gold Commissioner which creek it came from, and the Gold Commissioner at Barkerville was good. He recognized immediately that the dust sent by Rowland had been part of the shipment on the stage on the day of the robbery.

Based on the Gold Commissioner's testimony, Rowland was convicted only of possession of stolen gold. He hadn't been charged with the robbery because it had been dark at the time and the driver couldn't positively identify him.

Lone Butte to Kamloops

Lone Butte and Mount Begbie Tower

Turn left onto Highway 24, which goes from Highway 97 to Highway 5 at Little Fort (see p. 16), on the way passing through the Interlakes Area, where fishing for rainbow trout, canoeing and hiking are the favourite sports. In less than 1.0 kilometre (0.6 miles) from the junction there is a large sign that shows all the lakes and resorts in the area. At kilometre 9.4 (mile 5.8) you reach the sign for Lone Butte. Look ahead to see the extinct volcano core that forms the 'butte,' after which the hamlet was named, against the sky. To your left at kilometre 10.4 (mile 6.5) there is a water tank in a small park. This water tank, circa 1920, was built to supply water for the Pacific Great Eastern Railway's steam engines. Also in the park is a speeder used by railway crews to check the track, plus a speeder shelter.

Across the road from the water tank is the site of the Lone Butte Hotel, which was constructed in 1920 and burned down on January 13, 1998. In its heyday, Lone Butte was the largest town in the Cariboo. Return to Highway 97 and continue southward.

At kilometre 11.9 (mile 7.4) from Highway 24, turn left onto Mount Begbie Road to visit the Mount Begbie Tower. The parking lot is to the right just after you turn off. Walk across the cattleguard and take the steep, narrow path over uneven ground up the hillside to the tower. If the gate on the driveway is open, you may hike on it for better footing.

Once you reach the tower, you are 1276 metres (4186 feet) above sea level and you have a great view in all directions. If the tower operator is there, you can climb up the steps for a visit and to sign the guest book. It is open to visitors between 8 AM and 5 PM every day of the fire season, unless rain has allowed the lookout staff a few days off.

There has been a lookout on Mount Begbie since 1923.

View from Mount Begbie Tower.

83 Mile and Chasm Provincial Park

At kilometre 2.2 (mile 1.4) from Mount Begbie Road, the 83 Mile Restaurant is to your right. The restaurant has been renovated, but part of it is still Stoddart House, a roadhouse that dates from the 1860s. Behind the restaurant is the old barn from the roadhouse days.

To visit Chasm Provincial Park, take the road to your left at kilometre 27.8 (mile 17.3) from 83 Mile. In 2.5 kilometres (1.6 miles) you cross some railway tracks and just past them you turn left into the parking and picnic area. From here you can see the reds, yellows, tans, browns, and grays that make up the layers of the 120-metre (395-foot) high canyon walls of the painted chasm, a three-sided box canyon, as it goes 1.5 kilometres (0.9 miles) into the distance. A protective fence runs along the edge. If you go to your left at the fence, you can walk down a slight hill to the remnant of the formerly much larger glacial stream that formed this canyon.

Chasm Provincial Park was established in 1940, originally with an area of 141 hectares (348 acres). In 1994 it was enlarged to its present size of 2927 hectares (7230 acres). Although geologists state that the box canyon has been here for 10,000 years, local legend has it that it was dug by a Scottish miner who had dropped a penny and was looking for it.

To return to the highway, you can stay on the side road, because in 1.2 kilometres (0.7 miles) you cross the railway tracks again and then pass some acreages and ranches in the community of Chasm, to reach Highway 97 in 5.1 kilometres (3.1 miles) from the park.

Just 14.2 kilometres (8.8 miles) after you return to the highway you reach the town of Clinton.

Chasm Provincial Park.

Clinton and Hat Creek Ranch

The best way to see the sights and shops of Clinton is to park and walk down the main street, Highway 97. Beside Parkies Store on the west side of the road between McDonald and Lebourdais avenues you will see some posts with square wooden signs nailed to them. These signs were started by the owner of a campsite in the area who wanted to give his visitors something to do. He handed them each a piece of wood and had them carve their names into them. Then he tacked them up on a post. The campsite is long gone, but you can still read the names of some of the people who visited Clinton over the years.

Sign posts in Clinton.

Continue down the street. On your left between Lebourdais and Dewdney avenues is the Clinton Historic Museum, in a red brick building. This structure, built in 1892 from locally made bricks, was first a school and then, from 1925 to 1955, a courthouse. In front of the entrance are two millstones, circa 1868. In the yard there is a 1925 La France Pumper fire-truck, brought from Vancouver in 1958. Around back are some buildings, and inside one is a replica of the Clinton Hotel, which was built in 1860 and burned down in 1959. Clinton's annual ball, first celebrated in 1868 and still continuing these days in a new venue, was formerly held in the hotel.

Clinton Museum.

In another building there is a gang plow of the type used by the Gang Ranch. The museum is open from 8 AM to 6 PM Monday to Saturday and 12:30 PM to 4:30 PM on Sunday.

Clinton's current name honours Sir Henry Pelham Clinton, who served as Queen Victoria's Colonial Secretary from 1859 to 1864. The town was once called '47 Mile House' because of its location 76 kilometres (47 miles) from Lillooet, and also 'Cutoff Valley' and 'Junction.'

The arid land south of Clinton is coloured by turquoise to greyish-green sagebrush, brown ground, yellow grass and green trees. At the junction at kilometre 29.0 (mile 18.0), turn right onto Highway 99, which goes to Hat Creek and Lillooet, Mile 0 of the original Cariboo Wagon Road (see Chapter 8 of *Backroads of Southwestern British Columbia*).

About 0.5 kilometres (0.3 miles) after you turn onto Highway 99, turn left into the Hat Creek Ranch. Hat Creek was one of the stops on the Cariboo Wagon Road and today's access road to the ranch is still via part of that old road. The first stopping house at this location, 'McLean's Farm and Restaurant,' was established in 1860 by Donald McLean. His sons, Allan, Charlie and Archie, along with a friend Alex Hare, were the members of the McLean Gang, which murdered a police officer south of Kamloops. Donald himself, who is said to have killed 19 men, was killed in the 'Chilcotin War' (see the sidebar on p. 202). The present Hat Creek House was constructed in the 1880s.

At the parking lot you can pick up a brochure to use as a guide as you wander around. The ranch offers wagon rides on the historic Cariboo Road, tours of the Hat Creek stopping house, and a visit to a blacksmith shop. Stop in at the tea house for lunch after your tour. Then return to Highway 97 and continue southward.

Original Cariboo Wagon roadhouse at Hat Creek Ranch.

Cache Creek, Walhachin and Kamloops

The black plastic tarps that you see along here, as in Chapter 1, are covering ginseng (see sidebar on p. 218). In 10.3 kilometres (6.4 miles) from Highway 99 you enter the town of Cache Creek. At kilometre 11.2 (mile 67.0), still in town, you

Large piece of jade.

reach the junction with Highway 1, which goes to the left. Turn right onto Todd Road and the Cariboo Jade Shoppe is the second building on your right. The huge piece of jade in front of the store is 0.3 metres (1 foot) thick and weighs 1290 kilograms (2850 pounds). It took something like 200 hours of cutting with diamond field-saws to slice this piece from a boulder near Dease Lake in the northwestern corner of British Columbia (see Chapter 5).

Inside the store you can find shirts, handicrafts made by local Natives, jade carvings and all types of jade jewellery. Prices range from $700 for jade carvings down to $3 for a piece of polished jade.

Cache Creek, on the historic Cariboo Wagon Road, is said to have got its name after a bandit stole 36 kilograms (80 pounds) of gold from a miner and hid it here. He supposedly disappeared and never returned for the cache. Another story is that there were several robbers who hid their loot in the area before they were arrested. No one knows what happened to them after they were released from jail but they never returned for their gold—or so it is said.

If you like car racing and are here on the second weekend of June, take in the BC Oldtime Drags and Rod Run. You can see races involving hot rods from BC and the Pacific Northwest and watch a restored-vehicle parade. As well, you can look on as graffiti is being written on the walls of local businesses, with the permission of the owners.

Jade

Jade has been treasured for over 7000 years, even taking the place of gold in the ancient Chinese civilizations that used it to make beautiful carvings. Chinese miners found it in North America in the mid-1800s.

There are two minerals that are termed to be jade. Nephrite is the more abundant and is found in such colours as red, yellow, grey, dark green, white and black. The other, jadeite, is very rare and much more valuable than nephrite. Its colours are light green, emerald and lilac.

Jade is made up of interlocking grids of fine needles. Because of these grids, it is four times harder than marble. Many people claim that jade has the power to bring health and wealth to its owner.

Take Highway 1 east out of town to continue toward Kamloops. You will be surrounded by arid hills as you follow the Thompson River. The turn-off for Walhachin is to your right at kilometre 23.4 (mile 14.5). This paved road begins by going downhill. You cross railway tracks and take a one-lane bridge over the Thompson River, then rise above the river. In about 6 kilometres (4 miles) from the turn-off you reach Walhachin, which is spread out along the bank high above the Thompson.

In 1908, an American civil engineer began the task of irrigating thousands of acres of land around Walhachin on the Thompson River. He set up a company that bought 1,820 hectares (4,500 acres) of land and leased thousands more. Sixteen thousand apple, pear, peach and apricot trees were planted and 27 kilometres (17 miles) of flume and ditches were created to divert the flow of water from streams and rivers to the site. A townsite was surveyed and a packing house, a store, a hotel and rental houses were built. Brochures were issued in England and about 70 young men came to work on the land, some bringing their wives.

Cash crops—such as tobacco, corn, onions, beans and tomatoes—were planted to provide income until the orchards bore fruit. It was hard work, but a golf course and a tennis court—plus swimming and hunting in the summer and skating in the winter—gave the men and their families some relaxation.

However, when the First World War broke out in Europe, most of the young men returned to England to help fight the war. The wives and older men tried to keep up with the work, but there was too much to do and not enough workers to do it. An excess of rain clogged the ditches with debris and broke the flumes. One heavy rain finally ruined much of the system. In the heat of the following summer, the trees withered and died. The dream was over.

Today the flumes and orchards have disappeared and the hillsides are now growing the plants of Chai-Na-Ta Ginseng Farms. The plants, in various stages of growth, are protected from the sun by a black plastic covering. These gardens are on private property, so stay out of them.

Back on the highway, you reach Deadman/Vidette Road at 8.2 kilometres (5.1 miles) from the Walhachin Road. If you want to see 'the Columns,' an interesting sandstone formation, turn left. Deadman/Vidette Road, paved for the first while, takes you through arid land, with sagebrush on both sides. The colouring

Ginseng

The growing of native North American ginseng, *Panax quinquefolium,* began in the province in 1982. Ginseng grows in the cooler climates of North America and Asia and needs shade. Polypropylene is used to create the shade, and straw mulch covers the plants under it. After a seed is planted, it takes four years for the plant, which is grown for its root, to grow large enough to be harvested. The root, which looks like a many-rooted parsnip, is dug up and dried.

Ninety-five percent of the ginseng grown in British Columbia is exported to the Orient for use in medicine. The remaining 5% is sold in British Columbia and other parts of Canada in capsules or as a tea. It is believed to relieve stress and to help the body work more efficiently.

of the hills is lovely. At kilometre 4.9 (mile 3.0) from the highway you reach a sign titled, 'Deadman River, Stream Bank and Salmonid Enhancement Project,' which tells you about the fisheries and wildlife habitat.

You are following the Deadman River and you cross it just after the hatchery. Soon you reach the Skeetchestn Indian Band village, which has a store with gas.

You cross a couple of creeks, drive by beautifully coloured cliffs and at kilometre 17.5 (mile 10.8) you reach the Silver Spring Ranch, which is on the right. Although the Columns are on crown land, you have to cross the Silver Spring Ranch's land in order to get to them. Turn into the drive and go to the house to ask permission. The owners will allow you on their land if you stick to the path and do not leave any garbage behind. If you bring your dog, keep it on a leash to protect the fallow deer raised here.

The Columns.

As you leave the farmhouse yard, you cross a bridge and follow around a fence. Then you turn away from the fence and head into the hills. From here onward there is no marked path—you just have to observe where the Columns are and work your way through the trees and up the hill toward them.

There are five sandstone columns, four in a row, with the fifth one beside the last of the four. Sandstone weathers away relatively quickly, except where it is protected by harder rock. Over the centuries, the sandstone here has been worn away, leaving pieces of harder rock balancing on top of the Columns that they have shielded from the elements.

When you stop in to thank the ranch owners for letting you park on their property and walk across it, you will be asked to sign a guest book. People from across Canada, the United States and Europe have climbed up to the Columns.

After Deadman/Vidette Road, you work your way down into the valley of the Thompson River and can see Kamloops Lake. You cross the Thompson River at kilometre 4.7 (mile 2.9), just after it leaves the lake. After the bridge you can turn left onto Savona Access Loop Road to drive through the village of Savona. The hills around Savona are dry, with few trees and not much grass. This road takes you on a scenic drive past the residences of the village, with their well-kept lawns and flowers a contrast to the dry hills.

Follow the road back to the highway, where you turn left. You have Kamloops Lake to your left as you slowly rise above it. At kilometre 17.4 (mile 10.8) you reach the top of the hill. To your left is the Kamloops Lake Rest Area, a beautiful place to stop and have a picnic overlooking the lake.

From the rest area, you drive through the lovely, arid landscape on your way to the city of Kamloops. You enter the city at kilometre 23.3 (mile 14.5), thus completing your journey through the central and northern parts of British Columbia.

Index